TALKING
ABOUT
DIFFERENCE

TALKING
ABOUT
DIFFERENCE

Encounters in Culture, Language and Identity

edited by

Carl E. James
and
Adrienne Shadd

Published by:
Between The Lines
720 Bathurst Street, Suite 404
Toronto, Ontario
M5S 2R4
Canada

Distributed by University of Toronto Press

Cover and interior design by Artwork
Printed in Canada

"One Family. Indivisible? Or Me, and Two of My Children" originally
appeared in the *Canadian Forum*, October 1992.

Between The Lines gratefully acknowledges financial assistance from the
Canada Council, the Ontario Arts Council, the Ministry of Canadian
Heritage, and the Ontario Ministry of Culture, Tourism, and Recreation.

Canadian Cataloguing in Publication Data

Main entry under title:

Talking about difference: encounters in culture,
language and identity

Includes bibliographical references.
ISBN 0-921284-92-6 (bound) ISBN 0-921284-93-4 (pbk.)

1. Multiculturalism - Canada - Literary collections.
I. James, Carl, 1952- . II. Shadd, Adrienne L.
(Adrienne Lynn), 1954- .

FC105.M8T35 1994   306.4'46'0971   C94-932657-7
F1035.A1T35 1994

CONTENTS

v

ACKNOWLEDGEMENTS

We would like to thank all those who submitted essays, stories, and poems for this collection, whether or not they made the final selection process. All submissions were greatly appreciated, and your support and enthusiasm for the project are what kept us going. We are particularly indebted to Susan Ship for the extra effort she made in securing contacts in Quebec for us. Thanks also to Ayanna Black for her assistance during a crucial stage in the development of the book, and to friends Laura Cohen and Scott Milne for their support. We extend a special thank you to Between The Lines, in particular Carroll Klein for a superb editing job, and Marg Anne Morrison for both her invaluable reviews and comments on the articles and her overall contribution to the final product. We enjoyed working with you. Finally, a big hug and kiss to Kai and Marishana, who we hope will mature in a Canada that is truly respectful of difference and for whom all of our work is ultimately dedicated.

INTRODUCTION
CARL E. JAMES AND ADRIENNE SHADD

"Where are you from?"

"What is your nationality?"

"But, I never think of you as . . ."

"I didn't know you were . . ."

"You're different."

"I'm not racist, but . . ."

"It's just a joke."

"What does a white person know about racism?"

"Some of my best friends are . . ."

Some questions and comments are so much a part of our every day world that we rarely give them a second thought when we hear them or say them. But for some people these questions and comments are constant reminders of their race, ethnicity, and immigrant and/or minority status. These people may not regard such statements as a genuine desire to "get to know the person," but rather a reflection of the speaker's ignorance or insensitivity.

Being recipients as well as initiators of some of these questions and comments, and being unsure about how best to ask or respond to them, we were prompted to put together this book of readings. Our first goal is to have contributors share with you, the reader, their experiences—to say what these statements and questions mean to

1

them, and to help you begin to understand and appreciate the impact of such questions and comments. We believe that if we are to go beyond the cloak of stereotyping, we must share our experiences and backgrounds. Only then can we really begin to learn about and understand each other.

Second, we hope that this collection will reveal just how much we have in common, in spite of seeming differences. Our third goal is to reveal how our personal exchanges and interactions, that is to say, *encounters*, are critical to understanding the complex ways in which culture, race, class and identities find expression in our daily lives. We wish to make explicit how they intersect to influence each person's life experiences and relations. Ultimately, our fourth goal is to add to the debate on diversity, in the hope that the issues and insights raised in this book will lead in some small way to social action and change.

As you read these accounts, we are sure you will find your own experiences reflected in those of the various authors. We hope that this will empower you, the reader, by articulating some of the issues with which you too struggle.

In writing their articles, the contributors have placed their experiences at the centre of their discourse. We see this as essential to building awareness and initiating social action and change. We believe that social change results not only from policy reform and government enactments, but also from confronting our own attitudes and feelings, as well as those of others. This is not to limit analysis to individual experience but rather to illustrate how, through the understanding of individual experience, we gain insight into the social structure and how it shapes experience and interaction. Therefore, a change at the individual level can occur through increased knowledge of others, which then leads to changes in the social structure — a structure that excludes some, and prevents us from knowing about each other.

It is precisely because of the way in which the social structure operates that we remain misinformed, ignorant, and thus separate from each other. David Schoem, in his book *Inside Separate Worlds*, comments that "the effort it takes for us to know so little about one another across racial and ethnic groups is truly remarkable." Remarkable, because we live in the same country, are educated together and work together. Despite all this — despite the fact that our lives are so intertwined socially, culturally, economically and politically — we still manage to be ignorant of each other. Consequently, what little we know is shaped by stereotypes, gossip, rumours and fear. (We will save discussion of the media's conspiracy in this for another book.)

In this collection, contributors share their unique histories and perspectives, providing a glimpse into their respective worlds and a space for voices to articulate individual experience and interpretation. The authors provide information that many were reluctant to share because it has, up to now, remained the domain of our private thoughts and stories. If we are to bring about social change, however, we must take risks.

We ask that our readers compare the experiences they have had as members of ethnic or racial groups with the experiences of the contributors. In so doing, you will identify commonalities and differences. It is in recognizing the commonalities between us, even as they co-exist with our differences, that the many dimensions of our lives will be revealed and we will learn to be more respectful of each other.

Often when another person's ideas or information make us uncomfortable because they challenge our "truths" and/or "facts," we find reason to question their validity. A common response is to reject these ideas as unfounded or "biased"—while failing at the same time to consider the "biases" that result from our own vantage point or world view. However, this tendency must be confronted if we are to hear each other and build an inclusive and equitable society. In making an attempt to understand the contributors in terms of how we describe our realities, construct our lives and interpret our experience, you are, in a way, acknowledging and accepting difference—a process which is absolutely critical in fostering healthy and harmonious relations.

In this book, contributors have written in different styles and genres, which are indicative of the many voices that need to be heard in order to understand and appreciate our complex realities. These layered complexities are communicated through personal narratives, "academic" essays, short stories, letters, poems and journalistic articles. We present these diverse forms, not only to maintain your interest and attention, but also to legitimize the contributors' unique ways of voicing their stories, in order to communicate their points. While many of the articles in this book are thoughtful and based upon the authors' experiences, they are nonetheless controversial, and liable to provoke argument and debate. We do not see this as a negative, for it is our belief that discussion and debate concerning questions of identity, equity and inclusion in a changing society must necessarily include many voices and diverse perspectives.

The book is divided into six sections representing six areas of discussion and debate in today's Canada. Grouping contributions based on people's personal experiences around themes is always limiting and problematic. Nevertheless, it is one way in which to grasp meaning and sort out the different messages being communicated. Some of these articles might easily have appeared in several different sections, but in such cases we went with the category we felt was the "best fit."

The essays and poems in Part I are intended to respond to the question "Who's a Canadian, Anyway?" — a question we think needs to be posed. Particularly when people continue to be asked "Where are you from?" or are grilled about their accent, skin colour, language, name or ethnic origin, it suggests that such people are not viewed as Canadian. The articles in this section challenge us to think of Canadians as having different colours, accents and languages. No one is more "Canadian" than another. On the contrary, it is possible to conceive that individuals may be more consciously Canadian because they have made a deliberate choice to be here rather than simply being Canadian by accident of birth.

Growing up is an especially precarious time, when being seen as "different" or, worse still, viewing oneself as "different" can be quite traumatic. Most children just want to fit in and be like everyone else; children who are racially or ethnically different face a particularly painful time. The essays in Part II address, among other things, the issues and problems of growing up in Canada as a member of a racial or ethnic minority.

A constant theme in all of the contributions is that of identity. For this reason, many of the pieces could have been placed in the section entitled "Identities: Living in Many Worlds." However, the selections in Part III are intended to focus attention on how identities get constructed with regard to race, ethnicity, gender and citizenship. The authors demonstrate how their identities are a product of the way they view themselves as well as of how others view and interact with them on the basis of race, ethnicity, gender, language, colour, immigrant status and name.

Part IV, "Race, Privilege and Challenges," addresses the flip side of these issues by looking at how white, middle-class Canadians are attempting to deal with their race and class privilege in the context of a future Canada which truly celebrates and accommodates diversity. We also get a glimpse into the unbelievable contradictions of being a racial minority in a traditionally "white, middle-class" profession.

It is often said that "everyone stereotypes" because it helps us to categorize the vast amount of information about others that we must process. However, stereotyping often leads to blatant misrepresentation, which can have serious, negative consequences for individuals or groups. In the section "Stereotyping Is a Common Practice, But . . ." the authors expose the pitfalls of stereotyping, noting that seemingly innocent statements sometimes have racist and discriminatory implications.

Finally, Part VI reveals some of the ways in which people have dealt with racism or stereotyping, whether this has been in family or interpersonal relationships, or as teachers trying to impart a critical consciousness of "Euro-American ethnocentrism" masquerading as universal knowledge in Canadian school curricula.

Ultimately, one of our goals is to encourage a re-examination of existing ways in which we view and think about others. This requires us to transform not only how we interact with people who are different from us, but also the language we use to describe and define them. But language is problematic; it is not neutral. The words and terms we use reflect particular perspectives or frames of reference with which we feel comfortable. For this reason, we should say something about the language that appears in this collection.

We are aware, for example, that for some the terms "racial minority" and "ethnic minority"—used routinely by social scientists—marginalize groups identified as outside the mainstream or majority (white Anglo-Celtic) culture. The term "non-white" is objectionable because it defines people by a negative—white being the norm against which all other groups are measured. For our purposes, we use the term racial and ethnic minority to indicate the power relationship that is inherent in our society—"majority" representing not simply numbers, but the cultural group with political and economic power compared to the "minority" which does not have access to that power. Arun Mukherjee, in "The 'Race Consciousness' of a South Asian (Canadian, of Course), Female Academic" points out that she uses the term "non-white" in order to talk about the binary relationship of power where "white" is the dominant term because there is no denying the fact that we live in a racist world order. On the other hand, the term "people of colour" is used to apply to all people(s) who are not white. However, Rick Arnold and others, in their book *Educating for a Change*, quoted one person of colour as saying: "This term has gained credence and is widely used. Personally, I think it's a way the dominant culture lumps the 'rest of them' together. For me it is the acceptance of the dominant view (as espoused by the dominant culture—white) that everyone else is 'people of colour'. I guess white isn't a colour."

5

Clearly, whatever words we use will have limitations in that they are products of particular political and cultural arrangements that are rooted in classism, sexism, racism and heterosexism. When we talk about our personal experiences, we employ terms which best communicate our unique situations and political perspectives. Therefore, readers will not find a uniformity of terminology in the various selections of the book. As editors, we did not feel that we should change the contributors' terminology, for the use of language is a problem we do not know how to solve. We trust, however, that readers will bear in mind the significance and limitations of words as you follow the contributors' efforts to employ more inclusive and non-discriminatory language. Ultimately, we hope that this consciousness of the influence of language on our encounters and perceptions will mean that we use words and terms that are positive and inclusive rather than those that reflect and perpetuate negative stereotypes and attitudes.

PART 1
WHO'S CANADIAN, ANYWAY?

"WHERE ARE YOU **REALLY** FROM?"
NOTES OF AN "IMMIGRANT" FROM NORTH BUXTON, ONTARIO
•••••••••••••••••••••••••••••
ADRIENNE SHADD

When nineteenth-century Quebec historian François Garneau decided to write Histoire du Canada (1846), he deliberately suppressed the fact that slavery existed in New France, leading the public to believe that the "peculiar institution" never tainted our soil. Even though the fourth edition of his work was changed in 1882, the misinformation of a generation had effectively taken place, with a quite lasting impact to this day.

Until recently, tourist brochures and advertising outside Canada had never reflected the diverse make-up of this country. That is why tourists travelling to Nova Scotia, for example, always express surprise at the existence of a large and distinct Black community there. That is also why filmmaker Sylvia Hamilton's documentary Speak It! From the Heart of Black Nova Scotia includes a scene of the young narrator on a Halifax wharf while the famous Bluenose sails serenely behind him in the harbour. With this one brief image, Hamilton symbolically counteracts centuries of erasure of people of colour from the Canadian media.

9

A few years ago, my cousin Dolores Harold, who lives in Detroit, Michigan, was upset because a reunion booklet of the Chatham high school that she attended seemed to have omitted all of the Black students in its depictions of former students and their exploits. Given the artistic, scholastic and sports achievements of her friends and relatives at the school, it seemed so unfair that none of them was represented in the booklet.

As a researcher in African-Canadian history, I am constantly reminded that the four-hundred-year presence of Blacks has been written out of our history and obliterated from the Canadian psyche in general. First brought as slaves in the 1600s, later arriving as refugees or fugitives from American slavery (late 1700s to mid-1800s), and emigrating in the twentieth century from the Caribbean, Africa and elsewhere, people of African descent have been on the scene for centuries. Yet the very concept of a "Black" or "African-" Canadian is — in the public perception — a contradiction in terms. The opening examples serve to illustrate just some of the ways that this contradiction has been reinforced and perpetuated over time.

What is the impact of this kind of invisibility (note the irony here!), of being a nonentity in your own country? I will refer to my own experiences to illustrate how the denial and omission of the Black presence affects interpersonal interaction. I want to illustrate just how psychologically taxing it can be to be "Black" and "Canadian" in typical everyday encounters. For those of us living in large urban centres, there are constant reminders that we are not regarded as truly "Canadian."

In my case, I am a fifth-generation Canadian whose ancestors came here from the United States during the fugitive slave era, as abolitionists and free Blacks trying to escape racial oppression in their homeland. Yet, routinely, I am asked, "Where are you from?" or "What nationality are you?" as if to be Black, you have to come from somewhere else.

I respond that I'm "Canadian." Although light-skinned, I sport some form of "natural" hairdo, and therefore assume that my "African-ness" is apparent. This in itself is a gamble when speaking to most non-Black immigrants, because they perceive only the most "visible" African people (i.e. dark skin, thick lips, broad nose, very kinky hair, etc.) as being Black. I nevertheless play along. The scenario usually unfolds as follows:

"But where are you *originally* from?"

"Canada."

"Oh, *you* were born here. But where are your parents from?"

"Canada."

"But what about your grandparents?"

"They're Canadian."

As individuals delve further into my genealogy to find out where I'm "really" from, their frustration levels rise.

"No, uh (confused, bewildered) I mean . . . your *people*. Where do your *people* come from?"

"The United States."

At this point, questioners are totally annoyed and/or frustrated. After all, Black people in Canada are supposed to come from "the islands," aren't they? At least, that is the stereotype. One woman was quite indignant upon my telling her this, as her sneer seemed to imply that I had a lot of nerve not matching her preconceived image of whom and what I was!

Of course, there are variations on this theme, like the people who respond to my answer "Canadian" by hastening to point out to me that I couldn't be. As one South Asian man asked me after I told him I was Canadian, "But what about your hair?" "I didn't tell you I was a white Canadian!" I responded.

If I factor in race and ethnicity, whether one is Canadian- or foreign-born, recency of arrival in Canada, and so forth, the variations have a certain predictability: (white) English Canadians, when I respond "Canadian," rarely delve further into my background, and, I presume, take my response at face value. Perhaps they consider it impolite to ask the hard questions.

Among Blacks, it is the East Africans — the most recent immigrants — who most closely follow the above sample dialogue. This is because this image of Canada as a "white country" is so very pervasive. It is as prevalent in information disseminated about this country around the world as it is in our schools here in Canada. Long-settled Blacks from the Caribbean or West Africa are aware enough to know what I mean when I say that I'm Canadian, although some still believe that it must mean I'm a "Nova Scotian." (Because Nova Scotia has the largest Black population in Canada per capita, and the largest indigenous Black population, some believe that all native Black Canadians come from there.) Clearly, foreign-born non-Blacks remain the most intransigent on the issue of my origins; the more recently arrived they are, the more consistent with the above scenario.

These situations are usually very frustrating for me because, as the conversation develops, I realize that the individuals have not

11

grasped the very concept of what I represent, even when I go to the trouble of explaining it to them. Apparently, it is just too baffling to comprehend! And what about my reaction? Should I get angry and say something rude? Should I ignore their ignorant comments? Or should I give them a short history lesson?

I suppose humour is the best policy. I know people from Toronto who, when asked which one of the "islands" they come from, respond "Centre" or "Toronto." Based on my own experience, this would sail over most people's heads! I have tried becoming indignant. On some occasions, I have provided information on the history of Blacks in Canada. On other occasions, I have provided no information apart from responding "Canadian" to their questions. Yet for some, no answer I supply satisfies them. One dimwit even came back a few weeks later to grill me on this very same point!

Yes, I am Black, I am Canadian and I grew up in North Buxton, Ontario. This is a rural Black community near Chatham which was once a famous settlement of ex-slaves who escaped on the Underground Railroad. When I was a little girl growing up in North Buxton, I was very much situated in a particular family and community. We were part of the landscape of southwestern Ontario. Everyone knew the family name, and it was, and is, well-respected. In retrospect, it felt good to belong and not have to explain to anyone whom I was and where I came from. Even though racism was a fact of life, and we lived a quasi-segregated existence, I had a sense of being part of the fabric of the society. No one questioned our right to be there—at least not in that stretch of land we had staked out and claimed as ours.

Of course, whites, not knowing the history or significance of Buxton, believed it was the other side of the tracks, a rural Black enclave of "poor" or "underprivileged" people. This was brought home to me at a party a few years ago when a man, after asking where I am from and hearing me respond "North Buxton," excitedly informed me that he too was from the "wrong side of the tracks." I guess the poor fellow was trying his darnedest to establish a rapport but in his zeal he hadn't considered he might be insulting me.

No, it would be wrong to assume that Buxton was the "wrong side of the tracks." Not that Buxton didn't have its share of poorer individuals. It certainly had more than its share of town drunks! But it also held a middle-class rural gentry of farm owners/operators and their families; people who sent their children to university; people who were active in the church and community, CGIT (Canadian Girls In

Training), baseball, Home and School, the North Buxton Maple Leaf Band, community dances, Christmas pageants, and many other activities. The sons and daughters of Buxton have gone on to become teachers, doctors, nurses, school principals, labour leaders, artists, writers, and composers, to name a few. Many successful people have come out of this tiny community, even though historically many of these individuals had to go to the United States to be educated at segregated Black colleges and were obliged to practise their professions in the much larger African American community. There were numerous positive role models and institutions that we established and ran. In the minds of that man at the party and many others, however, the terms "Buxton" and "successful people" are antithetical.

I suppose that this is a perfect example of what happens when an entire racial group is oppressed and held at the lowest rungs of society, when caste and class almost completely overlap. By virtue of membership in the lower caste group, everyone is stamped with the badge of inferiority. Even those who have been upwardly mobile are "tainted" by the negative perceptions and stereotypes associated with group membership. This is precisely what is meant when Blacks tell the joke: "What do you call a Black doctor?" Answer: "A nigger!"

Yet, I dwell on this question of where I'm "really" from because North Buxton has even deeper, almost spiritual, meaning for me. It has come to represent a strong and visible symbol of our long and rich presence in this land. As one of the few remaining indigenous Black communities in this province, North Buxton has a history and culture which emanate from its unique vantage point as an "African" enclave in a sea of British culture and tradition. It is all the more important since this "other" aspect of Canada has been deliberately buried. Blacks (and many others) from across Canada and the world have flocked there to see for themselves this famous community which was the first to exercise Black power at the voting booth. Canadian-, American- and Caribbean-born alike are rallying around this symbol of Black Canadian tradition and culture which is uniquely ours. And the annual Labour Day Homecoming weekend, now a seventy-year-old tradition, is increasingly becoming a celebration which attracts more than just former residents and relatives. For Black people regardless of origin, it has become a celebration of our African Canadian roots in this country.

Perhaps the greatest significance of North Buxton, however, is more personal still, appreciated most by those who grew up there or in similar situations. In an essay entitled "Revolutionary Black

13

Women," from her book *Black Looks: Race and Representation*, feminist theorist and cultural critic bell hooks describes growing up in a segregated rural Black community that was very supportive:

> Our segregated church and schools were places where we were affirmed. I was continually told I was 'special' in those settings, that I would be 'somebody' someday and do important work to 'uplift' the race. I felt loved and cared about in the segregated black community of my growing up. It gave me the grounding in a positive experience of 'blackness' that sustained me when I left that community to enter racially integrated settings, where racism informed most social interactions.

Yes, this is Buxton's greatest legacy for me. It is the place where my positive sense of self was first developed. It is the place that encouraged and reinforced academic excellence, and where it was assumed that I was intelligent and an achiever. It was not the place where these characteristics were snuffed out because of the colour of my skin. Relatives who received all of their education in Toronto have not fared as well in the educational system, leading me to believe that my early "segregated" educational experience was crucial. Many Black educators both here and in the United States are coming to the realization that chasing after the "integrationist" dream was a dismal failure. This is why Black-focused schools have been proposed in Toronto, to great public outcry as a form of reverse racism. However, these educators are trying to address the tragedy of high dropout rates, streaming, etc., in creative ways that speak to the positive aspects of segregated Black schooling.

Buxton provided an excellent grounding for me in that it was there that I learned that somehow, some day, I would make an important contribution and make my community proud. Without it, I have to wonder how my life might have been different. It most certainly has been instrumental in the strong, positive racial identity that I have carried throughout my life, even in the days when the question of an African Canadian "experience" was unheard of, much less taken seriously by most Canadians. Ultimately, it has enabled me to come to terms with my racial being in a racist context in a far more effective way than if I had grown up in denial of whom I really was, something all too common for people growing up in predominantly white settings.

So you see why a seemingly innocent question like "Where are you *really* from?" evokes a very strong response in me. By asking it, you are unintentionally denying me what is rightfully mine — my

14

birthright, my heritage and my long-standing place in the Canadian mosaic. If nothing else, I hope that you have gone away with at least one message: if you see a Black person on the street, or if you are meeting someone for the first time, don't assume that he or she comes from some other country. They might just be someone like me, who is sick and tired of being assumed to be an immigrant. If you are bold and brazen enough to ask the impolitic question, and they tell you they're Canadian, trust that they know their own background better than you, a perfect stranger. Even those who have come from other countries get tired of being constantly asked the question, as if they have just stepped "off the boat." The President of the Canadian Advisory Council on the Status of Women, Jamaican-born Dr. Glenda Simms, remarked in a speech at a Women's Forum that she too was tired of this "immigrant" label that people want to slap on her at all costs. "We have to deconstruct these labels, stop hanging on to being 'immigrant women,' stop buying into the hierarchy of the oppressed and be proud Canadian citizens," she boldly told her audience.

In one of the many encounters around my origins, I had an exchange with a Guatemalan Canadian who had asked me "the question" at a streetcar stop one evening. On that occasion, I argued with him because of his insistence that I could not be a Canadian. In the end, however, he had the last word on the matter. "Except for the Native people," he stated, "the rest of us are just immigrants anyway." I couldn't argue with that!

BUT WHAT IS YOUR NATIONALITY?

SUSAN JUDITH SHIP

Like most other English-speaking Jews in Montréal, I had very little contact with francophone Québécois in my formative years. The linguistic divide was, and still remains, a geographic divide. Anglophones live in the west end of Montréal and francophones live in the east of Montréal. Most of what I knew about the francophone Québécois, then, came largely from my parents, who never missed an opportunity to remind us of the rampant anti-Semitism of the French and the English in the 1930s and 1940s in Québec. My mother always told me, "Just remember, in the final analysis, they will always call you a dirty Jew. And if they don't say it, they are thinking it."

I never really believed my mother. Or perhaps, I did not want to. I understood her fears, eminently justifiable, in the light of her experiences in Québec and the experiences of our family in Europe. But as I grew up in the Trudeau era in the large multicultural neighbourhoods of Côte des Neiges and Park Extension in anglophone Montréal, it seemed to me that the days of blatant anti-Semitism were precisely that: a regrettable part of our history, but history, nonetheless. The only time I had ever been called a dirty Jew was by an older boy at school; his father was a Nazi sympathizer. Gone were the days of discriminatory laws, quota systems and restrictive immigration policy designed to limit the Jewish presence and our full integration. Multiculturalism defined both my experience and my frame of reference and that, after all, is what it means to be Canadian.

The anti-Semitism of the francophone Québécois never seemed as malevolent as that of the English community. It was almost understandable. The French had been dominated for centuries by an English community that had always held economic and political power in Québec and in Canada. Most immigrant groups, certainly white Europeans, became upwardly socially mobile more rapidly than the francophones. Jewish shopkeepers, landlords, businessmen and professionals were the immediate competition for francophone Québécois and often their first and only contact with "Anglo" exploiters. As in the case of the Anglo community, much of the overt francophone anti-Semitism against Jews in Québec disappeared during the 1960s.

I cheered when the Parti Québécois came to power, although I felt a certain uneasiness. If historical experiences tell us anything, nationalism invariably seems to end up as racism and fascism. But it seemed to me that the Parti Québécois commitment to a social democratic platform would vitiate the potentially negative consequences of Québécois nationalism. And perhaps more importantly, unlike the old French-Canadian nationalism, the Parti Québécois wanted to include "les autres" (the others) in their "projet de société."

Contemporary Québécois nationalism and the new Québec are unquestionably more open and tolerant. However, it soon became clear that even in the New Québec, as an anglophone Jew born here, I am still an "other" for many Québécois. That sense of being an outsider is, at the same time, much more subtle and insidious now than it was when my mother was growing up. The dismantling of most forms of active discrimination against Jews in Québec has given way to more refined forms of exclusion and the social construction of "otherness."

My experience has been less one of outright hostility, rejection or exclusion, although that is not the case for the ultra-religious Hassidic Jewish community, whose relations with francophone Québécois have become increasingly acrimonious. I can't ever recall being called a "maudit juif," but old stereotypes about Jews die hard. "All Jews are wealthy and live in Westmount." "All Jews are cheap." "You are not like the rest of them." Repeated encounters with enduring stereotypes about Jews in everyday experience and speech serve as a continual reminder and reaffirmation of "otherness."

The reaffirmation of "otherness" is also conveyed in everyday experience and in the language of exclusion embodied in the collective representations of "us" and "them" that underpin the politics of national identity in Québec. I was enrolled as a student in the political

18

science department at the Université du Québec à Montréal in the early 1980s, and I can recall a heated discussion on the topic of immigrants and French language usage in Québec in one of my classes. The professor, a very sympathetic and open person, did her best to explain the complexities and difficulties of integration that newcomers to Québec face. I cannot fault her. However, in typically Québécois fashion, the terms "us" and "them" — "nous et les autres" — were bandied about. I suddenly wondered, as an anglophone Jew born in Québec, where am I in all of this?

That question was soon to be answered for me. When I was taking a course on Québec-Canada relations, Louise Harel, the Parti Québécois MNA and long-time ardent *indépendantiste,* came to our class to speak about the strategy of creating a federal wing of the Parti Québécois. While listening to her speak, I began to notice that she was directing most of her remarks to the right side of the lecture hall and rarely to the side where I was sitting. I wondered why she was ignoring our section of the room. When I looked around I saw that all the students of African, Haitian and North African origins were sitting together — with me — to her left. The message from her non-verbal behaviour and body language reinforced the growing discomfort I already felt. I understood. We were not "Québécois," but "les autres — les Noirs, les Arabes, les Juifs et les Anglais" — and we weren't really a part of their political project.

The issue of who is Québécois/e came up one day during a coffee break in the cafeteria, prompted by one of the African students at the table. I turned to the young Québécois woman sitting next to me and said, "I study at a French university, I listen to French radio, I watch the news in French, I go to French films, I have Québécois friends and my significant other is a francophone. Am I Québécois?" Without hesitation, she said, "No." I asked her, "Why am I not Québécois? What is Québécois culture?" She said that she really didn't know, but perhaps she didn't want to tell me.

I felt angry and hurt, if not betrayed by the new nationalism of the Parti Québécois, which, for me, at that moment, began to oddly resemble the old inward-looking French-Canadian nationalism. If the defining features of "la nation québécoise" are linguistic and cultural, that is, the French language and the French culture, then why am I not considered to be Québécoise? What does it really mean to be Québécoise anyway? Perhaps, it is the Myth of Origins.

A number of years ago, I was helping a friend move into a new apartment in the Parc Lafontaine area. The owner of the building, a

19

congenial sixty-five-year-old Québécois woman, was in the apartment at the time, making some repairs. We struck up a conversation. She asked me what my nationality was. Somewhat surprised, I said to her, "I was born in Québec as you were." "But what is your nationality?" she asked insistently. "I'm Québécoise, like you. I was born here," I replied. Changing her approach, she said, "You must speak many languages." "No, not really, I only speak English and French, like you," I said to her. Then she said, "Well, where were your parents born?"

Nationality, as I have always understood it, refers to formal-legal citizenship rights that are accorded by virtue of being born in a particular country or through the process of naturalization. In retrospect, I realize what the good woman meant. I speak French with a funny accent and I don't have blond hair and blue eyes. I don't look Nordic or Norman. Therefore I'm not "francophone de vieille souche," or Anglo-Saxon. I don't belong to either of the "two founding nations"; therefore, I must be in that "other" category—the eternal immigrant.

This woman is not alone in her ideas of nation and nationality. I cannot count all the times I have been asked by people, "Where were you born?" What is it about my appearance or manner of speech that gives the impression I was not born here? What is someone who was born here supposed to look like and act like? It makes me wonder about some not-so-subtle underlying physical and cultural criteria which define someone who is "of here" and "not of here."

Recently, *La Presse* ran a series of articles on the evolution of the Jewish community in Québec. The articles were informative, well-documented and positive in perspective. They bore none of the traces of the anti-Semitism of Lionel Groulx's Québec, which Mordecai Richler continues to see everywhere. Rather, they revealed the significant changes that have taken place in the status of the Jewish community in Québec and in its relations with the larger francophone society, which Mordecai Richler also ignores. Yet I still found myself disturbed by the articles. The Jewish presence in Québec dates back to 1738, the oldest synagogue in North America is in Montréal, yet they still speak of "les Québécois et les Juifs." At what point do we cease to be outsiders in the country where we were born or choose to live?

Everyday terms to distinguish Quebeckers such as "Québécois pure laine" or "Québécois de vieille souche," on the one hand, and "Québécois de nouvelle souche," "néo-Québécois," Jews or Blacks on the other hand, serve as continual reminders to those of us who are not of French or British Isles origins of our status as outsiders. The language of exclusion and inclusion is deeply embedded, not only in everyday speech and popular culture but also in the formal legal-political discourse.

Identifying social groups in terms of "nations" and "ethnic groups" or "cultural communities" is not simply about preserving cultural differences, the affirmation of the right to be different or the demarcation of the socio-cultural boundaries between groups. It also is a means of structuring and legitimating unequal power relations between groups, of creating and maintaining an operative ethnic and racial hierarchy. Formal political labels that distinguish social categories of citizens, developed by academics and government officials and enshrined in policy, carry with them attendant rights and privileges, establishing a hierarchy of belonging.

I was born in Québec and my roots are here, too. I am tired of being referred to as an ethnic minority. I am tired of being referred to as a cultural community. I do not want to be integrated as a member of a minority whose rights need to be protected. When do I cease to be a member of a cultural community? How many generations do I need to count back? What cultural characteristics do I have to acquire? When do I cease to be a Jew and become Québécoise?

If the new Québec nationalism is, as Daniel Latouche and Louis Balthazar assert, no longer an ethnic nationalism but a civic nationalism, then the prevailing concept of Québécois national identity will also have to be redefined to accommodate an increasingly multiethnic and multiracial society and policy. I, too, will have to be accepted as Québécois/e "à part entière," with my funny French accent, my Semitic face and my Anglo-American, East European Jewish and French cultural heritages. For this is also what it means to be Québécois/e.

That transformation of Québécois national identity has yet to begin. If the experience of Canadian multiculturalism can serve as a reliable guide, the transition to a widely accepted pluralistic concept of national identity will be a long, conflict-laden process.

The current moment in Québec is a critical one. Economic crisis has brought old fears to the surface yet again. Anti-Semitic and racist incidents have become more commonplace. Prominent Québécois politicians and journalists have voiced anxieties over Québécois collective identity. The resurgence of renewed hostility towards immigrants, particularly from Asia, Africa, the Caribbean, the Middle East and Latin America, coupled with the growing perception that these groups constitute a threat to social peace and Québécois cultural survival, resonates with a familiar distaste. It was not that long ago when the Jewish community in Québec and elsewhere in Canada was the prime target of right-wing reaction. They said we took their jobs and we were culturally unassimilable. The arguments remain the same, only the scapegoats change. If historical experiences tell us anything, the collective task of redefining our identity is but the first step in creating a more egalitarian and open society.

QUÉBÉCITUDE
AN AMBIGUOUS IDENTITY
••••••••••••••••••••
GUY BÉDARD

Accepter de réflichir sur les ressorts qui sont à l'origine de notre iden-
tité, c'est déjà un peu admettre que celle-ci est une construction de
l'esprit. À tout le moins, c'est reconnaître que ce qui va de soi, ce qui
semble appartenir à l'éternité, être déterminé par les conditions ob-
jectives d'existence des individus ou à l'évolution historique des col-
lectivités, a encore besoin de l'apport de la raison pour voir clairment
le jour. C'est aussi une manière d'échapper aux idées qui façonnent
notre être, s'expatrier de soi-même.

All identities are a construction of mind. The emergence of the
Québécois identity is a perfect example. Even though I readily subscribe to this identity, I must admit that, on a philosophical level, I
still have difficulty grasping the concept of Québécois identity and
how it is constructed. Through my life history and experiences, therefore, I want to explore this identity and how, at this stage in Québec's
history, it has become increasingly inconsistent and contradictory for
me.

For as long as I can remember, I have never identified myself as
other than Québécois. And yet, it is only recently that the term has
even appeared in the dictionary. Prior to the 1960s, I would have said
that I was French Canadian. In so doing, I would be defining myself
first and foremost as a French-speaking Catholic, and therefore as a

member of a community whose demographic boundaries extend beyond the borders of the province of Québec. My reading of Québec history also tells me that in another era I would have called myself *Canadien*, but in a particular way which most Canadians today would be completely unable to imagine. Up until the middle of the nineteenth century, the term "Canadian" referred almost exclusively to the descendants of the French colonists. (Jacques Cartier used the word "Kanada" to identify the Aboriginal peoples who lived in the St. Lawrence Valley. Shortly thereafter, it came to signify the inhabitants of French origin born in the colony.) Others preferred to call themselves British subjects: Irish, Welsh, Scottish and English. So how did the term "Québécois" come about? And why do I feel that I must now identify myself as a Québécois? No book has ever explained this to me.

To be honest, there was a time when I would never have called myself Québécois. This was during my childhood, when the parameters of my universe did not extend beyond family, the part of the street where we lived, the route I took to school, and the friends I made. After this early period, everything turned upside down.

Three incidents stand out in my mind: the parade down chemin du Roy when Charles de Gaulle travelled the historic route down the St. Lawrence River linking Montréal and Québec in the days of New France (this happened prior to the now-famous *Vive le Québec libre!* speech), a visit to Expo '67, and reading *White Niggers of America* by Pierre Vallières.

I was nine years old at the time of the first two events. I barely remember de Gaulle's visit. However, I do remember that my parents were very proud to have been there when de Gaulle passed through Québec City. This feeling, and perhaps the crowd's enthusiasm, as well as the obvious interest of my parents in all that spoke of our heritage, contributed to shaping a constant, but not well-defined, identity: an attachment to my roots, to my origins and to my ancestors.

The second event is much fresher in my memory; it also reveals the ambiguous character of my early identity. Leaving Québec City to visit Expo '67 in Montréal, I was to discover another country, a foreign land that allowed me to recognize my own. This was not China, or the USSR or Great Britain, or any of the countries that had built pavilions on Île Sainte-Hélène, where the international exposition took place. This was simply Montréal, the metropolitan centre. At nine years old, my sense of geography and space was still quite limited. The never-ending voyage, the turbulence and feverishness of a big city were impressive. At the very least, the distance that separated the two cities, as much a function of their differing lifestyles as the number of kilometres one had to travel between them, was enough to impress upon me the idea of difference. There existed a country called Québec (without a doubt, to avoid confusion, others called it Québec City) to which I identified and belonged. I became Québécois in the sense that I certainly was not Montréalais.

In retrospect, this anecdote might seem rather insignificant, the simple manifestation of the fertile imagination of a nine-year-old and his ignorance of the basics of geography. However, on further reflection, it brings out the ambiguous and changing character of Québécois identity. The increasing uneasiness that I feel each time I hear nationalists say *Le Québec aux Québécois* illustrates this in yet another way. In adhering to this battle-cry, some *indépendantistes* are necessarily forced to admit that there are certain individuals whose status as residents of Québec is not enough to qualify them as Québécois. Therefore, they adopt a logic of exclusion. But this is not what bothers me most. Is there an identity or a way of thinking that is not ultimately exclusionary? After all, those who call themselves Canadian do not treat other peoples of the world any differently. No! What profoundly embarrasses me about this slogan *Québec aux Québécois* is that it forces me to choose between a territorial concept of Québécois citizenship — a perspective which, let us remember, is defended by a good number of *indépendantistes* — and an ethnic definition of Québécitude based on race, culture and language: social markers for exclusion.

Somehow, I know that to say Québécois presupposes race, culture and language, or at least one of these elements. It implies that we need to find affinities with a group, a community. There would not be so much commotion about Québécois identity if we were living, as some *indépendantistes* insist, in a "normal country" — that is, an independent state. In other words, there would not be this dichotomy if Québec were independent. At least, the racism or xenophobia of this ethnic definition of Québécois identity would be completely clear. The problem is that, as things stand, there is a lot of confusion in this respect: it is often difficult to distinguish between the simple act of self-affirmation and racism.

Nor is the territorial criterion of Québécitude sufficient for me. After we agree on the boundaries of the territory concerned, we must then establish a full and complete definition of Québécois citizenship. Using ethnicity as a basis for identifying oneself as Québécois is too

25

dependent on the way each one of us envisages the criteria, and on our individual life histories and experiences. Imagine for a moment if I had kept the vision of Québec that I had when I was nine years old, and you get a sense of the breadth of perspectives on this issue.

For me, the real *prise de conscience* came when I was twelve. During his stay in prison, Pierre Vallières, the presumed head of the *Front de Liberation du Québec (FLQ)*, wrote a book about his childhood and adolescence, *White Niggers of America*. Vallières made me aware of a whole world of oppression, of the *porteurs d'eau*, the francophone proletarians of Montréal subjected to the "Speak White" dictates of the anglophone bourgeoisie. For the first time I realized that this city, Montréal, was also mine, was in some small way my home too. Oh! To be sure, there were enormous differences with Québec City: ninety-five percent of the population in the latter is francophone; the English presence is insignificant. But what Vallières described closely resembled my father's life. He had to quit school at the age of ten. He sweated for English bosses who couldn't be bothered to communicate with him in French. I couldn't help but notice that in one of the factories where my father worked for several years and where the overwhelming majority of employees spoke only French, signs were exclusively in English.

I do not know if this vision of my father's lived experiences is totally accurate; it may have been distorted and exaggerated by the eyes of the child that I was. However, it was enough for me to accept Vallières' vision of the world: *Vive le Québec libre!* and socialist to boot. The history books took care of the rest. They recounted a long series of events that marked the relations between the francophone and anglophone communities of Canada: the deportation of the Acadians, the English Conquest, the hanging of Louis Riel and the crushing of the francophone Métis rebellion in western Canada; the implementation of laws at the turn of the twentieth century prohibiting the teaching of French in schools in the other Canadian provinces, and so forth.

I felt that I belonged to an oppressed and persecuted people. I had the impression that the others, the anglophones with whom I had no contact other than what I read in books, were constantly seeking to annihilate the group to which I identified and belonged. The demographic decline of francophone communities outside Québec was ample proof.

And yet, these beliefs never fully rang true for me. To hold onto this perception of being an oppressed and persecuted minority, I had to appeal to experiences which frankly were foreign to me, that came from a history I had never personally experienced. I was a child of the Quiet Revolution; I lived in an era when the use of French was more prevalent than at any time since the Conquest. From this point of view, outside of Montréal, you could say that Québec has been reconquered. Since moving to the metropolitan centre of Québec — Montréal — I can see that French is well-entrenched here, too. The threat of assimilation has been reduced to the point where it is no longer feared. And if there is still oppression, it certainly does not manifest itself in the same way. Through the years, the Québec state has encouraged the emergence of a francophone bourgeoisie that knows how to exploit the country's natural resources as well as anyone. So why do I still have the desire to call myself Québécois?

It is perhaps the force of collective habit and the pressure of institutions. In thirty years, the term "Québécois" has become common usage. First affirmed by the poets, novelists, playwrights and *chansonniers*, the term is today used by virtually everyone. The media are its foremost proponents, where even the news coverage is influenced by its implications (everything that happens outside Québec gives the appearance of being somewhat foreign). Governments have also adopted it. I cannot think of a single politician who would dare not use the term. Even the members of the communities called anglophone and allophone now demand to be included in that so-named collectivity. The term is celebrated, emphasized, displayed and asserted.

However, this is not the only vision or perspective of the world here. As in all Western societies, identity has become considerably more complex and dynamic, crossing many boundaries. Certainly, the rise of advanced communication and technology has given birth to the concept of a global village. Moreover, I frequently have the impression that I have more in common with intellectuals in London, New York or Bangkok than with Québec workers or the convenience store owner in my own neighbourhood. To invoke the weight of habit or the power of institutions to explain why I identify myself as Québécois seems unsatisfying. It is to forget that this identity is in competition with other identities.

I do not know precisely what it is that makes me Québécois. All I know is that occasionally I feel as foreign in Paris or Toronto as in Amman, when the chanting from the mosques fills the small hours of the morning. It is difficult to understand. However, a number of events in the history of the Québécois community resulted in the

27

construction of a "collective imagination" that distinguishes this community from others, defining it vis-à-vis the rest of the world, whereby my diverse personal experiences have imprinted this "imagination" in my mind. In short, apart from the historical and cultural specificities, the process by which a Québécois identity was born is not much different from the formation of other community identities around the globe.

I WANT TO CALL MYSELF CANADIAN
KATALIN SZEPESI

I want to call myself Canadian, but I'm not allowed. My name is Hungarian by origin so therefore I am Hungarian. It doesn't matter that on my mother's side I'm seventh-generation Canadian and before that our family came from Great Britain. It doesn't matter that I can't speak Hungarian and have only a marginal understanding of the culture. It doesn't matter that I was born and raised in Canada. It doesn't even matter that I'm white. Katalin Szepesi is not a Canadian name, so Katalin Szepesi will never be a Canadian.

My cousins on my mother's side are Canadian. They have last names like Moreton and Thompson. People can spell and pronounce their names on first hearing, unlike my foreign name. Sometimes they call me Cathy. If my name was Cathy I could be Canadian as long as I didn't tell anyone my last name. I would also have the hope of becoming a full-fledged Canadian if I married a white person with an Anglo-Saxon name. My husband could have been born and raised in another country, but if he had an Anglo name then I would get my status.

My brother's name is Stan and my sister's name is Esther. Most people don't bother learning their last name since it's too much of an unnecessary challenge. However, both of my names are Hungarian so I am forced to identify with my Hungarian heritage. My mannerisms have become more Hungarian than those of my brother or my sister. Others have made me who I am.

White adult immigrants will never be Canadian because they will retain their accents. Accents are frowned upon in Canada unless they are British or Australian — then they are considered sexy.

However, if immigrant parents are white, they will still need to change their names if they want their kids to inherit the title of Canadian. As long as "ski" is at the end of a name, that person will always be considered Polish.

Native peoples don't want the title Canadian. Blacks and Asians will never achieve it. If being a true Canadian is being British and bigoted, then I'm glad that true Canadians are becoming a minority in this multicultural society.

HELLO . . . MY NAME IS . . .
KATALIN SZEPESI

Longing for it
not to happen
ONE MORE TIME.

And what's your name?

Wrinkled nose, puzzled eyes.
I must repeat.
Spelling not helpful.
Nationality then requested
to excuse the unintended butchery.
Comparing my identity
to objects and places
for the sake of memory.

Next, considered *interesting, different*
and sometimes *pretty*.

Last name not attempted.
Too difficult, not necessary.

PART 2
GROWING UP

MY MOTHER USED TO DANCE
VALERIE BEDASSIGAE PHEASANT

She was graceful and light. Her movements made the room disappear. There was only her. Every shift and swirl of her warp caused the air to move so that I could see the patterns in the air. I looked at her face. It was my mother's face, but it was possessed by a spirit that I had not seen before. She kept moving, without touching the floor. She smiled and danced. Her face radiated — my mother was free.

I sat on the banister railing for what felt like an eternity watching my mother. As silently as I crept to watch, I left. I wondered why she did not dance for us. That was the first and only time I saw my mother dance with abandon. What I did see was a gradual freezing of her emotions and a treacherous walk with silence. Her metamorphosis had happened before our eyes and we were unable to stop it. Why didn't she yell at them? Why didn't she tell them — no? Where did the fire go? When was it that the dancing stopped?

The cocoon that encased my mother was woven by inside thoughts that constricted her more strongly than anything tangible in the human world. Inside thoughts reacting to outside action generated towards our family's Nativeness. Blatant racist remarks and statements by women who did not care to know us. Each word, each comment diminished her capacity to speak — she moved slower and slower.

I went with her to different places. What I saw fuelled my anger. My anger was directed towards my mother in the beginning, because I could not measure her resistance. It was a strange relationship. We walked together, each of us trying to recognize and locate our safe space. There was none. Not there.

My mother liked to play Bingo at the church hall occasionally. I went with her. She paid our admission, and sometimes she bought us pop and chips. All expensive. On occasion we won. It was nearing Christmas and our hopes were high. It was hard to find seats. We found some. We looked around at the other women at the table. Nobody said hello. They looked and I looked back. My mother sat down and arranged the cards. We sat and waited. The other women talked amongst themselves in what resembled a huddle. They glanced furtively in our direction. We sat and waited—I watched. Whispers. Whispers coming from the huddle. Whispers that called out, too loud, clanging around in my ears, "Smells like Indians!" Instinctively, I breathed in deeply. Did they mean us? I could see them staring at us. My mother's head was down. Tears? I looked back at them. I knew it was us. We moved to another table. We do not speak about what was said about us. We do not recognize them. We cannot give them more power. My anger grows. My mother's spirit staggers.

My education began years before and was not always confined to the classroom. The real lessons took place outside the classroom—in this case, right outside its door. I have to accompany my mother to the school for parent-teacher interviews. We go from teacher to teacher. My mother glances at the report cards and listens to the teacher pass information to her about her children. Each in succession. We are almost finished. It is time for her to see the grade three teacher. I am instructed to wait outside the door. My mother is alone. In the stillness I can hear everything that my mother hears. I am afraid to move. The voice grows loud in my ears, telling her that her son doesn't know what to do. How can he pass? He has trouble reading. The voice grows louder, trying to convince her. I hear no response. Pages are being torn out of a workbook. The voice burns in our ears ... "He cheated. He could not have done this. This work will not count!" More pages being ripped. I feel the shame and the guilt. It grows quiet. A chair moves. The door opens. My mother walks out. I am waiting. I see the humiliation and the pain. My anger ignites, recedes and begins to smoulder. My mother is exhausted. We go to the next teacher.

More pressure is put on the older children to help the younger ones with their homework. We do it because we cannot allow people to think that we are "stupid Indians." I detest these people I do not know. How can they make a judgment about Native people without knowing or caring to know about us — judgments made in ignorance. I decided that someday I would tell them about things they did not want to hear, about things they were afraid to ask. I decided to talk back. There was nothing to lose. People hated us anyway.

We went on in a continuing fashion. My mother's walk slowed down. She stopped going out. When she did, it was with reluctance. I was cautioned to be quiet. I could, I might, get hurt. What did it matter? The hurt was not going to stop by itself. The hurt fuelled my anger. It grew inside me. I liked how it felt — powerful — but it was a power I instinctively knew would eat my spirit and leave me empty. My mother knew it too. We did not speak about it. I went out and she stayed inside.

I played with the idea of dropping out of school, but I wanted a good job. I wanted to have money. I wanted to have purchasing power. I was tired of watching my mother eat last. I stayed in school. My education continued. All the while I dreamed of leaving the small, ugly mining town that was teaching me. It taught me that if your father did not work for the single industry with the corporate monopoly, you were excluded from certain places. The income of your family categorized you as "rich," "not-poor" or "poor." If you excelled at something — anything — then others would make sure that it did not happen again. And I was also taught that girls were liked better when "they put out."

We were all working-class kids in a working-class high school. All subject to the rules, but for a few of us, there were more rules with unrealistic demands. I hated the rules and hated the kids that exalted "the mine." They fantasized about the money, the women, the cars, the notoriety, the shift work, the money, the holidays, the wife, the husband, the house, the kids, the, the, the, the. I hated the fatalism. Didn't they know there was more than the "mine," more to live for? Didn't they want to be free to see new places, meet new people? I hated them. I saw the trap. My fire raged.

My journey began to be a lonely one. I went on, unsure of my destination but knowing that my spirit was strong, that it would lead me. Without being given specific instruction, I had to walk through that raging fire. How? With what? I was afraid. I was unsure of when. It was foolish of me to worry. I had to keep on. As children we are taught that "You will know when it is time. Make sure you are ready." I was confused about how to get ready, but my spirit would be guided. The nurturing of my spirit began when I was born. In subtle,

37

sure and gentle ways, my family—mother, father, grandmother, grandfathers, aunties, brothers, sisters and cousins—gave. As my journey took me out of immediate contact with them, we met through other people we knew. I was still getting ready. You cannot measure time when "getting ready" is taking place. (Do not confuse this with preparation, which is structure.)

I went along. Times were becoming more confusing. Instructors of psychology and English wanted to know about my "fixation" with my mother. Why, they inquired, did I feel so loyal to her? Why couldn't I let go? Why did I feel obligated to her? Confusion. Static in my brain. Did I know I looked Oriental—not (gasp) Indian. Oh, your father is only half . . . (relief). But you read that aloud so well. So what do Indians do at home? Was your mom born in the bush? Bingo players—all of them. I watched and listened. These comments were petty and stupid. I would not waste my talk on them. Fuel for the fire or energy for my spirit, I did not know which.

I continued in formal education. A change would occur in desks only, from the student's desk to the teacher's desk. I was still learning. Teachers' College reinforced the knowledge that the classroom did not reflect society; did not reflect the values of all families; did not utilize stories of women and stories of non-white people; evaluated from one perspective only; did not justify our existence; perfected exclusion. I was inside, but inside what? Why was I here? Who was I walking with and where were we going? I allowed myself to be led. I questioned without articulating the words. I slowed down but did not stop. The assault on my spirit continued. Words. Words that burned me. Words that festered and left wide scars. From the Masters, more words. . . . Did I really think that I belonged at Teachers' College? Did I really think that I would pass? Did I really think that practice teaching in a Native school was a good idea? Did I really think I would get a job? I could feel my anger blazing, almost out of control. I was choking.

My mother telephoned the week before exams and asked when I was coming home. I went home for the weekend. After that I decided that I would hitchhike to the college and stay in Sudbury with a friend. The week's tests that followed were not in the written examinations, but in me. Each day I ventured out. Each day I wrote my examinations. Each day I was tempted to quit.

On the day after examinations, I caught a ride with a man travelling out West. It was a hot, clear day. He tried to make conversation. I was too tired to speak. We travelled along in silence. The car moved.

It seemed like the wheels were not on the ground. We were skimming along. The driver kept glancing at me. I moved close to the door and found the handle — looked directly at him. He watched the highway. My head began to dip and my eyes closed, but I was awake. I checked around the car. My eyes opened and I began to hear my name being called. I looked towards the driver. He was quiet, still looking awkwardly in my direction. No words were exchanged. I saw fear in his eyes. He looked back at the highway. We drove on in silence. The voice was calling. It was clear now. I wanted to sleep. If only I could close my eyes. "VALERIE! . . . VALERIE! STAY AWAKE. . . . LISTEN TO ME!" the voice demanded. I looked out the window. Something was outside, moving alongside us. I could sense its power. It was connected to me. The voice called me again. It was talking, soothing me, guiding me, warning me, containing me. From the other side of the car, the man was asking, "Are you alright? Do you want me to stop?" I could smell his sweat and hear the fear in his voice. I looked in his direction, my flames reached out to touch him. He became quiet and drove on, careful not to excite the flame with his breath. Outside the car, still beside us, the woman's voice familiar from the womb was again speaking to me. I talked back without words. My mother told me not to be afraid. I passed through the fire.

Parent-teacher interviews for my daughter. I go alone. I am afraid. Each time, I am afraid. I recognize the fear — we have met before. Now I am the mother. There is no child outside the door. I will not let her come along. The meeting is between adults — both trained in the same Bingo Palace. Only this time one of us refuses to be a player.

We meet. Cordial greeting. Forced pleasantries. I am asked what the problem is. Why is it that your daughter will not participate? Why does she think she can get away with this? How come she didn't finish her project on the family unit? I cut in. I willed my voice to an even tone. There are explosions in my brain. I refuse to have this woman speak to me in a condescending fashion. I inquire about my daughter's lack of participation; about the model of family structure that is being recognized and rewarded in class. Ours does not fit the mould. I explain. My words are vaporized. I ask about forms of resistance being demonstrated by other girls. None. I ask about the manner in which questions are directed at my daughter. The teacher's voice rises by several decibels. She yells, " I am sick and tired of hearing Athena this and Athena that. She is not that special. What's all the fuss about?"

I breathe in. I stare in disbelief. I refuse to accept the blame, and feel the guilt and shame this woman, this teacher, is trying to place on me. Sparks are flying. I must remain in control. I refuse to speak. I can only stare. She stops to catch her breath. She demands to show me her proof. I move the chair and stand up. She steps back. I look at her with disgust. I start towards the door. She yells out at me, "I am not finished yet!" I am overwhelmed by her bile. I begin to smile, the images of long ago play themselves out, and the anger subsides. The spectre of my younger self shadowed in the doorway looks on, lips up-turned and eyes strong and steady. I turn and distinctly reply, "Yes, but I am." My smile grows. I walk out on shaky legs. Somewhere music — and my spirit starts to dance.

Tears? Yes, there are tears. I cry for my mother, myself and my daughter. I cry because our children's spirits are still being assault-ed — not educated. My tears (I am reminded) are good. They help us to heal. They return to Mother Earth. They cleanse us, help us grow.

My anger is still in me. It is mine. I earned it. I share it. It belongs to all of us, collectively. The forces of religion, education, society, the judiciary, the media, make it a real, everyday occurrence. At times I do not realize there is a difference between being happy, being angry and being alive. I have had to make friends with anger. We are togeth-er when people continue to say — you sound so angry when you speak about the education system. Yes I am, because it continues to perpet-uate inaccuracies. I am angry when Aboriginal Peoples are labelled "Indians." I am angry when a person is devalued by the colour of their skin. Yes I am, when children are victimized. Yes I am, when I am patronized. Yes I am, when teachers continue to tell us that we were discovered out of our own savage chasm of non-sentience. Yes, I am angry when people are silenced. Yes I am, when people try to use me to justify their theories. Yes, I am angry.

Who says we can't dance? "Whoever pays the piper, calls the tune" — well — we've paid the piper for half a millennium. It's time to call the tune. It's time to dance.

ZEBRA
GROWING UP BLACK AND WHITE IN CANADA
••••••••••••••••••••••••
LAWRENCE HILL

> Eenie meenie minie moe
> Catch a nigger by the toe
> If he hollers let him go
> Eenie meenie minie moe
>
> — school yard rhyme

The White, churchgoing people of my neighbourhood may have supposed that I, having atheists for parents, revelled in freedom from the burden of Commandments. Not so. We had two.

Under the roof of my parents, the Penultimate Commandment posed no constraints on my life. I had no reason to violate it. It was: *Thou shalt not utter the word nigger.* The Ultimate Commandment, however, caused me great anxiety over the years. It was: *Thou shalt not fail to rain the fury of hell upon anyone uttering the said word.*

As the light-skinned son of a Black man and a White woman, I felt safe from the word *nigger* during my boyhood. Nobody aimed it at me, in my first ten years. And when I did hear it used generally, I did not feel singled out. Somehow, it didn't apply to me. I recognized it as an attack on a whole race of people — including my father, his parents and their ancestors. But years would pass before I saw myself as belonging to that race.

41

Nevertheless, I understood the Ultimate Commandment at an early age. I remember standing nervously in a school yard during the spring of my second grade, while classmates were about to determine who would be "it" to start a tag game.

I knew how their rhyme went. I knew it couldn't go unchallenged. But the prospect of losing new friends terrified me. So I jumped in to recite it myself, changing one key word as my parents had suggested:

Eenie meenie minie moe
Catch a tiger by the toe
If he hollers let him go
Eenie meenie minie moe.

Again and again in the following years, I sanitized that rhyme before the offending word could be spoken, secretly grateful for the chance to avoid confrontation.

People rarely called me *nigger*. But the word had a way of vaulting into conversation at times when nobody—not even I—was conscious of the racial difference between my White friends and me. I would object to the word, but that drew attention to my own racial identity—something I would take years to define.

In the 1920s, Langston Hughes wrote "Cross." It began:

My old man's a white old man,
And my old mother's black . . .

and ended:

My old man died in a fine big house,
My ma died in a shack.
I wonder where I'm gonna die,
Being neither white nor black.

I first read "Cross" as a young teenager, and identified with the lament of the young man with no clear fix on whom he was. I still love the poem. But now I see in it an irony that Hughes must have recognized: although the narrator didn't know where he would die, he couldn't have had any doubt where he would be buried—in a cemetery for Blacks.

In the United States—the country of my paternal great-great-grandfather, who was born a slave—anyone known to have any African ancestry has been defined as Black. In the past, that definition stuck for the purposes of slavery and segregation. Today, it still holds true for subtler forms of discrimination. Where many of my relatives live—New York City, Washington D.C., Baltimore and North Carolina—Americans are accustomed to noting slight traces of African heritage. People as light-skinned as I am are frequently identified as Blacks.

Not so in Canada. Certainly not in Don Mills, Ontario, where I grew up from 1960 to 1975. Most people assumed I was White. Some Blacks thought so too. In 1975, for example, I had a summer job washing floors at Sunnybrook Hospital in North York. Most of my co-workers were Caribbean immigrants. One day, in the locker room, I told one of them that my father was Black. He said I was lying. I showed him a photograph. By the next shift, every West Indian in the hospital knew who I was.

"My father is Black." That's quite different from saying, "I am Black." I thought of myself as Black at the hospital. I usually thought of myself that way in the company of Blacks. But in the locker room of the hospital, surrounded by dark-skinned West Indians, I didn't say it outright. Imagine the laughter. *Hey, George, do you hear what this man's saying?* So I eased in the back door. By saying "My father is Black," I was saying "Decide for yourself what that makes me."

Why did I lack the confidence to call myself Black?

Part of it had to do with growing up in neighbourhoods, attending schools and competing on sports teams in which I was usually the only person of colour — and my colour, such as it was, generally went un-remarked. On the whole, White people paid little attention to my racial background, and I tended not to think about it as I played and studied. I saw myself as the same as the White people who surrounded me.

On the other hand, sometimes I was proud of my Black ancestry. Such moments came when my parents drove us to visit relatives in Washington, D.C. I'll never forget playing tag in a park off Chain Bridge Road, wondering whether my cousins would accept me. Some of them were also light-skinned. That made me feel better. It gave me hope that they would see me as one of them. I remember noting that my mother seemed whiter than ever before. Still, she mingled easily with my Black relatives. They accepted her! Surely, I reasoned, they accepted me too!

Other moments of strong racial identification came in the intima-cy of our house. Hearing about Muhammed Ali and Martin Luther King, Jr. had something to do with that. So did welcoming Black friends of my parents. But the most powerful influence came from my father.

He pointed out Blacks wherever he saw them ("Larry! Did you see that Negro doctor?" or "Hey! A coloured bus driver!"). He had many contacts with Toronto's Black community.

43

My father never sat me down and said, "You are a Negro." He didn't tell me, or my brother or sister, what we were. He let us work it out for ourselves. He made only one type of reference to my race, and it was in jest. Occasionally he called me a zebra, which I thought quite funny. Within our family, it became a private expression for people of mixed race.

Living among and accepted by Whites, I often spent weeks at a time without thinking of myself as different or thinking at all about my own race. Yet when those moments of introspection took place, I thought of myself as Black—but only timidly. It was hard to see myself as Black when nobody else did.

At the age of fourteen, I entered a private high school so exclusively White that it made me more conscious—and proud—of my own background.

I joined a music class and decided to play the saxophone. But the teacher told me that Negroes lacked the correct facial structure to play the instrument properly. My first thought was, "I can't tell my dad about this because he'll storm into the headmaster's office and demand that the teacher be disciplined. Everybody will hear about it and I'll never live it down." I kept the incident to myself. I knew the teacher was an idiot, but he was my teacher, and it was my first week in school, and I didn't have the courage to argue with him, or to tell him that I had grown up listening to Black saxophonists such as Illinois Jacquet and Coleman Hawkins.

I merely insisted on taking up the saxophone. Unfortunately, though, I had puny lungs. No rhythm. And when I fought to hold long notes, my cheeks felt like they were stuffed full of gum. But I stuck with the instrument. I held on for a year, signing the sax out after school and dragging it home on the bus. I practised and practised to prove my teacher wrong. He gave me an average mark at the end of the year. I felt relieved to pass the course, and I never studied music again.

I began thinking much more about race. I wrote a short story, my first, about a Black youth who runs away from a bigoted North Carolina town with his White girlfriend. I wrote an essay about Langston Hughes. I began reading other Black literature—and it troubled me.

Soul on Ice, by Eldridge Cleaver, suggested that Black men sought White women only because they were forbidden fruit. Cleaver wrote powerfully. But he was unable to convince me that interracial relationships were inherently flawed. He couldn't rebut the protest rooted in my own upbringing—a protest that sprang to mind as I read his book: "But what if they LOVE each other?" *The Autobiography of Malcolm X* also fascinated and upset me. During his most militant phase, Malcolm X insisted that White people were devils. I rejected the idea outright. "How can he say that? My mother is White! She's no devil!"

In the summer of 1974, when I was seventeen, I travelled in Europe. In Belgium I saw signs posted outside night clubs saying "No Blacks" or "No North Africans" or "North Africans Must Be Accompanied By Women." The signs horrified me. But even more repugnant was the reaction of Belgian acquaintances, who defended the rules as necessary to prevent Blacks from acting up.

That same year, I took my mop of tangled curls to a Black hair stylist. I had worried about it for weeks in advance, uneasy about how the hair stylist would see me. Definitely not, I hoped, as some curly-haired White kid who thought an afro would look cool! Cliff, the stylist, was too professional to make me uncomfortable. He merely grumbled about the hour it took to untangle my mop, sold me a pick and sent me out with a modest afro.

At school, most people looked but said nothing. A few teachers said kind words about the new look. Only one student, whose name was David, gave me a hard time about it.

"Jesus, Larry, you look like a French poodle!"

"It's an afro. It's common among Blacks."

"Black! How can you say you're Black? You're not Black! You're barely darker than me!"

My mouth dropped, but I said nothing. The words made me burn with anger. They rang in my ears for weeks to come. I wanted to wrench out David's hair and yell: "Yes I am! Yes I am Black!" I wanted to scream that Blacks had been defined for centuries on the basis of their racial origin — something not necessarily emphasized by skin colour. I never did speak to David about it. But by challenging my racial identity, he helped drive me to a more insistent self-image. Periods of time still passed during which I gave no thought to race. But when I did, my thoughts turned to my own sense of Blackness.

In Canada or Europe, racism — even when directed at other people — reminded me that I was Black. Something else did that too. After I left home to study and work in other cities, people began asking, "What *are* you, anyway?"

In English Canada I heard this question only occasionally. But from 1978-80, when I studied in Quebec City, people asked me every week about my "national origin."

In the winter of my first year there, transit workers went on strike. I began hitchhiking daily from my bachelor suite on Cartier Avenue to Laval University. I found that Quebeckers readily picked up hitchhikers. I also discovered that they felt no compunction about grilling me about my racial origin. I must have had this exchange thirty times:

"Where are you from?"

"Toronto."

"You don't look like someone from Toronto."

"Well, I am."

"But what is your nationality?"

"Canadian."

"But where were you born?"

"Just outside Toronto."

"And your parents?"

"The United States."

"Ahh, the United States."

But still, they weren't satisfied, and wouldn't be unless I described my racial makeup, which I usually refused to do — not because I was ashamed of it, but because I resented that it was demanded of me.

In the summer of 1979, at the age of twenty-two, I spent two months in the West African country of Niger. I travelled with a group of six Quebeckers, as part of a cultural exchange that involved living with young people from Niger. Together, we planted trees to help protect fertile lands from the expanding Sahara desert.

I liked my fellow travellers. Today, twelve years later, three of them are still among my closest friends. But there was a time, shortly after my arrival in Niger, when I wanted nothing to do with them. Their presence made me feel White. And that summer, with an intensity that I had never anticipated, I wanted to be Black! Welcomed and loved as a brother.

I dove headlong into learning to speak Djerma. I ate and drank whatever was offered me. I held hands with African men, as is the custom there between male friends. Most people of Niger offered me great hospitality, but they appeared to see me as White. Before I could summon the nerve to tell people that I was one of them, I became sick. I was overtaken by vomiting, diarrhea and a fever that climbed out of sight. Hospitalization followed, and a blood transfusion, and days of intravenous feedings. I lost twenty pounds in a week.

My friends from Quebec slept on the floor by my hospital bed, carried me to the toilet, and fed me when I could eat again. They never left my side. I loved them and left the hospital a changed man.

I discovered that bringing my White friends into conversation with Africans was more rewarding than hoarding new friendships to the exclusion of the Quebeckers. I knew what I was, and I felt it tranquilly. I was both Black and White, and this was irrevocable, whether other people noticed my colours or not.

Years have since passed, but I still feel that way. I'm a man of two races.

"Zebra," of course, sounds faintly ridiculous. I wouldn't use the word in a serious conversation, but I do prefer it to "mulatto." Indeed, "mulatto" offends me more than "nigger." To say "nigger" is to say, "I hate you because you're Black." At least I know where I stand. But "mulatto" reduces me to half-status — neither Black nor White.

Even as a boy, I sensed that terms such as "mulatto," "half-Black" and "part Black" denied my fullness as a person. I recognized the absurdity of calling somebody "one-half" or "one-quarter" or "one-eighth" Black. Ancestral identity, I knew, couldn't be apportioned mathematically. One couldn't assign this colour to the heart and that to the liver. And at the same time, a person like me couldn't be all white and not Black, or all Black and not White, unless society imposed one colour on me.

I didn't grow up under apartheid, or slavery, or racial segregation. I grew up in a country in which I had a say in what I would be. That meant periods of ambiguity. It meant confusion. It meant anxiety. But it also meant the opportunity to come full circle and to decide, years after my father first poked me in the ribs and teasingly called me a zebra, that I truly was both Black and White.

Two years after my first trip to West Africa, I returned, this time to Cameroon. I met the French-Canadian woman who is now my wife. We now have two young daughters. I hope to infect them with enthusiasm for the many wings of their family. I don't know how old they will be when they start asking questions about the meaning of Black and White, and about how they fit into the picture. I'll answer what I can, and share with them what I know. But I won't tell them how to think. When they are old enough to play with the big questions, they will be ready to start moulding their own answers.

GROWING UP UKRAINIAN IN TORONTO

••••••••••••••••••••

JERRY DIAKIW

I was born in Toronto in 1936. I lived above a hairdressing and barber shop run by my mother and father, an aunt and two uncles, at Queen and Seaton streets. in Toronto. The smell of fingerwave solution and the unique odour of a permanent wave still trigger an eruption of memories of playing in the shop. I spoke no English until I went to Duke of York public school, nor did I need to. Playing on Seaton St., I wasn't aware that English existed. There were enough Ukrainian families on the street that it was like a tribal village or circle of tents in the desert, so oblivious were we to the surrounding population.

Our Ukrainian community was so safe that I could play on Seaton St. all day while my parents worked. If I didn't come home for lunch it hardly mattered. I simply ate with all of the other kids at the home where we happened to be playing. Warm, wizened old babas shrouded in black seemed to be everywhere.

On Sundays and feast days, the Ukrainian tribe trudged to the Holy Eucharist Ukrainian Catholic Church on King St., near the Don River. Today, forty-five years later, when I exit the Don Valley Parkway from the Richmond St. ramp and pass over the former site of the church, I'm flooded with memories of weddings, plays, christenings and religious celebrations. I swear the smells of incense, wax and the stale odour of the basement hall are still there twenty years after the church was demolished. I sometimes still hear the priest's deep booming voice chanting *Hos podi pomelui* as he swings the cadillo of smoking frankincense on a golden chain.

At eight, I survived the terrors of Saturday Ukrainian school where I was threatened with life in eternal hell if I didn't agree to become an altar boy. I remained steadfastly opposed under relentless pressure from two large nuns. My parents were never able to get me to return to Ukrainian school after the nuns forced me to try on the altar boy robes to show me how beautiful I looked in them. They promised me a life in heaven where, as one nun said, "You can have an apple any time you want one." I can still see her bulbous, scrubbed face framed by her white habit as she leaned close to mine and whispered this holy secret.

When I was five, I was hospitalized with a serious case of strep throat. No one understood me as I whined and complained in Ukrainian and my condition deteriorated. Frustrated, my parents whisked me out of the hospital, vowing they would never speak Ukrainian at home again. They never did, except when Ukrainian visitors came by from the old neighbourhood. I slowly became aware that not all Canadians spoke Ukrainian.

I never realized what a poor student I was until just recently. After my dad's death, I came upon some of my old report cards from grades four and five among his documents. Report cards then contained only rank in class, one subject after another; no grades, no marks, just rank in class, and a section at the bottom to indicate the number of students in the class. I noted that there were 44 students in the class and my rank for the academic subjects read 44, 43, 38, 41. While I was never required to repeat a grade, my parents were upset when the school wanted to put me into a special program for slow learners. But it was wartime and the placement never materialized.

I've learned since it takes a second-language student seven to ten years to approach the level of his peers in the ability to use English. My poor reports in grade four represented my functional level after five years of learning English. By the end of grade eight, after nine years of English, my grades were sufficient to gain admission to, and eventually graduate from, Upper Canada College. Later I completed B.A. and M.Ed. degrees from the University of Toronto.

I am amazed at how long it takes to learn and understand a language well enough to compete with one's peers, even when one is born in Canada. The streaming of children of newly arrived immigrant groups into terminal programs or vocational programs repeats itself over and over again.

Neither my mother nor my father ever learned to read or write English. There were no newspapers or magazines in our home. I never had a story read to me nor do I recall being told any stories. *Goldilocks, Winnie the Pooh* and *Hansel and Gretel* became known to me only as an adult, and there are innumerable references to children's literary characters that crop up in daily conversation that pass right over me.

I remember two books that came into the house. One was a tattered old book of poems by the Ukrainian patriot Taras Shevchenko. The other was a second-hand book on the diseases of the eye — a medical book my father bought for my older brother Walter. He was told to read it because he was going to be a doctor, just as I understood that I was expected to be a lawyer. I never saw anyone pick up either book. But my father constantly proclaimed the importance of education. He never went to school in the Ukraine but he was determined that his sons would make up for his lack of schooling.

My father and eleven silent partners bought a beer parlour, the Riviera Hotel on King St. near Sherbourne. Our family moved in upstairs, and my mother and father ran the hotel singlehandedly. Frankly, it was a whorehouse and a hangout for the legendary Mickey McDonald gang. My father was granted a temporary three-month licence on the condition that if he could clean up the prostitution and get rid of the gang, he would get a permanent licence.

I watched many a fight through the banister posts, and I'll always remember the night my father locked the Mickey McDonald gang inside the hotel until the police arrived. He stood defiantly at the door, bloodied, shouting in his thick accent, "You wouldn't leave when I asked you; now you stay till I let you leave!" He got his permanent licence.

Life started to settle down a bit. Like clockwork, my father opened the hotel doors every day at noon. The workers from the Christie Biscuit factory across the street poured in for lunchtime brews. One gentleman stood out. He wore a black homburg hat, a black overcoat, a black suit and black tie. Every day he ordered a draft, opened up his newspaper and read for about twenty minutes, finished his beer and left. One day my father, in his broken English, said, "Sir, you look like smart man. My son is in grade eight. I want to send him to good school. The best in Canada. Can you tell me good school?"

The man didn't like being disturbed. Abruptly, he replied, "One of the best schools in Canada is right here in Toronto. It's called Upper Canada College." The newspaper snapped open between them.

"Where is this school, sir?"

"On Lonsdale Road," came a curt reply from behind the newspaper. My father arranged to make an application for my brother Walter to attend the school. In time, my father received a letter that Walter was not accepted.

Towards the end of June, as my father delivered the ritual draft beer, the man in the black homburg lowered his paper and said, "By the way, did you ever apply to have your son attend Upper Canada College?"

"Yes," my father said, "but they say no."

This piqued the gentleman's interest and he questioned my father further. At his request, my father rummaged around in his cubbyhole of an office and produced the letter. One sentence said: "We do not feel your son would fit in well here." The man asked my father if he would still like to send his son to Upper Canada.

"Sure, if you think it's good school, I send!" my father replied.

He asked my father if he could keep the letter for a few days, and then he left.

About an hour later, the headmaster from Upper Canada College arrived in the men's parlour of the Riviera Hotel to inform my father that an opening had just come up and that the college would be delighted if Walter would accept the vacancy.

The man in the black homburg turned out to be a governor of Upper Canada College, who took time out from his law practice to enjoy a beer and a quiet read at lunch.

Though my father could ill afford it, we three Diakiw boys began fifteen years of roaming the hallowed halls of Upper Canada College.

What a strange quirk of fate! What a bizarre shift in cultures! My five years at the college were a combination of joy, pleasure, boredom, humiliation and anger. I revelled in the sports and other extra-curricular opportunities available there. Despite the strong loyalty I still have for the Upper Canada College, the appalling boredom and monotony of my classes hardly justified its first-rate reputation. Parents paid exorbitantly for the reputation, and students didn't dare question the teaching staff. Yet in many ways, away from the school, I acquired status. When adults learned about the school I attended, they gave me an unwarranted elevated social status, not unlike the deference they might have shown to an Oxford or Harvard graduate.

Until I entered Upper Canada College, I never realized how Ukrainian or, rather, how non-Canadian I was. Attending the college exposed the socio-cultural hierarchies to which I had been oblivious. For me, this privilege was not without its price.

In 1957, two years after graduating from Upper Canada College, I served in the Royal Canadian Navy's summer training program (UNTD) for officer cadets. I arrived at the Officers' Mess in Montreal, shouldered my duffle bag to my assigned quarters and introduced myself to my roommate, Milton Zysman, who was stretched out on his bed reading. "What kind of name is Diakiw?" he asked.

"Ukrainian," I said.

"Ah! Another Black man," he boomed.

I looked at him — stunned — as lights flashed in my mind and memories tumbled and unfolded like a kaleidoscope. I had never thought of it that way, yet he had exposed a central truth about the way I felt and the experiences I had had. What did a Ukrainian and a Jew have in common with a Black man? Why did I find it so easy to identify with that statement? While the differences in experiences were vast, we had all known intolerance, prejudice and second-class status. For Milton and me, this status was confirmed by law. Our parents had immigrated to Canada at a time when the rulings under the Immigration Act of 1923 classified European immigrants as preferred (northwestern Europe), non-preferred (eastern Europe, including the Ukraine) and Special Permits Class (southern Europe and all Jews except British subjects, regardless of their nationality).

The day that I arrived at the naval base in Montreal, I no longer spoke or understood Ukrainian. I was born in Canada and I had never visited the Ukraine. I had had no association with the Ukrainian church since the age of ten. I belonged to no Ukrainian club or organization, celebrated no Ukrainian holiday or festival. I was almost not a Ukrainian at all, except that my identity was defined and affirmed for me by English Canadians. They defined the group to which they had determined I belonged, and that group was somehow inherently inferior.

I was not aware of this inferior status until I went to Upper Canada College, where I was confronted with the impenetrable wall of white Anglo-Saxon Protestantism. I don't recall being insulted personally, apart from one French teacher. He regularly kicked and pushed me out of my seat and onto the floor while shouting how I was born out of my mother's deep black Ukrainian swamp.

Otherwise, I was treated as an equal and fully accepted into school life. No door or opportunity was closed to me. I was accepted by my classmates as one of them. And yet I felt like an alien. The culture of the college was English public school. This tradition was so highly guarded that the school always imported an English headmaster to guarantee that these central values were maintained. (A few years after I graduated, the school appointed its first Canadian headmaster.)

In being accepted, I came to learn how my culture, my parents, my lifestyle, my past were not acceptable. I believe that I hid this knowledge well from my classmates — they just never knew. As such, they revealed their feelings and attitudes. Even today I can't share with my close friends from those years the subtle and unconscious distinctions they communicated to me. They wouldn't remember, or would suggest that I was overly sensitive — I'm sure they just wouldn't understand. The distinctions were relentless: ethnic jokes, the derision about the way ethnics talked or dressed, their language about immigrants — "those bloody DPs are ruining this country" — the belittling of other cultures — "the only cultural achievement of the Ukrainians is the decorated Easter egg." A remark about an Italian, a Jew or a Hungarian painted me with the same brush. They accepted me as one of them, but when they joked about ethnics, they defined me and it belittled me.

At the college, we were trained to emulate proper Englishmen. We were taught Latin and the classics. We committed to memory, during daily Church of England prayers in the chapel, such patriotic English hymns as "Jerusalem" — "*Nor shall my sword sleep in my hand, Till we have built Jerusalem in England's green and pleasant land.*" I learned about Empire and about all the "pink bits" on the map. Through the Upper Canada College Cadet

Battalion's affiliation with the Queen's Own Rifles, I learned of that regiment's gallant history in creating, defending and protecting the Empire. Prince Philip, our royal patron, made periodic visits to the school to affirm our connection right to the top.

My classmates and I learned about power, and that power was in the hands of English Canadians; we were trained to be proper English Canadians. Many of those same classmates dominate in every corridor of power today.

This was not an environment in which I was able to talk proudly about my heritage. I retreated and assimilated as fast as I could. I was very ashamed of my background. I was particularly embarrassed about my parents. Compared with my friends' parents, mine seemed ignorant and crude. Not one classmate ever met my parents or visited my home during the five years I attended the college. I visited in their homes but not until the end of grade thirteen did I invite any friends to mine. Only then did I begin to realize that despite the differences in culture and wealth, my parents were among the best.

To me, my mother and father were largely without prejudice. (My wife maintains that I delude myself.) But the one ethnic group that bore the brunt of slurs and castigation by my parents was that of English Canadians with English accents. My mother always felt embarrassed and humiliated in their presence. When one of us put on "airs," acted overbearing, pompous, opinionated or domineering, they would say "Don't act like a 'Bronco.'" A "Bronco" was an English person, and in our house it was the most scathing insult you could make. As a youngster I never understood this hostility. But at Upper Canada College and in the years that followed, I began to understand the impertinence of "the dominant culture."

I came to understand and sympathize with angry Jews who stereotype gentiles, with Blacks who lash out against whites, with radical feminists who demolish men. Reverse discrimination, the slow-brewing reaction to inequality, is often accompanied by anger and hostility. I remember when my older brother Walter was dating an English girl my mother warned me not to marry a "Bronco" because "whenever you have a fight she'll throw it in your face that you are not a real Canadian." (All three of us married "Broncos.")

How many times will I hear "Why don't they just become Canadians?" uttered in dismay and frustration by a WASP referring to a hyphenated Canadian. It's always a WASP who understands what a Canadian is. They want us to be like them.

Even a friend, who lives in Metropolitan Toronto where the majority of residents are from a non-English-speaking background, when discussing a draft of this memoir asked me, "Do you feel more Ukrainian or more Canadian?" The depth of misunderstanding revealed by this question staggers me, yet it typifies the suspicion and misunderstanding that English Canadians have of immigrants. Even my father, a Ukrainian patriot, born and raised in the Ukraine, a man who loved his heritage passionately, loved Canada foremost. He considered it an honour and privilege to be a Canadian. He would not have understood my neighbour's question. It's like asking someone if they are more white or more Canadian.

I still struggle to control and understand my own prejudices. Though I have few remaining traits normally associated with belonging to a cultural group, such as language, religion or customs, my pride in my Ukrainian roots runs strong and deep. I somehow feel connected to the men and women in sheepskin coats who settled the west in endless waves. I still somehow feel that a stirring Ukrainian cossack dance is my kind of dance.

I AIN'T SITTING BESIDE HER
SHYROSE JAFFER

I can still vividly remember my first home economics class in Canada. It was my first week in grade seven, and I remember walking in late because I was still trying to figure out how to find my way around the school. Most of the students were already seated waiting for the class to begin and I confidently chose the first seat available and sat down. I hadn't even sat down properly when the Chinese guy beside me got up so forcefully that he knocked down his chair with a loud crash behind him.

"I ain't sitting beside HER!" he yelled scornfully, with disgust written all over his face.

It took me a few seconds to register the fact that he actually meant me. There was something about me, something that everyone was aware of, judging from their faces, that was terrible enough to make someone want to avoid me.

I still can't understand why I did it—maybe it was some kind of pride—but I actually stood up, collected my books and walked over to another chair (one that was sufficiently far from the others) and sat down without a word. There was pin-drop silence in the room for a few seconds and then, as if the incident had never occurred, class began.

Later, I walked home and I remember playing the scene again and again in my mind. I was crying because I had been rejected, but I honestly didn't know why that kid had done such a thing to me. I

57

was thirteen years old, and until that day it had never occurred to me that I was different. It wasn't that I had led a very sheltered life when my family had lived in the Middle East, because I had gone to school with a mixture of children of all colours, from different countries of the world. It was simply the fact that I had never before noticed the "difference" between people of other colours and me.

It may seem hard to believe, but I was actually unaware of the notion of racism. No one had ever prepared me for the concept that some people in the world consider themselves to be better than others. Until that point in my life, I had thought of myself like any other thirteen-year-old in the world. In that symbolic event at class, my sixth day in Canada, I experienced a certain change in my self-concept. It was a moment of disillusionment in what it meant to be me. To an innocent preadolescent, there was no comprehension or insight that this was what it meant to be oneself in a predominantly white society. It simply meant, "This is what it means to be me. I am different. I am undesirable."

We lived in downtown Toronto at that time. I still can't get over the fact that children of many races, Chinese, caucasian and Black, found me an object of ridicule. I dressed like them, my English was at times even better than theirs (my accent wasn't that pronounced, even then) and yet they called me names and rejected me. It just served to bring home the fact that everyone thought I was distasteful. I cried each and every day of my first three months in Canada. I was too ashamed to tell my mom. How could I, when I had spoken to her with so much enthusiasm about how much I would like school here? I had boasted to her that I would be the smartest in my class.

One day I was sitting in English class and "Rick" kept calling me names across a few desks. Suddenly, I could take it no longer. I began to write in my English book. I wrote of all the things that people were calling me, how much it hurt, how much I hated Rick. Then I ripped off the page, walked over to the Black supply teacher we had that day, handed it to her and went back to my seat. I just felt so good to get it out of my system and I wasn't a bit remorseful when she called me over and told me that the principal was waiting to see me in his office downstairs.

I can't remember his face, but I do remember that he put his arm around my shoulder after he finished reading my letter. He asked me to fill in one of the blanks I had left in a sentence. I told him the missing word, but I remember that I didn't even know the meaning of that swear word at the time. We spoke for a while and he was kind, but none of his words had any impact. All that I remember is the comfort I felt in having his arm around my shoulder. Next day, Rick wasn't in class. He had been suspended for a week, and when he came back he never said a word to me again. My parents were never notified and I don't think I ever told them about the incident.

Just when I started making friends (I let them cheat off my paper on tests to get them to like me), my family decided to move to Unionville, which is right in the centre of Markham. My whole public school was full of white children whose parents made over $35,000 a year. By the end of grade eight, I had encountered three more "Ricks" and I did the same thing again; I spoke to my teacher who gave them and the class a big lecture and made the offenders speak with me privately and apologize.

When I started high school I was full of renewed hope and enthusiasm. I had won the coveted "Actress of the Year" award in public school and had become quite popular. Little did I know that my troubles were just starting. I was the only "brown person" (there was one Black guy) among 2,500 high school students, but that didn't really bother me until one day in grade nine.

I had almost reached my locker when I saw something written on it in huge black letters.

"Go home Paki," it read, "back to India where you came from."

I was trembling with rage and tears and I found myself unable to go near the locker. It would be so embarrassing if anyone realized that those words were for me. I wasn't even from Pakistan. Besides, Pakistanis aren't from India, anyway. All sorts of thoughts were flashing through my mind—I was trying to console myself but it wasn't working.

Almost every day, throughout grade nine, I found myself at the principal's office, complaining about various sayings that kept appearing on my locker door. They would send a janitor down to wipe it off. Then it appeared as if someone was trying to break into my locker: I would find my combination lock malfunctioning or half-broken. I must have gone through at least ten locks that year (I even tried key locks or using two locks at a time but nothing helped). Then my tormentors started covering the locks with masking tape, or taping all the edges of the locker closed. Sometimes they would spray the lock with shaving cream, and once I reached out unsuspectingly to touch my lock and found it covered with spit.

Life became miserable. My self-esteem deteriorated and I had to face the shame of walking up to my locker and having people stare as

I'd try to deal with the latest "prank." The principal told me to report my suspects to him but that was useless. Could it be the girl in my phys. ed. class who was always making comments about "Pakis"? Or the kids in English who made me trip whenever I walked into class? Or the boys in physics who spoke in a funny accent and joked about wearing turbans and living in straw huts? Each one of these people was sent to the principal's office and still no one owned up to being the culprit behind the "pranks."

I started having nightmares about finding my locker full of snakes and spiders; my nightmares almost came true when I found my locker without a lock one day. I didn't have the courage to open it myself because I was afraid of what I'd find in there. When my friend opened it for me, she found nothing inside: all my books had been stolen, and exams were in two weeks.

It didn't occur to me at the time, but I wonder why it didn't strike the principal to change my locker number or provide a guidance counsellor for me. Why did I spend my class times doing surveillance of my locker in the hopes of finding the culprit instead of the high school providing someone to do this for me?

I guess everyone thought it would stop someday, but did anyone ask me how I was feeling during all this? Did anyone notice that I was becoming depressed, that I would shuffle my feet and look down when I walked or that I didn't say much because I was afraid that people would laugh at my accent? Did anyone bother telling me that it was the racists who had a problem and not me?

Sadly enough, no one bothered to do any of this. I had to help myself. And I didn't know how. All my life I had been taught to turn the other cheek and to ignore rude people because they'll soon get tired and stop. But none of these sugar-coated philosophies worked. No one stopped.

I tried to ignore it when boys in the bus seat behind me pulled my hair and called me names, but it didn't do any good — it simply resulted in them laughing as I covered my face and cried into my hands in front of everyone. I went through many stages and conflicts in dealing with my experiences. I would plead with God to help me, and my faith would keep me going.

Then I would go through a period when I'd scorn God and question His existence, telling myself that if there was a God then He would not have left me this long in so much pain. I believed that I was ugly, that I had nothing worthwhile to offer to anyone.

Then I would feel delusions of grandeur and think of myself as above everybody else. I'd want everyone to give me attention, to see me as my family saw me: a beautiful, talented, intelligent, interesting person.

In the end, I found myself arriving at a new philosophy: "God helps those who help themselves."

I found the culprit who was doing all those things to my locker. (I saw him while I was doing surveillance and grabbed the girl standing beside me in the hall, pleading to her to be my witness.) When the principal arranged for a meeting between "Mark," his father and me, I brought my brother along as moral support.

In that tiny office I looked Mark in the eyes and spoke with confidence and sincerity. The odd thing is that I felt compassion for Mark as he sat there in his leather jacket, his fists clenched as he struggled to get the apology out. He just couldn't say it and his eyes looked watery. I found myself crying for the person who had made my life so miserable.

"Mark, I don't want you to go through this," I said. "It doesn't make me happy to see you get in trouble. I just want you to understand and I want you to tell your gang, too, that what you did to me was wrong. It hurt me so much. And it was unfair. What have I ever done to you? I don't even know you. And you don't know me . . . so how can you know how clean I keep myself or whether my father wears a turban or even where I come from?"

Mark and his friends never bothered me again. But I found myself attempting to change and be more like everyone else. I don't know if it was for the better, but it helped improve things in my life. I began to dress in a trendy style and memorized the pronunciation of various words to improve my accent. And one day, when a guy (who seemed to have sworn an oath to yell "Paki" across the hall whenever he saw me) did his regular routine, I turned around and held up my middle finger. He actually bumped into someone, he was so shocked. He never did that again.

I have grown up a lot since then. Today, I can say with conviction that my experience made me into a very strong and confident person. Instead of letting racism push me into a little shell, I used it to grow as a person. I have made myself ask questions in class and speak in front of large audiences. And instead of letting myself feel shame, I have developed a love and pride for my culture and religion, and I often try to dispel myths and educate people about them.

My ten years in Canada have taught me that racism will always haunt and follow you around. There is a lot that needs to be done to educate some people, even at university. The trick is to fight it. You can't let racism swallow you and make you a part of itself so that you start viewing yourself like it views you. You have to believe in yourself. And you have to use it to make it into some sort of a positive experience so that you can grow from it. It's not easy at all, sometimes it's downright impossible . . . but you have to keep fighting.

Because often enough, everything in your life depends on it.

PRESENT COMPANY EXCLUDED, OF COURSE...

STANLEY ISOKI

It wasn't until I was in school that I realized I was both highly visible and also totally invisible. It was a lesson learned in the subtlest way; a lesson taught by a series of the unlikeliest teachers; a lesson incapable of being unlearned. It has made an impact upon all personal and professional aspects of my life.

One of my first lessons occurred in the corner store in Thunder Bay (then Fort William), Ontario. Non-metropolitan Canada abounds with across-from-the-school, corner variety stores where one can purchase almost anything from pantyhose to penny candies. They have a character and ambience not found in Toronto or Montreal or Vancouver. The regard their patrons have for this type of entrepreneur is reverential. And the backbone of the institution is the child. The child who, clutching pennies, nickels and dimes, represents most of the profits. No wonder then that a special relationship exists between the proprietor and the prepubescent clientele.

Trying to break into this special relationship was impossible for me. My "Excuse me, sir, can I have three cents worth of bubble gum?" was usually met with a hostile glare or, worse yet, an indifference which negated my existence. At seven years old, I couldn't understand why my three cents wasn't as valuable as that of my friends who always seemed able to get the owner's attention. I most often resorted to having my friends buy my candy for me from this same man who taught me that in some way I was less valuable and valued than my peers. I'm not talking now about the kids-versus-adults kind of invisibility. Kids are used to being ignored by store owners when a more lucrative transaction with an adult can be made. I'm talking about the kind of invisibility that set me apart from other kids in my own age group, an invisibility that sapped my fragile self-esteem and gave rise to self-doubt.

Another assault on my self-image occurred when my grade five teacher, a woman whose apparent wisdom and stature were unquestionable, put me and the only other "different-looking" child in the class on either side of the front row in order to take the class picture. I felt honoured to have been chosen for this special place, but I also felt a little confused. In every other class picture, I had been placed somewhere near the middle because I was usually the smallest kid. Later, when the anxiously awaited picture arrived, the reasons for her actions became graphically apparent. Neatly framed between two different-looking children was the "real" class, those children for whom the school system existed. I think I realized even then that my humanity was, at the very least, inferior. I felt that I had been left on the periphery, looking in. I have that picture still. It serves to remind me not only of the subtlety with which a teacher or parent or adult can harm a child, but also of the vigilance that must be maintained in order to avoid the damage which can be so easily perpetrated.

Other examples of failed attempts at assimilation (and at that age I wanted nothing so much as to "fit in") seem insignificant by themselves, but cumulatively they had a devastating effect on a child's developing psyche. It is easy to doubt one's worth when there is what appears to be overwhelming evidence that one is invisible. I remember a birthday party where I was the only non-white child. What fun it was to watch the children bob for apples and to make hilarious, uncoordinated attempts to pin the tail on the crudely drawn donkey. But when it came my turn, what a disappointment to discover that the cake was in need of cutting at that precise moment and that we would have to wait to complete the game. Inevitably, the game was never completed, nor was the elusive tail ever pinned. When my mother came to pick me up and asked the obvious question, my reply was an enthusiastic, "Yes, I had a really good time, Mom." I couldn't admit that I had been overlooked by the parents of my friend.

It was around that time, or perhaps a little later, that I began to question my rationalizations about what seemed to be a series of coincidences. Store managers seeing through me, friends' mothers ignoring me, playmates often not knowing me when other friends appeared, were all occurrences far too apparent to ignore. Did I exude a peculiar odour? Was my breath inordinately foul? Was I just plain stupid? These were questions I asked myself in my futile attempts to deny the obvious. And yet . . . and yet. . . .

And yet, I had friends who never denied me as myself. The small town and smaller community in which I spent many of my formative, impressionable years had a relatively large proportion of Canadians of Japanese descent. It was with these friends that I felt most comfortable and most valued as a person. Perhaps it was because I was so young that I did not realize that my comfort came from their unconditional acceptance of me. I was being treated as though I belonged; as though my being whom I was mattered. And I was denying a fact I did not wish to know. People treated me differently because I was different; my culture, appearance and attitudes were different. But at that age, I wanted nothing more than to be the same. I had internalized the values and norms of a society that systematically denied the validity of my cultural heritage and that denied me access to the opportunities for success that are purported to be the right of all Canadian citizens.

One of the last incidents that led to my realization that I was invisible came as a Scout. The Boy Scouts of Canada is an organization devoted to making responsible, dutiful, loyal, honourable young men out of boys. The problem with that definition is that it omits the word "white." In order to be successful, one must subscribe to the ethical values explicit in the Boy Scout motto and attempt to live by them. I was able to pass without much effort the tests required to attain the badges, and I enjoyed immensely the diverse activities sponsored by the organization. But again, I was troubled. Was I required to believe every word of the motto? I had also been taught that by dint of hard work and striving, I would rise quickly and become a leader among the boys in my troop and that eventually I would be able to help with the younger boys in Wolf Cubs. Now, having risen as far as I could and become a Queen's Scout, I was still not asked to lead the Cubs, although I had made my willingness well known to the Group Committee which ran our section.

In retrospect, my naivete is appalling. How could I have expected an organization whose poet laureate could pen the words "Take up the white man's burden" to recognize any leadership potential in a non-white person? Or, more insidious still, were the parents afraid that I might instil unacceptable cultural values into their children?

But these questions were too perplexing and, with the optimism of youth, I thought that I would have many, many years to answer them.

For me, other, more direct examples abound throughout my life, but I have deliberately chosen to outline the more obscure ones from childhood memories because they seem to me to be the ones that only the victim will remember as significant. The perpetrators would have almost certainly dismissed them as unnoteworthy or, at the very least, as having had a different intent.

I feel it is important to note the dichotomy existing between intent and result. Most Canadians have good intentions. I believe that their intent is not to willfully harm another individual. The results of some thoughtless actions or words, however, are far different from those anticipated or unperceived by the instigator. From my recollection and analysis of the feelings associated with those recollections, I can assure anyone that the child, and later the man, who was forced to deal with those feelings was lonely and confused. Invisibility is not a happy state; it embodies isolation, self-doubt and often despair.

There was one incident which, I remember, left me agitated and confused for months. I couldn't understand, given my transparency, why I had been so ill-used. More often than not I was accustomed to being seen through rather than being noticed. I was about fourteen years old and, like most teenagers, had begun to feel the first vague stirrings of rebelliousness that characterizes that age. Several of my friends and I had decided to "play hooky" and skip classes to go to a movie that was playing in a downtown theatre. In order to get there we had to take several buses and make two or three transfers. The second time we changed buses, the driver informed me that my transfer was invalid. I explained in a less-than-obsequious tone that since he had accepted my friends' transfers and since the previous driver had punched all of them together, I couldn't understand why he would not accept mine. His loud retort that "You people are all alike — trying to get something for nothing" left me speechless and I immediately retreated into invisibility and meekly paid another fare. I was faced with an apparent duality in my existence.

Looking back, I weep for the child whose attempts at assimilation, whose desire to be like everyone else was one of the dominating factors of his childhood. How could he realize that the act of assimilation in itself is a concession to the systemic racism that pervades our society as well as a denial of our own culture which, for better or worse, has shaped our psyches? In the desire to be accepted by the dominant culture, minorities willingly accept an inferior position that maintains the status quo. "Let's live in harmony" translates to "Don't rock the boat" which in turn means "Keep your rightful (inferior) place in our society and we can all live in harmony."

Several decades after my recognition of invisibility, I learned that not only was I not invisible, but also I was, in fact, a member of a visible minority. This has been the underlying contradiction which has informed my life — I was both visible and invisible at the same time. Of course, there had been times as a youth that I had had my different-ness thrust on me, but I wasn't ready to recognize that my life had any more facets than I could understand.

Much later, as an adult, I began to build expectations and foster hopes for myself and for my family. Having gained some measure of success, I optimistically began a conscious effort to bolster my self-image and to succeed in my society. During that period, my visibility and self-esteem grew.

Armed with fledgling confidence, I sought work and there encountered more striking examples of how my society perceived me. In the final year of my undergraduate program in English language and literature, I looked for a teaching position with one of the school boards in Metropolitan Toronto, secure in the knowledge that the dearth of teachers would help me find a position for which I was qualified. I went to the "cattle auctions," the mass hiring procedures of the day, at Don Mills Collegiate and was promptly offered several positions in Toronto. Unfortunately, none of them were ones I could accept. The interviews began with the usual background questions but ended abruptly when, in every instance except the last, the hiring official asked me whether I was interested in teaching mathematics or science. Here were high-ranking school board officers who automatically, and to them quite naturally, assumed that because I was Asian, I was a math or science major. All stereotyping has a negative aspect. Expectations, the way we view others, how we react to others, are all shaped by what we think we already know about one another. What if I had not been able to acquire a position because people in power made those assumptions about me?

Finally, however, I managed to obtain a job. I mark the beginning of my second, more painful "education" from that moment. Less than two weeks into my first term, one of the more experienced teachers, possibly in an effort to make me feel accepted and at ease with the faculty, related a "humorous" story dealing with a common stereotype about Asians who, according to him, because of their slanted eyes couldn't tell the difference between a harbour in Hawaii and a human being and therefore ended up bombing the human. As if noticing me for the first time, he said, "Present company excluded, of course." These words have come to symbolize for me the insidious affliction that permeates our society. This educator, this shaper of our children's minds, this well-educated man felt that by mouthing those five meaningless words, and by dint of his maleness and whiteness, he had earned the right to disseminate a racial stereotype that was both harmful to the whole race and demeaning to the individual in whose presence he felt no discomfort in telling the "joke." Looking back, I recall that I laughed harder than the others and I am shamed at my naivete and my relief at what I thought had been acceptance by the faculty. I felt much like Dudley Moore's character in the movie *Arthur*, who in a drunken state was informed that he was with a prostitute and exclaimed, "Are you a hooker? I thought I was just doing great with you."

As my years of experience in teaching grew, so also did the stockpile of present-company-excluded jokes, anecdotes and generalizations; so also did my realization that I was not, in fact, "doing great." I learned through experiences, sometimes humiliating, sometimes bitter, often humorous but always enlightening, that somehow I needed to try harder in order to achieve the same successes that seemed to come so easily to those for whom the rules of my society had been made. I had been optimistic enough to imagine that merely by trying harder, I would be rewarded for my efforts. And now, I am constantly saddened by many of my "visible" students who believe, infused with the freshness and optimism of youth, that our existing institutions and networks have changed sufficiently so that they will be given the same opportunity as everyone else. I am consumed by the ambivalence of teaching these young people, without fostering a sense of hopelessness, that we live in a country which still requires a great deal of learning, maturing and changing before it can live up to its claim that we are all equal. The task often seems overwhelming and I feel much like the politician who would have his country go to war for peace.

But the essence of the human spirit is to strive, and in that striving I encountered another type of behaviour from a source, although obvious, I had not anticipated. In the staff room of my high school, I was being subjected to yet another generalization about how "all

Asians whom we allow to come to our country take the jobs away from our own unemployed" when our principal came in. The speaker immediately enlisted his complicity but the principal refused to participate. Instead, he hastily excused himself and left the staff room. The incident itself was, I am certain, insignificant to both administrator and perpetrator. It served to reinforce for me, however, the latitude that our educational institutions allow in interpreting what appears to me to be a straightforward document, the Ontario Human Rights Code. If silence implies consent, and even if it doesn't, did that principal's silence not give the appearance of agreeing with an unfair and inaccurate stereotype? It is unconscionable that through inaction a respected figure, who possesses the power to discriminate, was party to the dissemination of harmful stereotypes. By that time in my career, I was secure enough to voice my disagreement with the stereotype, but I was dismissed as "just another malcontent who can't take a joke." And he was right! I cannot, nor must I, listen to another joke or generalization that impugns or discredits another person. It is my responsibility, as a teacher and as a member of the human race, not to allow such thoughts or attitudes to go unchallenged.

In case I sound like I'm condemning all educators or the entire educational system, let me explain that the examples cited are from my life and are particular to me, although I believe that any person of colour can corroborate, and indeed add to, this compilation of incidents. The point, I think, is that none of these situations should have occurred, nor would they have had I not been a member of that part of our society which, through racial background, manifests a discernible difference in habits, looks, speech, or method of worship. Of course, to be different implies a "norm" from which to differ; and that "norm" in North American society is white and Eurocentric, and it has dominated this continent since it was forcibly imposed upon the First Nations of this country. That "norm" carries with it all the privileges which our society has gone to great lengths to deny it possesses.

I have stated before that I believe most people would not intentionally hurt another human being, and it is my fervent hope that explaining the degree of unintentional anguish caused by the privileged position of some unthinking individuals will serve to enlighten them and provide some insight into the repercussions of their thoughtlessness. Most teachers I know are sensitive and kind, but even they have difficulty recognizing that if they are white, of European descent, and additionally male, they are endowed with privileges which, having

69

been scrupulously hidden or assumed for so long, have become, for them, a right. For example, I am curious about how many white, Anglo-Saxon Canadians have been asked to speak for people of their race; or to write an article explaining their experiences in our society; or to go into a history class and explain how their parents were interned by their government; or to Anglicize the spelling of their names or even change their names so they could be more easily recognized and pronounced; or how many opportunities were made available to them through no virtue of their own. However, the controversy over what is a right and what is a privilege is easily settled if one remembers that in our democracy, the rights of one must be the rights of all. And that reality is patently a myth.

Yet another, more recent example provides startling insight into how some people think. Not long ago, as a former internee in a British Columbian internment camp, I received the Canadian government's redress payment along with a letter of apology and a formal acknowledgement of the mistake that had been made. Having been born in Canada and considering myself Canadian in all respects, I was thrilled at the thought that my government had been capable of admitting error and was taking measures to rectify the injustice. Naturally, I felt that other Canadians would share my elation and perceive the action as right and just. Unfortunately, I had overestimated the vision of some of my acquaintances. In an initially casual conversation about the redress issue, one individual in our group remarked that it was only because "we," meaning white Canadians of European descent, had allowed the Japanese Canadians to assimilate so easily that "they" had managed to bring the issue to a beneficial conclusion. When some others, perceiving the unreasonableness of the assertion, would not allow that he was correct, he immediately shifted to another line of attack, which was to point to the inequity of redress for only one group. We all agreed and stated further that if the Canadian government was serious in its efforts to be equitable, it should consider redress for all the groups who had been wronged, especially those who had the least influence. He persisted by stating that it was only the Japanese who would take advantage of having been educated in "our" country and then would use that education to subvert Canada. My argument that rather than subverting the country, we had made it more truly democratic and responsive to the needs of its people fell on deaf ears, and I was left with a feeling of frustration and despair.

70

It was obvious that my antagonist had no interest in an intelligent discussion, but that he was interested only in expressing his views and having them accepted by the present company. However, in this case, the present company had not been excluded; it was, in fact, the very target for his vituperation. As is so often the case when discussing matters pertaining to race, ethnicity and who belongs, his emotions rather than his intellect had seized control of his arguments and rendered them easily assailable. But he was adamant. No amount of arguing or reasoning would sway him from his convictions. His philosophy that Canada would be a much better place if "those other people" had not been allowed to immigrate was as hard and unshakable as the lump forming inside me as I listened, by now silently and sadly.

Perhaps because it occurred relatively recently, perhaps because the person involved is well educated and holds a responsible position in our society, this particular incident left me unusually depressed. Had we come such a short way in such a long time? Can we ever hope to generate an understanding that will attenuate the rift between the ideals of our nation and the reality of discrimination and prejudice that still flourishes here today? I still believe we can. I believe that education is the route and I believe that true strength does, indeed, lie in diversity. As a teacher, I have attended many workshops and teacher-in-service sessions dealing with anti-racist education and equity issues. I have been astonished at the vast numbers of well-informed and well-intentioned people from all cultures, ethnicities and races who are working together to re-create a vision of Canada which is truly multicultural. Much remains to be done, but with current Ministry of Education mandates to school boards on equity issues, as well as the growing awareness that our educational and other institutions systematically exclude a wide variety of individuals from enjoying the advantages of other groups in our population, we have begun a process that could lead to a truly equal society. I'm not sure how long the process will take but I do know, to paraphrase Bob Dylan, that the norms, they are a-changin'. And the people, we are a-waitin'.

I hope that no one any longer believes that there are no racists in Canada and that all Japanese Canadians are inscrutable, polite, and humble . . . present company excluded, of course.

MY NEW HOME
DENNY HUNTE

They met us at the airport — my parents, that is.
Fortunately for us, we recognized them,
as they had left us for "the promised land" only one year earlier.

I knew I would be coming to Canada
but each day's wait seemed like an eternity.
Canada, the land of plenty (where things were either free or cheap),
the land of fourteen-lane highways (at least that is what my uncle said).
And when my aunt from Canada visited
she had such a "nice" Canadian accent.

I was excited about moving to Canada,
but I was also afraid.
I would be leaving my family and friends and my "cricket,"
but I would gladly give it all up
for whatever sport they played in Canada.
It is Canadian . . . so it must be better.

It was November 20, 1967, at 3:15 p.m.
From 80+ degrees to 20 degrees,
from the constant heat to steady cold.
From a lot of us and a few of them,
to a lot of them and a few of us.
Somehow I thought that only pets and
inanimate objects were "cute."
But now I was also commonly referred to as "cute,"
and oh! how I hated it.

From day one when I attended school
I did not fit in.
I was afraid
I felt alone
I was alone
I was petrified and insecure.

I was the only one who could not skate.
I did not know anything about ice hockey or Gordie Howe.

I felt like an outsider listening in,
like the fourteenth man at the last supper.

They said that I spoke with an accent,
they said that I spoke rather quickly.
I stammered.
This condition increased or became more pronounced when I was
nervous,
and I was nervous all the time.
I hated school — it constantly reminded me
Of how different I was.

Oh my God! I hated this place,
but who was I to tell that my dream was now a nightmare.
My friends and neighbours back home would give
an arm and a leg to be in my shoes.

We had music theory classes every day in the late afternoon.
The teacher, a balding man who never smiled much,
assigned musical notes for all the students to read aloud
except me.
From December to June, when my turn came,
he skipped to the next student.
I was relieved not having to read the music notes to the class,
but I felt in my gut that something just wasn't right.
Never once did he take a minute to teach me to read music.
In June he gave me a "C" grade.

Spring came and I went out for track and field.
Lo and behold, I was the fastest kid in the school.
I was relieved to have beaten everyone,
but better yet I did not run with an accent.
While in the classroom I was timid, afraid, insecure,
on the track I was the best.

The gym teacher took a liking to me.
He took the time to help me with long-jumping techniques.
I wish my music teacher was like him
I swear I would have long-jumped in perfect pitch.

GRADE SIX
KAI JAMES

In school, I don't learn much about my ethnicity,
Because of the school board and its eurocentricity.
White students often ask me annoying questions with regards
to my colour.
They do not know of our achievements or our culture.
Is it ignorance or arrogance
That makes them this way?
They should think before they speak,
If they have something to say.

PART 3

IDENTITIES: LIVING IN MANY WORLDS

REVEALING MOMENTS
THE VOICE OF ONE WHO LIVES
WITH LABELS
••••••••••••••••••••••••
DIDI KHAYATT

Moment # 1

The year was 1981. I was a graduate student at the Ontario Institute for Studies in Education, working on my Ph.D. I was also a novice feminist, listening to the words of my professors and of my fellow students, and absorbing the ideas that were changing my life and my thoughts. We were being taught to attend to the words of other women, and to locate ourselves in our research. That day in class, the discussion centred on immigrant women. Students were attempting to grapple with the new (to us) sociological methodology that began from the standpoint of the oppressed, in this case, "immigrant women," and not from a defined sociological category. The debate had been raging for close to an hour when finally the professor was asked to give her opinion regarding what constituted an "immigrant woman." The professor smiled, looked in my direction, and said, "We have an immigrant woman in our midst, why don't we ask her what she thinks?" Following the professor's example, the whole class focused on the space where I was seated, and, likewise, I, too, glanced behind me, trying to find the "immigrant woman" to whom the professor was referring. In my astonishment at being included in that category, I was rendered speechless. It had never occurred to me that I could be perceived as an "immigrant woman," a category which, to be precise, did include me because I had emigrated from Egypt in 1967, but one which did not fit me any more than it did our "immigrant" British professor.

Why did I reject being included in the category "immigrant woman"? Why did I feel the label did not fit? We had just been told that people who originated from white, Western, industrialized countries were not considered "immigrant." I came from Egypt. Why did I think I did not qualify?

The term "immigrant" technically refers to any individual who has a legal status in Canada of landed immigrant or permanent resident as opposed to being a citizen. It is a temporary category intended not only as a period of adjustment, but also as an interval during which those who are being considered as potential citizens can be evaluated. Individuals are given the rights and privileges in areas of work and education but are not yet able to vote or to carry Canadian passports. Indeed, historically, immigration policies were traditionally tied to labour needs and the political and economic imperative of populating certain areas of Canada with communities of skilled and unskilled labour. However, as Roxanna Ng suggests, the term is used in government documents to suggest all persons who are "foreign-born," regardless of their citizenship status. She continues: "In common sense usage, however, not all foreign-born persons are actually *seen* as immigrants; nor do they see *themselves* as 'immigrants'. The common sense usage of 'immigrant women' generally refers to women of colour, women from Third World countries, women who do not speak English well, and women who occupy lower positions in the occupational hierarchy." I agree with Roxanna Ng that there is a disjunction between the legal government definition and the common sense notion of what comprises an "immigrant woman."

Moment # 2

I was recently going up the elevator with one of the cleaning staff of my building. Since I often saw her, smiled, and always greeted her previously, it was appropriate that in the time we had to go up nineteen floors we would engage in a short conversation. I asked her where she was from. She answered, "Me from Korea." I informed her that I was from Egypt. She smiled at me and said, "No, you Canadian, me Korean." I laughed and insisted that I was from Egypt. She was adamant. She kept shaking her head and repeating, "You Canadian, me Korean," right up to the floor where I got off.

What had this woman seen in me that was Canadian, that denied my assurance to her that I came from Egypt? Evidently, she perceived me as assimilated, as having power, and, in her eyes, as undifferentiated from those people who fit her notion of "Canadian." Although not all immigrant women are "visible minorities" (another state-originated term) like this Korean woman, and not all visible-minorities are foreign-born, often both categories are *perceived* as almost interchangeable. Frequently, as Roxanna Ng points out, the situation of Canadian-born visible minorities and that of immigrants is similar in many respects because of the race and class biases inherent in the social structure.

In her analysis of theories of race and class oppression, Caroline Ramazanoglu argued against the notion that racism can often be reduced to class. She rightly points out that Black women and, I add, women of colour, "are not uniformly oppressed and they can have contradictory interests in which race, class, ethnicity and nationality cut across each other." Furthermore, she asserts that colour "is not a static or universal category of disadvantage that transcends all other sources of social difference which determine the quality of people's lives." Although I agree with Ramazanoglu's position, I suggest that colour is *perceived* to be a category of disadvantage, as are other labels, such as "immigrant," "visible minority," "refugee," "person from a developing or Third World country," and so on. This perception does not just stem from bigotry, but is in keeping with official government ideology that has currently designated individuals who fit into state categories of gender and/or of multiculturalism[1] as disadvantaged minorities who should be protected from discrimination and assisted in maintaining equal access to Canadian standards of living. The state, for the most part, has defined those categories, and as such they have entered the currency of institutional language. They each have a state-produced definition which is designed to signal difference, but at the same time to protect those included in these classifications from social and economic discrimination in this society.

It is precisely because of the perception that these categories are of disadvantage that I am concerned with indiscriminate labelling of individuals. To call me an "immigrant woman" or a "woman of colour" is to trivialize the very real oppressions of those who are within these categories and who are disadvantaged. Moreover, those "benign" categories themselves, although useful for state-supported policies of employment equity or legal bases for human rights complaints, are not as effective for the individuals themselves who are named within them. They often do not locate themselves in that manner precisely because the categories emphasize what seems to be an inalienable difference between themselves and the rest of the population. These classifications are significant when they are appropriated to provide a feeling of belonging to a community, where this self-labelling may develop into an accepted identity, or whenever these terms are taken up by the women so identified and transformed into a political identity. For instance, being referred to as a "woman of colour" because a person merely belongs to a particular ethnic group, regardless of whether this individual shares any common concerns, becomes more a means of slotting people to force containment; whereas in self-labelling even if the same term is applied, it is used by the people themselves to achieve a cohesive community of support based on shared concerns or political perspectives.

Here I want to use my own experience to discuss the intersections of sex, race, class and ethnicity. I am interested in examining how, in the process of assimilating into a new culture, one finds the self-definitions that will eventually comprise one's identity. I shall also investigate the distinctions made between the various expressions of dominant white culture and minority groups within the social contexts of Canada. Finally, I shall demonstrate how the categories used to describe race and ethnicity operate differently to keep certain groups oppressed when particular elements are present. These include such factors as sex, religion, sexuality, class, language, financial situation, education, and relative darkness of skin, combined with an individual's particular history.

I came to Canada in the late sixties to do graduate work. At the end of my first year in this country, I decided I wanted to stay and I applied for immigration status. At that time, the process included an application form, a set fee, and, most important, an appointment with an immigration officer who would assess, based on a predetermined point system, whether I, as a candidate, was suitable to become a landed immigrant. According to Alma Estable, this hurdle consisted of assigning points to different categories, the most significant of which were employment skills and professional qualifications. Immigrants were also "assessed on the basis of their personal characteristics (such as age, and professional qualifications), education, possession of a skill in demand." Because it was quantifiable, this system was supposed to be neutral and equitable. However, it should be noted that the linking of citizenship with occupation points to a system which is located within the dynamics of capitalism. Canada needed (and still needs) young, skilled immigrants; therefore practical training and work experience comprised the category that yielded the highest points. For my appointment with the immigration officer, I dressed up and made a special effort to look "good," not that I had any idea what would really make a difference. I presented myself at the appointed time, and we proceeded with the interview. On the one hand, my age, my very fluent English, my education, as well as my knowledge of Canada's second official language, French, gave me a certain number of points. On the other hand, my chosen field of anthropology did not rate at all on the priority list of needed skills, nor did I gain any points because of professional capacity. I had never worked in my life, not even at a summer job. The education officer questioned me regarding sponsorship by a relative, an organization or a company. I had none. Did I presently have a job? No. What kind of work was I capable of doing? I was a cultural anthropologist; my choices were limited. The poor man obviously wanted to give me the points, but I was clearly ten short of the required number and no amount of prodding into my professional experience could produce one single point more. Finally, he just looked at me, smiled, and said, "I know. I shall give you ten points for charm."

Would I have obtained these points had I spoken English haltingly? Would he have had the same measure of patience with my lack of skills and work experience had he perceived me as a visible minority? The accredited "charm" that the immigration officer appreciated relied on a combination of social relations which are not quantifiable, nor were they meant to be. Points were based on very practical state-defined occupational categories as well as potential characteristics which would eventually lead to job proficiency. I was assigned ten points based on nothing more functional than class and gender. I was located as a woman with no colour. My different-ness was invisible. I was perceived as posing no threat to the ruling white system. As a woman, my potential for work was trivial when compared with my youthfulness, and thus my procreational capacity. Therefore, I would suggest, what he saw was a woman of the right age and class to marry well, after which my assimilation would eventually be complete.

The assumptions implicit in the categories of "immigrant woman," "woman of colour," and "visible minority" conceal real differences in experience and do not account for or distinguish between the various levels of oppression. They assume a homogeneity of background amongst all people who fall into those various groupings. As Linda Carty and Dionne Brand point out, these terms are "void of any race or class recognition and, more importantly, of class struggle or struggle against racism." Who is entitled to determine who we are? How are those labels made to apply to various people? What do the labels really signify and how does that translate itself in the experiences of the individuals to whom they are applied? The question becomes not who we are, but who are we perceived to be. It is not my identity that is of concern, but the appropriate label that can be attached to me and can decipher what I represent. The labels are applied by those in power to differentiate between themselves and those they want to exclude, and they accomplish this on the basis of race, class, ethnicity and other factors. Or, as Carty and Brand suggest, "State policy around issues of race, class, or sex can be characterized as policy of containment and control."

When asked how I identify myself, who I am and where I come from, my responses vary: a) according to the questioner (who is asking me, what I perceive is her/his interest in knowing, how she/he is going to use the answers and how I think they will be used, what the relations of power are between the questioner and myself); b) the context of the questions (an interview, the topic at hand, the discussion which frames the question); and c) the circumstances under which the questions are asked (friendship, intimacy, making acquaintances, first meeting, family, etc.) In each case, my answer will be different, and the differences will be generated from the relative safety of the situation and the interest of the questioner. My answer will contain elements of pride, uncertainty, political correctness, concealment of aspects that can be misconstrued, or that are threatening; in the same way, it will include aspects of my social self that I feel will make my listener think the best of me — at least for a moment.

Therefore, in disclosing my identity to you, I will say this: I am a woman. I am an Egyptian Copt. I come from the upper class. I am a feminist. I am a lesbian. Your labels for me may include: woman of colour, immigrant woman, Third World woman. When I asked a friend recently what she thought the difference between "identity" and "label" was, she answered with little hesitation, "Identity defines, labels limit." To me, identity is that part of me that needs to fit into a group, the need to see a reflection of myself in that group. It is the safety of belonging. What you choose to call me, the label by which you refer to me, may have little to do with what I call myself. It has more to do with how you treat me, with how you treat the group with which I identify. Mistreatment on the basis of a label is discrimination. It may be against one individual or aimed at all those included within the disparaged category. However, the distinction between identity and label may become blurred when the label is threatening in a way to marginalize or exclude the one labelled. For instance, I may have been sexually involved with women, but have chosen not to

82

identify as a lesbian. Or, conversely, I may identify as a lesbian, but be afraid to disclose it publicly.

Moment # 3

Several years after I obtained my landed immigrant status, I was finally granted citizenship. By that time I had qualified as a secondary school teacher and had been gainfully employed by a northern Ontario board. The day I was supposed to be sworn in was finally at hand and I presented myself at the local courthouse. The judge had come all the way from Toronto for just this occasion, to oversee the transition from immigrant to citizen of several people. There were only five of us: a Chinese family of three, an Italian man and myself. After the ceremony, we were all invited to attend a tea given by the I.O.D.E (the Imperial Order of Daughters of the Empire) where they were to present us with a few mementoes, a Bible and a Canadian flag, to commemorate the occasion. I crossed the street from the courthouse to the church basement and found myself surrounded by older women bent on making me feel "welcome to Canada," my new land. Since the other four people had great difficulty with English, I became the centre of attraction, the one queried about conditions in my "old" country. The gist of the conversation was to make me articulate how I had left behind a dreadful situation to come to this land of plenty. The questions revolved around how we dress in Egypt, what and how we eat, do we have cars or is our public transportation based on camel power. I thought they were joking. I believed that they spoke in stereotypes on purpose and I played along. I laughed at their references and exaggerated differences, all in the name of fun, until the moment I left. Since I was the only Egyptian for miles around in that northern Ontario town, people often made humorous allusions to pyramids and camels in order to tease me. It never occurred to me that these women were deadly serious. I did not take offence at the conversation.

I did not translate the exchanges as a level of racism. I knew my background and therefore I did not perceive their presumptions about Egypt as anything more than lack of information. Many years later, when I understood the language of racism, this incident fell into place; I recognized their benevolent attention, not as welcoming me, but as relegating me to my "proper" place as grateful immigrant. Racism is not about colour, it is about power. Racism *is* power. It is not only a recognition of difference, but also the explicit emphasis on difference to mediate hierarchy based on colour, ethnicity, language and race. Those women would probably not have seen me as particularly distinctive if I had met them socially without mention of my cultural background. Within the framework of my class, they had no power

83

over me, which is why I took no offence at their words. I was neither destitute, nor was I essentially dependent on Canada for my well-being. I had emigrated for personal reasons which had more to do with the necessity of finding myself than the urgency of earning my living.

In a recurrent discussion with my friend Marian McMahon (where she plays devil's advocate) she suggests that just because I am not conscious of racism does not mean that I do not bear the brunt of racist attitudes and remarks. When I interject that racism serves to place an individual in a vulnerable position, that, like sexism, it is flagged as a fundamental difference to highlight hierarchy and therefore justify discrimination, she agrees, but argues that as with those women who say they are not oppressed, my inability to feel oppressed is a denial of my status as a woman of colour, indeed, is in itself a form of internalized racism on my part. I take up her discourse seriously. However, I see that because of my privileged background, I can hardly qualify as "a woman of colour" and it would be inconsistent with the spirit of the common-sense usage of the word for me to assume that label when I have never been submitted to the anguish of discrimination, the alienation of being slotted without my consent, or the experience of being silenced.

Moment # 4

In 1967 I enrolled in graduate studies at the University of Alberta, Edmonton. I was twenty-three. My entire formal education had been in English up to this point, and I spoke French and Arabic as well. Shortly after my arrival, the chair of the department in which I was enrolled invited all new graduate students and faculty to a party at his house to meet the rest of the department. I attended. I mingled. I exchanged pleasantries with many people. I answered innumerable questions about my country, our traditions, our ways of eating and dressing. When I thought it was appropriate to leave, I went to my host, who promptly accompanied me to find my coat and boots, scarf and gloves. It was late October in Edmonton. At the front door, in full view of a room full of his guests, after he turned and winked at them in collusion, he offered me his hand to wish me good night. Since I was already dressed to go out, I tendered my gloved hand and, following the rules of formal social conventions I had been taught, I said, with all the dignity of youth, "Please excuse my gloves." At which point the entire room full of people who had been watching our exchange burst into laughter. I looked at them in surprise, and left without bothering to give or receive any explanation. To my youthful naive eyes, these people proved to be boors without redemption. Not for a single second did it occur to me that my behaviour was inappropriate, or that I needed to feel self-conscious. To me, they were simply amiss in their manners.

Laughter and humour, when aimed at a certain person who is not "in the know" because she is new to a culture, or is different from the rest of the group in some way(s), is a method of ridicule or mockery. It is particularly so when the person being laughed at is not included in the jocularity. If I had not had the assurance of privilege, the knowledge that my manners were impeccable, the assumption that my class background transcends most Western cultures, I would have withered in shame, wondered at my possible faux pas and wilted from the insensitivity of these, perhaps, well-meaning strangers. However, I did not give them a second thought. In the same way that I knew the term "immigrant woman" did not quite apply to me, I did not experience this incident as a humiliation or as a negative comment on my race or ethnicity. Even though I had just arrived from Egypt, a country considered "Third World," even though as a new graduate student I was at the bottom of the intellectual hierarchy in that department, and even though I was probably perceived as non-white, I had the composure of class and the confidence of privilege to protect me from the exclusion to which I may otherwise have been subjected and of which I may have been made an object.

From a very young age I was taught that I was a daughter of privilege, from a family of a certain class, from a particular city in the south of Egypt. Managing class is not just the knowledge that one is born to privilege, but also the understanding that this privilege may transcend different social and cultural changes. For instance, it did not come as a surprise to me when one day, as I was shopping for a sofabed in Eaton's department store in Toronto, the salesman recognized my family name. He came from Egypt and asked me the inevitable question to verify whether I came from that certain city in Upper Egypt and whether I was a Copt. Even though I was living on the limited means of a graduate student, he was immediately deferential. It was not me personally that he recognized, but how class operated in Egypt. The major discount he gave me was, perhaps, a reflection of his acknowledgement that, even in this new country, he had not forgotten the conventions of our past lives, that we both belonged—if differently—to a distant past, that in the vast sea of Canadian foreignness, we shared a common history.

The formation of my identity includes my class, my colour, my ethnicity, my sex, my sexuality and my religion. These factors seem to have been constant since I was old enough to identify myself. They

85

are my location. However, other elements which are as important are variable, their relevance modified by changes in personal politics, circumstances, age, career, current ideologies, the general political climate.

I came to this country over two decades ago. I could speak both official languages very fluently and with minimum accent. The relative lightness of my skin colour combined with my privileged class background have spared me from experiences of discrimination or prejudice. At best, I intimidated people around me; at worst, they found me exotic. Even though "exotic" is, broadly speaking, a form of racist categorization, the word is often used to imply a kind of difference which is coveted rather than scorned. Although I claim not to have suffered racism, I am often made to feel aware of my different-ness. Strangers regularly mispronounce my name, but then people in North America often stumble over names that are not simple to spell or are uncommon. When I refuse to use my first name, Madiha, it is because of the way it is frequently butchered, and because it is seldom remembered (even when people comment on "what a pretty name" it is). Moreover, as a result of its foreignness, if my name is being called out so I can take my turn at being served, it is often presumed that I do not understand English (especially if I hesitate before answering). I am addressed, therefore, in that loud, over-enunciated diction which assumes that volume will make up for language. But it takes only a moment to set people straight. I would maintain that those incidents are very minor, that if they constitute racism they, essentially, do not have any recognizable consequence on my life.

I have been assimilated well. I do not stand out. I have had to adjust to Canadian cultural significations, not to prevent discrimination against me, but to avert feelings of inadequacy which may spring from lack of communication. I have had to alter my British accent, to tone down my formal manners, to adapt to many Canadian customs and traditions. I have learned to use cultural referents to project the messages I want to convey. Consequently, I become invisible because I am recognizable. What is concealed is my history; what is hidden is my Egyptian-ness. However, I am in a position to produce my history when it suits me, when it adds a new dimension to my qualities, and certainly not when it can be held against me. Can it be said that my very insistence on assimilating is itself a response to levels of internalized racism? Is the invisibility of my foreignness precisely an indication of racism? I have argued that I do not suffer racism because of class and skin colour. This does not deny that racism exists, but it does suggest that, given certain other factors, I am not touched by its virulence. My assertions contain elements of contradiction because they stem from a complicated issue. The fact remains that I am spared, that in the ability to define my own identity, to convey a specific persona, to contain these contradictions, I can control how I am perceived. I choose to make myself invisible only in that I want to blend; I do not want to stand out. Consequently, although I can be heard, a part of me is silenced.

Rigid definitions of race and ethnicity, which do not account for the fluidity of the categories, are not useful in that they mask the differences of class and location. They fail to respect individual identities or to take into account lived experiences. Conversely, gender as a category, when considered a basis for discrimination without accounting for class or for race, conceals distinct and intelligible levels of oppression within the category. And yet, Catharine MacKinnon reminds us, "to argue that oppression 'as a woman' negates rather than encompasses recognition of the oppression of women on other bases, is to say that there is no such thing as the practice of sex inequality." It is also difficult to forget an early comment by Audre Lorde, who informs us succinctly that "Black feminists speak as women because we are women." Feminism transcends yet recognizes difference. As a feminist, I bring to the discussion of race and gender the specificities of colour and class. Unless the boundaries of race, gender, class and sexuality intersect to make visible the various nuances of each category, the usefulness of each becomes lost in a hierarchy of oppressions. In other words, if we isolate each characteristic in an attempt to make it visible without taking the whole framework into consideration, we are, in effect, rendering invisible the significant factors that combine to produce situations of oppression and discrimination. We are reduced to piling one oppression onto another to show the extent of discrimination, or we attempt to debate which form of oppression — race or gender or class or sexuality — is more potent. Gender, race, class and sexuality have to be considered together and at the same time. They must each convey specific location without denying the distinctiveness of individual experiences.

If I have personally ever felt the alienation of national identity, it is not in Canada but in Egypt. Egypt, situated in what Europeans called "the Orient," is anchored in people's minds as "a place of romance, exotic beings, haunting memories and landscapes," but, as Edward Said continues, "The Orient was almost a European invention." In Egypt, where colonization by the French and English has

87

reworked class structures to incorporate Western notions of "culture" and "education," upper-class society demands an understanding and consideration of, and an affinity with, the conquerors, with their locus of power. Some of the questions Said addresses in his book are appropriate: "What . . . sorts of intellectual, aesthetic, scholarly, and cultural energies went into the making of an imperialist tradition . . . ? What is the meaning of originality, of continuity, of individuality, in this context? How does Orientalism transmit or reproduce itself from one epoch to another?" I am a product of his problematic. Despite my pure Coptic origins, each one of my family sports a European name: my father Andrew, my uncles Albert, Maurice, Robert and my aunts Edna, Margaret, Dora. My generation was defiantly christened with Arabic names, another conqueror, but closer in geography and culture. It is in Egypt where I have never properly learned my native tongue that I feel like a foreigner. I have never read Egyptian literature except in translation. The literary imagery that informed my youth is that of distant lands. I recited poems on daffodils when I had never set eyes on one. I described fields, streams and forests while living in a land of intensive agriculture and wasted deserts. I knew of snow but had never experienced it. I enjoyed Western toys, bought real estate in London playing British Monopoly, and donned clothes made in Europe. I attended French and English schools, and an American university. I walked the streets of Cairo and felt I did not belong because I spoke my own language with the exaggerated enunciation of one who is not using it continually; my idioms are outdated, my expression forgotten. When I return to my native land, I stand as foreign, am perceived as alien. I was never assimilated because class demanded a perceived difference from the masses. In Canada I am integrated because my survival depends on my being like everybody else.

Finally, living in Canada, I have had to adjust to Canadian culture so as to be seen and as a way to be recognized. However, for me to include myself in a category such as "immigrant woman" or "woman of colour" would be to deny the very real experiences of oppression suffered by those who are truly disadvantaged within those labels.

Furthermore, within the framework of politically correct discourse, I would be given legitimacy to speak if I were to mention that I am a woman of colour. I would be granted even greater licence as a lesbian woman of colour. However, I do not believe in a hierarchy of oppressions. I do not want to be heard through a label imposed on me, through white guilt, but rather because of the validity of my words — whether I am a woman of colour or not. I do not want to be erased as a consequence of an assumed identity. As a woman, I have too often been silenced. As a lesbian, I have frequently been paralysed. As an immigrant, a woman of colour, I might be given a voice because of the current political climate. But this voice is not mine; it belongs to those who live with the daily burden of those oppressions.

Acknowledgements

I gratefully acknowledge the support and ideas of Marian McMahon, Frieda Forman, Linda Carty, Peggy Bristow, Mary Lou Soutar-Hynes and my sister, Dina Khayatt. They should get the credit for refining my thinking, although I take the responsibility for my words.

A version of this paper appeared in *Canadian Women's Studies Journal*, Spring 1994 (Volume 14, Number 2).

Notes

1 "Multiculturalism" is a term that expresses the varied ethnic heritages of Canadians. *The Collins Dictionary of Canadian History, 1867 to the Present* by David J. Bercuson and J.L. Granatstein (Toronto: Collins, 1988, p.143) states that the term was first heard in the 1960s "as a counter to the emphasis on Bilingualism and Biculturalism that characterized the Liberal Government." The authors explain that the "ethos of multiculturalism is that every Canadian, whatever his or her origin, has the right to honour his or her heritage in Canada." However, the dictionary also notes that government policies of multiculturalism were subsequently perceived to be a political tool to remove francophone concerns from the limelight by introducing those of other rapidly growing ethnicities. This strategy promoted a politics of divide and rule by using federal funds. Marjory Bowker distinguishes between two versions of multiculturalism, in the first of which "all cultures are allowed to prosper and flourish amongst their followers; that nothing in the law be allowed to impede the personal enjoyment and enrichment to be derived from one's ethnic heritage." The other version, like the above, "concerns government funding for ethnic programs which tend to divide rather than unite, resulting in a loss of cohesiveness and eventually a fragmented Canadian culture." (Marjorie Bowker. *Canada's Constitutional Crisis: Making Sense of It All*. Edmonton, Alberta: Lone Pine Publishing, 1991, p.87.)

IS IT JAPANESE ARTIST OR ARTIST WHO IS JAPANESE?

LILLIAN BLAKEY

About twenty years ago, *he* changed my name. And I became a split personality. All my life, I had been called by various forms of Lillian—Lil, Lily, Liliane, even Lilika—all of which were more or less acceptable to the real me, all of which identified me as myself, to myself. One's name is intimate, a cocoon that gives comfort, familiarity and security in a world that can be hostile. It is with you all of your life, or so I thought before I met *him*. Even changing my surname upon marriage did not affect me a great deal, but allowing someone to change the name that is the essence of me was like giving all of myself away. "Wait!" I cried silently in panic, "I've changed my mind. I don't want my name changed!" Too late. He told everyone he knew immediately. I felt myself slipping away, like a mist dissipated by the sun's over-powering heat. And the people who had known me before this name change looked at me in amazement, as if I had had a sex change.

He was my first husband. He was quite a forceful individual in his own way. On first impression, he appeared to be like a clumsy teddy bear who somehow inspired everyone around him, especially women, to look after all of his needs. We *all* gave in. I fell into the trap of agreeing to the change of my name, even though I was, deep down inside, very unwilling.

Right from the beginning, he felt that my Japanese name, Michi-ko, was much better than my English name, Lillian. And he decided that the shortened version, Michi, was the best of all. The only problem was that he changed the pronunciation to Meeshee, because to his ear it sounded more poetic. To my ear, this name was weird and foreign; it was not even Japanese. But like hosts of women before me, I allowed myself to be manipulated. I could not bring myself to contradict him because he was so pleased with himself. The truth is, I did have a choice, but I blew it. Because I said nothing, he interpreted my silence as approval. I now know that being Japanese had a lot to do with my choices, and less to do with his pushiness.

It's funny that, although I am so far removed from being "Japanese," much of my behaviour is still influenced heavily by a Japanese mentality and code of ethics, which can be a handicap in this country, where people's values differ so greatly. What can be good manners to one group of people can be insulting to another, because common understandings of appropriate behaviours are lacking. Of course, now the problems are compounded because of the increasingly large number of races, religious beliefs, attitudes and cultures that make up Canada. However, for most of my experience, there were white people, and then there were a few of us who were not white. I always felt as if I had one foot in the boat and the other foot on land. Very odd, at times. Most often, I found myself taking the role of observer in both worlds, rather than as a full participant in either.

The Japanese mentality obviously took over when my husband announced the name change. I found myself deferring to the male, who makes all the decisions in a Japanese household, where it is the women, not the children, who should be seen but not heard. All my life, I had watched my father decide what clothes my mother should wear, how she should wear her hair, what furniture she should have, what her job should be, and who her friends should be. It is no wonder I grew up thinking that men should make up my mind for me. My only saving grace was that my father had no sons. I became the son he should have had; therefore, the message was unclear whether I should behave as a Japanese male or as a Japanese female — or both, depending upon the situation or my father's inclination!

In addition, Japanese manners also dictate that, when confronted with a particularly embarrassing situation, you are not supposed to mention the problem. Embarrassment is to be avoided at all costs, even if it means disaster to you personally. You must allow the offender to save face because it is a matter of preserving his honour. Honour is so important that even enemies are courteous to one another. Hence, the inscrutable Asian! For a long time, my feelings used to be hurt by non-Japanese because I did not understand that people have some very conflicting modes of behaviour which can lead to enormous misunderstandings. And obviously, although I am not Japanese, I had inherited this very deeply ingrained mentality without even realizing it. It is only now that I am beginning to understand my cultural inheritance and to deal with it successfully in my life.

And so, I had allowed the name change because I would rather have had him do this than point out his insensitivity to my feelings and his blatant lack of respect for me. The way he looked at it, though, was that if I did not like what he was doing, I should have said so. Instead, my resentment seethed under the surface because I felt he ought to have known how I really felt. The marriage did not survive.

It was only a matter of time before I exploded and stopped repressing my real self, because the other half of me was pure Canadian. This other self had very strong beliefs about equality for women at work and at home. I was among the earliest advocates of equal pay for equal work. Not quite a suffragette, but not a doormat either! This duality of Japanese female subservience and Canadian feminism has continued to haunt me to this day, and it has taken me all of my adult life to come to terms with it. It has deeply affected my attitudes, my beliefs and my relationships.

Growing up, I had taken virtually no interest in things Japanese. As a child in Toronto in the fifties, my sister and I were the only Japanese Canadian children around for miles. My parents had avoided having much close contact with the Japanese community because of their reaction to the violent discrimination they experienced in pre-war British Columbia. My father always felt that part of the problem there was that the Japanese were such a close-knit group that they attracted suspicion and resentment to themselves. He decided that the best way for our future was to assimilate into the dominant culture. We were among the first to come to Toronto, and we lived apart from other Japanese Canadians, who obviously had the same idea. Unlike the Chinese, or the Italians, or the Greeks, or the Blacks, there is no definable Japanese community in Toronto even today. We had learned our lesson well.

My sister and I behaved like perfect children because we were encouraged to be invisible, to think white outside the home and to think Japanese in the home, and not to draw attention to the fact that we were Japanese. We were loved by our teachers and well-liked

93

by our friends because we worked harder than everyone else, so that we could be model citizens in a white society. Like the Toyota slogan, "We try harder!!"

As a result, the only culture I really know is European. Somewhere in the process of growing up and being educated, I had learned to deny my Japanese cultural heritage and to reject an integral part of myself, a part which, sadly, can never be regained. Although in later years I have explored Japanese philosophy, art, social and economic structures, and cultural traditions, it is always as an outsider looking in — never as one who belongs.

The experience which first awakened my curiosity to explore my heritage took place at the Japanese Canadian Cultural Centre, which I had visited only once before, to attend a wedding reception. The Japanese Canadians in Toronto erected this sanctuary at great expense to preserve their cultural heritage. When you think of the effort, it was quite a feat to get people who were not a community to work so long together to fulfil a common goal. I remember my father contributing to this undertaking for years, although I do not recall his ever going there. He always used to say, "When I retire, I'll have time to go there." He never did retire.

One thing which has always impressed me about the second-generation Japanese Canadian people is their incredible solidarity on matters of loyalty and reverence. Never mind that they have never been to Japan. These people are more Japanese than the Japanese in Japan. Their lifelong dream is a pilgrimage to the land of their fathers. And even if they do not see each other for years, they are fused together in a bond of kinship, a part of the cultural link which is so precariously thin in the land that is home and yet is still alien to them. As a result, they rally around the flag with the rising sun in undertakings such as the building of the Centre, which is almost a shrine embodying Japan, the homeland they will most likely never see. Similarly, when one of their own passes away, as did my father a decade ago, suddenly, out of nowhere come hundreds of people to pay their last respects. I remember thinking, "I don't know any of these people. When did he know them? I've been with him for thirty-five years and I've never seen them before."

The Japanese Canadian Cultural Centre itself inspired pride, partly because of its understated beauty and elegance, partly because it was designed by one of the sons of the Japanese Canadian community who had "made it" in a field dominated by white society. It was one of the earliest works of Raymond Moriyama, who has since become one of Canada's foremost architects. The building and its surrounding gardens were a true reflection of the serene, low-lying structures of Japan, and every feature of it spoke of good taste. Moriyama had envisioned a building that was in harmony with nature in the abundant use of beautifully crafted wood and stone surfaces throughout the inner and outer spaces. Behind the building was a lovely garden which inspired contemplation and inner harmony. In front of the main entrance was an incredible cantilevered fountain with a spiral of layered slabs of natural stone, landing as if flung by the hand of God Himself. Now, the beauty of the place has been marred by the addition of a paved parking lot around the fountain instead of a crystal clear lily pond with goldfish. People rush into the building without even a glance at the creation that stands before them with mute pride.

Perhaps it was the aesthetic beauty of the place which inspired me to agree to take part in the annual Arts and Craft show. As an artist, I could not resist the temptation. Ordinarily, I would never have agreed to create craft instead of art. But I thought to myself, "This is not your everyday craft show. After all, the surroundings are truly a work of art. It certainly is not your church basement craftsy show." What a terrible snob I was to distinguish between art and craft. I now realize that my vision was clouded partly by the brainwashing of the institutionalized Western philosophy of art education I had received at university. I also now realize, upon reflection, that this philosophy also casts doubt on the validity of all art forms not in the Western tradition. But it has taken me almost a quarter of a century of soul-searching to realize that that tradition always looks after its own and makes no room for the new kid on the block.

At the time, I felt a little odd about taking part in the show. My feelings were mixed as I became acutely aware that I was not one of "them." And I certainly did not want people who came to the show to think I was one of "them." Inside, I had become white and I felt very uncomfortable in the presence of other people of my race. I was a closet racist. I had prided myself on my acceptance of other people's beliefs and values — people other than the Japanese, that is. Today, when I look back at myself, I am horrified at this totally insensitive me.

And so my art career was launched by this craft show. I decided to create "soft sculpture." They were really soft toys, but I called them soft sculpture, to elevate their status to the level of art. I literally threw myself into my work, sewing frantically eight hours a day in

95

between running, like a fiend, after my precocious twin daughters. When they did sleep, they usually did so for four hours at a stretch. As they were being revitalized, I was creating art as if I were possessed by a demon. In one month, I designed and sewed eighty pieces, each one unique, each one a work of art. No patterns for me. After all, if you were going to be an artist, reproduction was forbidden.

A few days before the show, I suddenly thought I would like to create a real art piece, an appliquéd wall hanging, which would form a suitable eye-catching backdrop to my display of soft sculptures. In a fit of inspiration, I was transported into a fantasy world of underwater splendour with imaginary schools of fish, plants and coral, all positioned carefully to look spontaneous in a flowing design filled with movement and vibrant blues, purples and greens. At that time, I had no idea that this wall hanging would change my life.

As I was sitting by my display during the show, a very chic woman in an immaculate cream-coloured suit, dark glasses and a hat, which was tilted at precisely the right angle to give an air of mystery, approached me. I could not see her eyes behind the dark lenses. She reminded me of Ingrid Bergman in *Casablanca*. She glanced at the work and surreptitiously handed me her card. I looked at it. *Evans Gallery 123 Scollard Street Toronto Ruth Levinson, Director.* I looked at her. Without a hint of a smile, she said, "I'm interested in your work. Do you do anything besides children's themes?"

I replied, "Yes. I don't usually do children's art. I did these only for this show."

"Good," she answered tersely. "Why don't you bring me some of your other work. I'm looking for a fabric artist. By the way, what name do you go by?"

I do not know why, but when she asked me, I had a moment of anxiety. Which name should I give her? Instinctively, I knew that my professional name would be important. I blurted out "Meeshee, spelled M-I-C-H-I," and in a very small voice gave her my surname. I do not know why I said Michi and not Lillian, or why I was reluctant to give her my married name. Perhaps I subconsciously did not want to be tied to *him*. What flashed through my mind was that none of my fine art friends would know who Michi was and that it would be very difficult to change a professional name after a reputation was established. I probably chose Michi because it is the sort of name that could be used by itself, with no surname, but Lillian by itself would look stupid. However, as time went on, I regretted my decision, for each time I had a show, people would stumble on the pronunciation and ask me what it meant. All I knew was that the literal translation of Michi was road, and ko meant child; so I replied, "I guess it means child of the road." But in my mind, this response always evoked connotations of being a streetwalker's child and I would feel a smirk forming on my lips each time I was asked this question. In actual fact, I discovered a far more esoteric meaning much later. Michi is the way of the cosmos, not just a set of ethics for the artist or priest to live by, but the divine footprints of God pointing the way. I like this interpretation much better!

My heart was pounding as the chic lady walked away. I could not believe that someone actually thought that my work was good enough to display in one of the Yorkville galleries. I felt like Eliza Doolittle being discovered in *Pygmalion*. Things like this simply do not happen in real life.

Right after the show, I got busy with my first real art piece, producing it within a week. I am still mystified why I chose to create a non-representational piece of art. "White Night" was an abstract landscape completely created in varying tones of white fabric. Upon reflection today, I find myself thinking that this is an odd way of representing night. The other strange thing is that the abstract expressionism of the sixties had never been of intrinsic interest to me. As I grew older, I searched for meaning increasingly in the world of realism. Today, I paint only those images and people who are special in my own life.

There were many things which struck me as superficial in the art world. After the sale of that first piece, which really reminded me of an interior decorator's choice for an all-white room, it was decided that I should be half of a two-man show. Today, the word "man" would be replaced by "person," of course, but at that time, women were not exactly plentiful in the world of art. Another thing I found objectionable was the fact that I was now part of a "stable" of artists. It made us sound as if we were livestock to be disposed of at will. The director also decided that we had to get rid of any implication that my work was craft; therefore, my work was advertised as stitched fabric sculpture. They were not really sculptures. Stripped of all embellishing descriptions, they were appliqué wall hangings which were puffy and would pass as sculptural, perhaps. But being Japanese Canadian, I said nothing and smiled politely.

One of the most difficult things I had to do was to play the role of artist on display on the opening days of my shows. People come to drink wine, ask questions, see who else is there, be seen and perhaps

97

buy a piece. Being a very shy person who values private space, it almost killed me to be packaged, publicized and put on display for public scrutiny.

One absurd question repeated by many people, after the initial fumbling with the pronunciation of Michi, was, "And how long have you been in this country, dear?" to which I replied, "I was born here. So were my parents. And my grandparents, all four of them, came when they were very young." The answer was invariably, "Oh, my goodness, that is a long time." What this question had to do with my artwork defies logic. Perhaps it was the choice of the name Michi which triggered the train of thought that led to things foreign. It seems as if people automatically assume that one is a foreigner when one does things such as showing artwork, looking as I did, and with a name that they cannot pronounce.

Curiously, for ten years after the show, no one asked this question; now suddenly it is being asked again quite regularly. The people who are now asking me are the new Canadian Asians. It took me a while to catch on to why they were asking me where I was born. I kept on saying, "I was born here." And they would walk away, looking puzzled. I realized after a time that what they are searching for is another familiar person with whom they might have something in common in this totally alien culture. At first, I was reluctant to say that my family originally had come from Japan when the question was asked by a Chinese or Korean person, because of the inhumane treatment their countrymen had received at the hands of the Japanese. But I was relieved to find that they harboured no resentment. Any Asian, even a Japanese, was better than none!

A few years before this art opening, I had experienced the same odd feeling that this question had evoked. It was in my first year of teaching art that I was confronted by the night school pottery teacher, a nosy, chatty Englishwoman in her fifties, who always knew what everyone else should be doing.

"Why aren't you doing work that is more Japanese? Japanese art is so lovely. It really is a shame that you are not following your own heritage."

Immediately, I felt a prickling sensation on the back of my neck. Why should I be producing a hollow imitation of Japanese art when I am not Japanese? I merely happen to be an artist who looks Japanese. I found her suggestion patronizing, even a little insulting, for in her zeal to praise Japanese art, she had assumed that all artists who belong to a specific racial group should adhere to the art styles produced in their native country. Each to his own! I guess she felt that all Blacks should do African carvings and masks, all Ukrainians should decorate eggs, and that all Egyptians should make pyramids!!

What people like this woman fail to understand is that we are all products of an extremely complex set of influences, and that we are changing all the time. Nothing stands still, frozen in time. What she failed to see is that I was the product of two cultures, neither wholly of one nor of the other, and therefore my work, which is the expression of my particular view of the world, is bound to be different from the art of my ancestors. In fact, all true artists aspire to make an original contribution to art, not to rework glories of the past. It is absurd to think that I should be producing eighteenth-century Japanese woodblock prints.

The Japanese mentality in me was at work again as I answered politely that she was right. One should never ever criticize or disagree with someone older. Age gives a person the right to say the most outrageous things while maintaining a position of honour and respect. I still have trouble dealing with older people who are wrong.

Ironically, while I never attempted to make Japanese woodcuts, I did eventually try to resolve the dilemma of being two people in one through my art and, ultimately, my work does have a Japanese quality about it. By the time my first art show was launched, I had gone through much soul-searching in a variety of ways, ranging from trying out a few religions to writing poetry, but for me, the most meaningful way was through my art. Thus, two pieces in that first show marked milestones in my gradual self-awakening.

The first piece, "After the Fall," was a dark, romantic work which depicted Eve after she had fallen from grace. I was under great stress in deciding whether to present a naked Eve because, as strange as it may seem, the Japanese are extremely modest about nudity, though they think nothing of taking communal baths. My father thought nothing of walking naked to the bathroom when I was a child, but when my toddler twins tried to peek in, he would roar with panic, shouting to get them away from the door. Even erotic Japanese art does not reveal completely naked figures. There is usually a veil or some other strategically placed prop. Sexual matters are implied, not blatantly flaunted, for such immodesty would cause embarrassment. It was extremely important to me that my parents should not be embarrassed at my show.

My fears seem, in hindsight, to be ludicrous, because for years in my Fine Art studio classes I had drawn nudes, and I certainly was not embarrassed. We simply looked on nudes as subject matter, the same way we looked at bottles or flowers. Finally, I convinced myself that it would really be silly to cover Eve with a dress, or with leaves. This thought made me giggle, as it immediately brought to mind Dürer's "Expulsion," which shows Adam and Eve being hounded out of Eden, covering their private parts. Whenever I showed this work to my art students, they would roll with laughter. I am sure that Dürer never intended this reaction. All he was probably thinking about was the tragedy of loss of innocence.

What surprised me most about "After the Fall" was the review it received in the *Globe and Mail*, which described my work as appearing to be "heavily influenced by the surface decoration techniques of art nouveau. But closer inspection shows they go directly to the source that inspired art nouveau in the first place: Oriental art."

The strange thing about this observation is that I was not consciously following the conventions of either art nouveau or Asian art. All I was trying to do was to create harmony of design in establishing the profound sadness when one loses innocence and things can never be the same again. Hence, the dark, rich tones and the repetition of the lines mirroring the stillness, the timelessness caused by the guilt Eve felt after the sin. Perhaps there is a part of me which is so Japanese that it haunts my subconscious mind and manifests itself in the way I perceive and interpret the world in my art. My second husband believes in the reality and persistence of race memory. Maybe there is something in his theory, after all.

For me, intuitively, the most important element in my work has always been spatial relationships. Not the actual subject matter. Not the colour. Or the form or line. The handling of space is what conveys the meaning. I have always concentrated naturally on the negative space, the space around the figures which, to the Western eye, is the space left over, the space which does not count. I feel that awareness is heightened if you concentrate on that which is not obvious. To some people, this is a very odd way of looking at things.

Perhaps this ability to focus on relationships is a gift from my Japanese heritage. The Japanese have always been masters at manipulating space in a peculiar way. In a tiny country so incredibly crowded with people, they are able to find enough private space to make tiny gardens and create the illusion of vast expanses—raked sand that appears as a wind-rippled beach where no man has trod, a tiny pool that takes on the dimensions of a large pond complete with fish, reeds and lily pads, bonsai trees that are only a few inches high, but deceive the eye and make you think they are full-grown trees.

I will always remember an artist friend's description of his first attempts at learning ceramics from a Japanese teacher. After many, many frustrating tries, the teacher took my friend aside and demonstrated. "What you are doing wrong," he said, "is that you are trying too hard to control the outer shape of your pot. Concentrate on the shape inside the pot, and the outside shape will follow naturally." Sometimes a different way of looking at a problem makes all the difference.

The second piece from my first show, "Mirror," is really a portrait of my two selves. At the time, I felt I had to write a preface to the work. In it, I explored my dilemma of being two people in one:

> "Mirror" is an introspective piece which attempts to express my ambiguous feelings resulting from belonging to two very different cultures. It is a highly symbolic work. The two women are really one, as if one of them is looking at a mirror image of herself. Both are Oriental. One is in Western dress and the other is in a Japanese kimono. But who is the real person and who is the image in the mirror?

I have had many shows since this first one, and exhibited with many other galleries, but in 1980, with the death of both my father and my marriage, I decided that Michi must also die. I removed everything from the gallery and never really said goodbye. I simply said that I would be in touch sometime. It has been over ten years since I walked out of that gallery to begin my new life.

Since that time, I have experienced much, but I have never sewn anything again. And it is probable that I will never sew again, because I had never really wanted to become an artist known for wall hangings. I had never wanted to be Michi and I had always thought of myself as a painter. At the present time, I am painting images of people and situations that are part of my private world. Now I am faced with a dilemma of a very different nature. To show my work again means that I must be prepared to share my work with strangers and, eventually, to part with it. At the moment, it still belongs completely to me.

My work remains a study of space. I once wrote, "In silent spaces between the notes, I stand outside myself and watch." And it is the poignant space between the figures that carries the essence of the message I wish to convey. Am I, then, a Japanese artist, or am I an artist who is Japanese? Perhaps, ultimately, the answer to that question is heavily ironic; perhaps, ultimately, there is no distinction.

BEING GERMAN,
BEING CANADIAN
GOTTFRIED PAASCHE

I

In response to an attractive offer of a teaching position at a Canadian university, my wife, two small children and I moved to Canada in the summer of 1966. My wife had been born in America, and I had been in America since I was almost eleven years old. Moving to Canada had never been something we had thought about. At the time, the people around us considered the move rather risky from a professional perspective. It looked to them as if we were abandoning the benefits to be reaped from obtaining degrees from major American institutions in fields that offered great opportunities. I was headed to a newly founded university in a country in which my field of expertise had a shorter history and, although also expanding, was much less influential and prominent.

Why did we make this move early in our careers? First of all, although it became a permanent move, that was far from our minds. It was a professionally mobile era, and we assumed we would be elsewhere, most likely back in America, in a few years. For my wife the attraction was that we were moving to a major city, Toronto, which offered her many professional opportunities and promised to be a good place to raise our children. It was also closer to those parts of the United States in which she had grown up, and with which she wanted to maintain close links.

My mind set was a little different. I had joked that it was better to live beside a super power than in it. This was not a reflective comment, just something I found myself saying. My roots in America were in California. Because I had moved around even in America, I had no special need to be in any particular place (although I favoured an urban location at the time). In that sense, I was loose. I was also not deeply committed to a professional life, to a productive life yes, but not to a notion of career. On the other hand, I had an image of Canada as a peace loving, United Nations supporting country. I was aware of Lester Pearson, the UN, and of his Nobel Peace Prize.

In retrospect this may have been more important than I realized at the time. Twenty-five years later I had an experience which clarified my move to Canada for me. It was the winter after Saddam Hussein had marched into Kuwait, and the Americans were escalating their threats of retaliation. I found my spirits falling every time President Bush hurled an ultimatum at Saddam, even though I had no sympathy for the Iraqi. I told my friends that my America was a kind, generous place; Americans were not a warlike people. Later, as I was walking across the campus of the university at which I teach, the realization struck me that I myself had once been conquered by the Americans. I had been identifying with the object of American wrath! Immediately my spirits lifted, and I assumed a more rational stance towards the conflict. In other words, I was finding out that I had quite an ambivalent, conflict-full sense of identity when it came to America.

II

I was born in Japan to German parents and had lived there during the Second World War. At the end of the war, I embraced my American conquerors as all good, in order to come to terms as a child with the defeat of Japan. My parents withheld knowledge of their own loyalties from me, and had also not given me any help in making my own belated transition once the war had ended. Many years later, Canada seems to have been a kind of solution for me, unwittingly grasped, because it was neither Germany nor America. I had laid to rest my earlier Japanese identity. In this article I want to explore how I got to where I am today in terms of my Japanese, German, American and Canadian identities.

III

In March of 1948, three years after the end of the Second World War, my family emigrated to America. I spoke Japanese before either German or English. I had learned German in the family, and English in nursery school in Tokyo. Although I've lived significant segments of my life in Japan, America, and Canada, one constant throughout has been the German language.

It was part of the Japanese ethos of that time that foreigners in their land maintain their own language and identity, in effect, their own place. One of the first decisions a foreigner made in Japan was whether to live in a Japanese or in a Western-style house, and whether or not to live in a part of town or a region in which there were many Western homes and institutions. My parent's inclinations, and the circumstances which brought them to Japan, predisposed them to live only marginally amongst other Germans. It led them to live among and associate with the Japanese themselves, and with others from non-German, or non-conventional (e.g., non-Nazi) German backgrounds. Hence my early acquisition of both the Japanese and English languages.

My memory of playmates and friends begins mostly after 1941, when all those foreigners whose countries of citizenship had declared war on Japan and who could leave had left Japan. I had one playmate who had German parents (of a family that had roots in Japan), and the rest were Japanese. I don't recall being aware of being German, or of being different from the Japanese. I grew up identifying deeply with Japan. The isolation of war, and the difficulties of daily living that we shared with the Japanese around us, probably made it easier to be and to feel Japanese.

On the street we played with neighbourhood children. There were all kinds of games to be played. However, our more intimate family associations tended to be with families who had Western educations and connections. For instance, we were very close with a family that was a leader in the local Christian community. Although we were not particularly Christian, it did serve as a common bond in opposition to the majority Japanese society. I spent endless hours in the midst of this family that lived completely in the Japanese manner.

I was sometimes thrown into conflicting situations. On the same street along which I joined village children in playing highly dramatic and intense war games, I was also followed by gangs of children yelling "gei jin, gei jin" ("foreigner, foreigner"). Somewhat later, when I

105

was of school age, I would sometimes be the centre of attention because of my exotic, in the Japanese context, physical features. I would
be asked to close my eyes only to be greeted by a burst of giggles, or
entreated to allow schoolgirls to touch my soft, blond hair. I don't recall these experiences causing me any distress. I felt Japanese. War
time is a time of mobilization. I read the Japanese children's comics
which featured the struggle against the "foreign devil." I had an older
friend in the army, and when he came home injured he visited me.

An additional but crucial context for my childhood in Japan was
my parents' own particular relation to Germany and to Japan. My
parents had left Germany in order to distance themselves from the
Nazis. My mother's father was prominent as part of the German military opposition to Hitler and the Nazis, while she herself had a wide
circle of Jewish friends and acquaintances. In 1934 she went to Pales-
tine with my father to visit her Zionist friends from Berlin and to explore emigration. She soon found herself under increasing pressure
from the Gestapo. Had she stayed in Germany she would have had to
choose between endangering her family, her father in particular, or
betraying her Jewish friends and colleagues. My own father, on the
other hand, had a Jewish grandfather. When the first Nazi anti-Jewish
laws were introduced, he had to give up the study of law. Instead he
turned to the study of Japanese. After my father decided against Pales-
tine, they made up their minds hurriedly in 1935 to travel to Japan.
They were attracted to Japan by my father's interest in the language
and culture, as well as its position in the world. They did not anticipate Japanese military ambitions and Japan's alliance with Germany.

Although my parents managed to leave Germany in the early
stages of Nazi domination and the realization of military ambition,
they did not manage to leave Japan in 1941, when it attacked the
United States, and many of their closest friends departed. They had
begun as exiles from Germany and ended up in internal exile in
Japan.

IV

Among the Germans in Japan, a portion were Nazi sympathizers. My
parents had to guard themselves against these people. Once the Japanese were allied with Germany, my parents had to guard themselves
against representatives, open or hidden, of the Japanese government.
The situation for them was fraught with danger. One protective strat-

egy they used was to maintain total silence about the nature of their sympathies with respect to the combatants in the war. As children we grew up knowing little about our parents' politics. As a child during the war, I did not know that my parents hoped and prayed for German defeat or, more importantly, that a Japanese defeat was linked to German defeat. My sympathies, in so far as I was able at that age to understand the situation, were with the Japanese. And, partly because we were separated from our parents' families, and also partly because of the caution of my parents, I knew almost nothing of my families in Germany. I was not given a sense of who we were.

My parents' difficulties with the other Germans in Japan had an impact on us children. We were aware very early on that my parents were shunned by them. We didn't know why, simply that our parents were not accorded the respect we felt was due them. A particular experience had occurred in the one year in which I was sent to a German school. My older sister tells me that I was called names and that stones were thrown at me, and that she had had to defend me. We did not finish the school year. My parents subsequently hired private tutors, or simply gave us lessons themselves.

I have had a life-long ambivalence about my German background as well as a fascination with it. I think this is rooted in these early experiences and circumstances in Japan. My Japanese identity was more clearly available to me than was my German identity. When we left Japan in 1948, when I was ten years old, I went through deep mourning; I assiduously studied my Japanese characters on the ocean passage. I consumed every scrap of Japanese news for several years and cried over the terrible natural disasters that hit Japan so severely in the post-war years. I tried to speak Japanese in California to people I thought were Japanese only to find that they would hurry away. I hadn't known of the wartime internment camps for Japanese Americans.

There was a specific day when I knew that my ability to speak Japanese was slipping away. It was the verb forms that I lost first, followed by the nouns. I have retained an interest in and admiration for the Japanese and things Japanese. However, what I learned after the war has also made me critical of Japan during the war years. I have retained the language of gestures: body language. I often find myself misinterpreted because I sometimes respond in situations of social interaction in a Japanese fashion. For instance, I laugh in situations in which it is culturally inappropriate here, that is, when I am feeling discomfort or sense discomfort in others. I find myself bending my upper body forward in the Japanese fashion when I say goodbye, and so on.

My Japanese childhood has taught me how to make foreigners feel at ease, especially in adapting English speech patterns in such a way that I am more easily understood by non-English speakers. I speak a somewhat differently intoned English when I speak to someone from Japan or from other non-English-speaking countries. Part of my Japanese heritage is that I feel at ease with people from other cultures, and am able to make some of the adaptations necessary for easier communication.

My later ambivalence about being an American and living in America was rooted in my years in Japan and in the nature of my contact with Americans. As a Japanese (and a German), I had been defeated by the Americans, but in no time I had joined them and then ventured into the "belly of the beast." In Japan I had started visiting the U.S. tank company that had set itself up not far from our home in Chigasaki. A kindly, older sergeant had a uniform, complete with insignia, made for me. I became a regular. I helped out with English-Japanese translation at the gates of the camp. I was allowed to use the mess hall and the club, enabling me to bring food to my family each day. I rode around in tanks and jeeps, unless forced out by an officer. In this way, I was, at the age of nine, an eyewitness to a major military exercise simulating the American invasion of Japan (only a short distance from where we lived!). Because of my connections, I was able to arrange our transportation to the ship that carried us to America. My father had found work in the headquarters of the American Occupation in Tokyo, and later decided that in order to complete his university studies, we would emigrate to the United States.

I was ten-and-a-half when we landed in San Francisco. Overnight my Japanese background became largely invisible to others. I was never asked in school about my knowledge of the Japanese language or culture. I may have collaborated here. We were keenly aware that Japan had just lost a war to the United States, and that our Japanese background might meet with hostility. People knew us as refugees and as Germans.

My German identity was a kind of void at this point. I spoke German within the family and could read and write the language, although my formal German schooling was limited. I doubt that I knew where Germany was, nor did I know any of its history, including its immediate past. And I knew very little of my own family history.

I found myself poorly prepared for suddenly having my German background highlighted in America. I was at an age, however, when I needed a sense of family and background. I began by inventing a past. I recall, when I was about twelve, telling an older girl (in an effort to impress, undoubtedly) that I was related to the German imperial family. I did this on the strength of the name "Maximilian" that I had heard in connection with my father's family, and my mother's own aristocratic origins. There was, in other words, an emptiness that I was taking the first steps to fill. This has turned into a lifelong quest.

There was also the headlong rush to be an American, indistinguishable from other Americans, at a time in history when there was absolutely no doubt that to be in America was to become an American. It was seen as natural to become "naturalized." There was never any question in other people's minds but that we would become Americans. I suppose that it had something to do with California itself. People did not concern themselves with our past, only with our present and future. Except that it was also the dawn of the Cold War and the fear of Communism: the Immigration Service and the FBI did take an interest in us.

My parents were repeatedly questioned by agents of these services. They were especially interested in my mother's purported Soviet Communist connections. I still marvel at the image of my mother sitting in a simple California living room, in a rundown house, in a rundown part of town, being questioned about reports that in the early 1930s she had run off to the Soviet Union with the military attaché of the Soviet Embassy in Berlin. The agents were basing their information on Soviet diaries later proven to be fakes ("disinformation").

There was also the situation of my mother's older sister, who had chosen to live in the German Democratic Republic (as the Soviet zone of occupation was later to be called), and who earned her livelihood there as a lawyer. It was always said that this circumstance blocked my father's career in the United States. He later worked in the Chinese-language section of the Library of Congress in Washington D.C., but without the the possibility of security clearance, and hence advancement.

My parents had been suspect first in Germany, then in Japan, and finally in the United States of America. Actually, given the historical circumstances of the twentieth century, this was a solid accomplishment on their part, it seems to me.

V

This history and predicament of my parents had certain consequences for me. Although my family lived in California, I spent my high school years at a boarding school in the state of Vermont. In my senior year I was embarrassed when my father wrote a letter to my history teacher complaining about what he viewed as a pro-Communist bias in the list of course readings. Most dramatically, in that last year of high school, I found that I had to answer questions from the FBI about my senior project in history. I had made a study of Lenin and the Bolshevik Revolution; the FBI had obtained a copy of my essay. In that same California living room in which my mother had faced interrogation, I was interrogated by two agents. This happened a year after I had become an American citizen in a proud ceremony in a judge's chambers, in San Francisco. I had been pleased that I was able to answer all his questions concerning the American Constitution and form of government, such as, "How many senators are there?"

A lasting legacy for me of these dimensions of my parents' lives was a caution about joining any organized groups. For many years I worked on the margins of groups like the NAACP without actually joining. In the fall of 1956 during my first year at the University of California, Berkeley, for instance, I became interested in the work of the local chapter of the American Civil Liberties Union. The chapter president had asked me to take on the office of treasurer in the organization. My mother and father came to visit me on the campus; my father implored me not to join. I did not argue, or resist him. His experience with, and fears about, political persecution were in my bones. I continued to work for the ACLU, but without formally joining or accepting a title.

VI

In spite of these experiences and the ambivalence and confusion they must have sown, I embraced America with open arms. America was to be our future. And at every turn in America we met with generosity from strangers, new friends, teachers and many others. However, my parents had an exceedingly difficult time after coming to the United States. They were in mid-life with a family of four children, the oldest almost a teenager and the youngest a preschooler. After one year of full-time work, they entered into the life of graduate students. My father studied and worked part-time, while my mother worked full-time. My father worked nights in a tomato canning factory, and once as a butler. My mother had various jobs. She worked as a cook, a house cleaner, a secretary, and finally as a research assistant. Later I felt a bitterness at the harshness of the life my parents encountered in America. I learned that emigration favours the next generation, the children, not the parents.

But I plunged into believing in America. The country that had defeated my "team" had to be perfect. Paul Robeson's singing of "The Ballad for Americans," a poignant and expressive celebration of American ideals of diversity and equality, captured my imagination and feeling about my new country. I encountered contrary evidence in books. My eighth-grade teacher gave us Steinbeck's *The Grapes of Wrath* and Richard Wright's *Native Son* to read. I was amazed and moved by what I learned in these books about American life. And there were personal experiences with poverty, and the difficulties my family had with housing, health, and the finding of decent work.

Ten years later, in 1959, when I made my first trip to Germany, I was struck by how thoroughly I had drunk of the "American Dream." It was the era of American school desegregation (on which I was to base my doctoral work), and of racial violence against Blacks in the South. America was uniquely a society, I tried to convince my German acquaintances and fellow students, that had the capacity to overcome all social obstacles.

VII

In the early years in America, although I was busy creating an American identity, I was also groping towards my German identity. I struggled to keep alive my ability to communicate in German. I did not present myself as German; I kept it very close to myself. In my teenage years, when I found myself far from my family, I would go alone into the woods to practise my German. I avoided situations that would draw out my German background. It was a kind of secret. It was almost as if by exposing it, I would lose it. My German identity was a fragile thing. I recall learning about the Holocaust in high

111

school and finding it totally incomprehensible. I had no context for it. Who were these Germans responsible for such unspeakable crimes? What was my connection to them? I had not yet fully understood my parents' own background in Germany and why they had left for Japan in 1935. At this time I remember the high school being shown a film about cultural differences narrated by Margaret Mead. I silently noted that the German children shown in the film were characterized by obedience. It ate at me. I was inwardly ashamed that the whole school saw this as what was typically German. Just as in Japan, I was finding that identifying as a German in America was a double-edged sword.

I also recall feeling irritated by an American stereotype that I often encountered of Germans as loud, beer-drinking, sauerkraut-and-sausage-eating boors (Oktoberfest Germans). In university I was to learn that this caricature of Germans grew out of a conflict in the late nineteenth-century between newly arrived German immigrants and native supporters of the so-called "Blue Laws" (e.g., restricting the purchase and public consumption of alcohol). However, at the time I responded by having nothing but contempt for any such Germans. I had known very few Germans and had never lived in a fully German environment, and none of the Germans I had known fit such a stereotype, least of all my parents.

I still remember my first encounter with Germans that seemed to fit some of these stereotypes. It occurred when I had arranged for a stay in a cabin in the Blue Ridge Mountains of Virginia, and had joined my parents for a brief vacation there. A group of Germans who seemed to me to be behaving just like the stereotype passed us on the trail just on the other side of the cabin. I was mortified. Incidentally, I learned later that my father had agreed to vacation at the cabin only because it had been the time of the Berlin Crisis, and he had found it wise to get out of Washington for fear of a Soviet attack!

In my last year of university, I chose to do my main project on a history topic, this time, under the influence of my professor, on the foreign policy views of the nineteenth-century German daily newspaper in Dayton, Ohio. This was part of a pattern in which others would assume I had an interest in things German or would mobilize me because of my German language skills. I resented this, but it was a no-win situation. I was interested, but found it irritating when others took the initiative. I wanted it both ways, but only I could decide when I was to be German. This history project, as it happened, taught me a great deal: that large parts of America had once been heavily German in their institutions (schools, newspapers, churches), but that the First World War had wiped all this out. And while doing my research, I came upon a notice announcing a talk in Dayton by my great-grandmother Paasche, during a North American tour with my grandfather, on the evils of nicotine and alcohol.

VIII

An important chapter in my struggle with my German identity occurred during my 1959 first trip to Germany. My ship docked in Rotterdam and I made my way by train to Bonn. As I stepped off the train, I found myself looking around for Nazi soldiers, just before being welcomed by my mother's brothers.

The ostensible purpose of my visit was to study at a German university. My underlying intent was to try to find out whether, and to what extent, I was German. Over the ten months I spent in Germany, I concluded that I had become a North American in several important respects. I felt the shortness of the distances, and saw the extent to which young people my age were already tied to a particular career track. I found that I had been shaped by the geography and the flexibilities of culture in North America. For example, I was dumbfounded that after several weeks visiting my grandmother in Berlin, the police came around and informed me that I had to register if I intended to make my stay longer. At the time I felt this to be very contrary in spirit to my American experience.

Being in Germany for the first time was also an opportunity to strengthen my ties to family and place. Of this I took full advantage. I discovered what it was to have an extended family, and to have my family name recognized and respected, even sometimes by perfect strangers. One of the things I missed in living in America and later in Canada was the absence of any kind of name recognition. In other words, the history of my family, or even just the names we hold, had no meaning for anyone. At times this was also liberating, of course.

In the German university where I studied for two semesters, I took part in the first set of lectures and an accompanying seminar that focused specifically on the Nazi era. To have been among German students being confronted for the first time in an intimate and thorough way with the historical materials of those years was a rare privilege. I found myself able to take both the insider and the outsider position. My own parents had left Germany as opponents of the Nazi regime, while my grandfather and several other relatives had

113

participated in the resistance. The seminar leader commented after the conclusion of the course that I had seemed to feel free to identify sometimes as a German and sometimes not, depending on the issue and historical moment. He had picked up on the love/hate relationship to Germany that I felt at the time, and still often feel today. I am fascinated and drawn to my German background, while at the same time repelled and distanced. This tension has surfaced in a variety of ways over the years.

IX

Years later, during my first years in Canada, I had experiences which also bear on identity. For instance there was one quite trivial, but for me eye-opening, situation. In the first telephone call I made to the university library I was responded to in German. I was taken aback. Something like this had never happened to me in America. I had felt completely American in this respect. Suddenly this stranger had felt free, unasked, to respond to me in German. Here I felt was a Canadian difference with America. It was all right to speak in other languages. This was a revelation.

Another experience that reflected my ambivalent sense of German identity resulted from a senior professor at my university presuming that I would want to do research on the recent German immigrants in Toronto. I was hurt. I felt he was imposing in an arena in which I wanted to be free to make my own decision. However, I went along. I was a junior member of the research team and had much to learn. This research had the unintended consequence of allowing me to make peace with "ordinary, beer-loving, sauerkraut-and-sausage-eating Germans." Although I had learned about the pleasures of beer a few years earlier, I actually became fond of sauerkraut, sausages and other German foods as a result of the field work I did. Later, in another context completely, a descendent of prerevolutionary German soldiers and their families, who settled in the Mohawk Valley of upstate New York, taught me how to make sauerkraut, and I have been making it every August since. The research project also taught me something about the variety of backgrounds, including Germans from the Volga region of Russia, among the Germans emigrating to Canada in the postwar years.

X

Being of German background is, in my case, a rather complex matter. The effort I have put into knowing and understanding my family history, as well as German history itself, has been motivated by my desire and need to come to terms with my German-ness. Could I have simply turned my back on it? I don't think so. That initial void, the departure from Japan, as well as the particular circumstances of my immediate and extended family, impelled me to take on the challenge of my German background.

I have often wondered how I would have responded and coped had my parents or grandparents and other relatives been Nazis. Everything would have been different for me. My family has served as an island of safety for me. It insulated me from "ordinary" Germans. Recently I have become more aware of this, and have tried to extend my network in Germany, and among Germans in Canada. I am privileged to have been born into my German family. It has enabled me to find and cultivate a connection with Germany. It has also at times made me feel superior to other Germans in a way that has not been constructive, and has prevented me from knowing people I might have learned much from. In Canada I often seek out conversations with travelers from Germany, especially young people. I find them quite fascinating, even exotic. This, of course, suggests that I am the outsider looking in, but a very particular kind of outsider (the "outside-insider"?).

XI

The theme of this article has been my German identity. But in the process I have had to come to terms also with my American identity. I came to Canada from America after all, not Germany. In the 1970s, when there was great agitation in academia about the threat of American domination of Canadian universities, I tended to be sympathetic. And I quietly became a Canadian citizen. But it was a low-key event. I did not take any family or friends along. Impulsively, as I watched the proceedings in the court room, I resolved to take advantage of the right to swear my allegiance to queen and nation in the French language. French had always held a privileged position in my father's family. By doing this, it seems to me now, I was, in effect, distancing myself once again from a firm identity, this time the Canadian one.

Or was I just emphasizing a difference with the United States? That I did not bring anyone else along, most of all my children, also suggests something of my feeling about citizenship in general and Canadian citizenship in particular. My motive in becoming a Canadian was that I did not want my American citizenship to become an issue for my students. For it to become an issue would have been ironic given my underlying ambivalence about America. I did not intend to make any public statement about America when I became a citizen of Canada. I was making a personal statement; my relation to America was even more complex than I myself was aware of at the time. But I also had wanted to spare my students in Canada my own condition. They were to have a solidly Canadian education. I did not want a passport to come between me as teacher and my students.

My German identity has served as a constant in my life. It has been the thread tying together past and present. So what does it all mean for my routine life in Canada now? Most of the time it is probably irrelevant. There are other things which impact more heavily on my life, issues such as profession, income, gender, age and so on. However, issues around my German identity crop up unexpectedly even in very small ways. Just recently I collided, unwittingly, with the issue of identity. I was calling a business that repaired telephone message machines. I noted that the woman at the other end had a distinctly non-English accent, but one that I could not place. When I brought my machine in and gave my name, she said to me, "European, isn't it?" I concurred, but left it at that. I had suddenly become guarded; what if she was Jewish, or even a Holocaust survivor? For me to have added "the name is German" would have been to take the risk of offending this person, or at least of putting her off. Later, when she volunteered that she was Greek, I felt a kind of relief. In other words, I had felt it necessary to hold back the knowledge from her of my German background. Lots of people have German surnames without having any German identity, or background. Why was I so guarded? The answer probably lies in its importance to me, and the continuing tension between what attracts me to it and what repels me about it. I still want to be free to pick and choose the moments when I am German and am not German. But I also want definitely to be both a Canadian and a German. I do not in any sense feel like a "German-Canadian." I see them as distinct and separate identities.

XII

Being German is for me an open-ended identity. By this I mean that I am continuously learning about, and feeling through, my encounter with the German in me. That German in me impels me to learn more of German history, as well as to confront the contemporary face of Germany. It is a living thing. I have a love for language, and being familiar with more than one feels like a blessing.

I am also not a German. I am a Canadian, and even sometimes again an American. Canada has grown on me. When I travel elsewhere, I take the Canadian in me along. I have learned something of its history, and of its struggles. I know my way around in this Canada. Many of the landscapes of Canada have become dear to me. I glory in its seasons. I have some thoughtful things to say about Canadian issues. I associate certain qualities that are important to my well-being with Canada. The dualities of Canada, and especially of the French and the English languages, give me a sense of room to move around in, and of safety. Canada has much that is unique and important to contribute to the rest of the world. We have much to accomplish here. I want to be a part of this.

WHY ADMIT YOU ARE AN ESKIMO?

DORIS J. SAUNDERS

Labrador's first inhabitants were the Inuit and Innu who freely roamed the vast and beautiful land. They took what nature provided for all their needs, depending on no one for help. Archaeologists have given some idea of the lifestyles of these people, based on artifacts retrieved from prehistoric sites. It makes sense that they existed in relatively small groups, large enough to make viable hunting parties, yet small enough to prevent starvation when fish and game were scarce. This was the pattern up to and even after Europeans came and "discovered" our country.

Many of the first European whites who came to Labrador came initially to stake a claim on the territory for a foreign ruler; the next wave of Europeans came to greedily take the riches of the land and sea. They considered the Aboriginals they encountered to be savages and placed them on a level beneath the animals whose pelts they coveted. The last group of arrivals during those early times were the men and boys who stowed away on ships to escape the hard times in their home countries. Most would have been of low rank in the class-structured systems of their homelands, and most, if not all, would probably never have survived without the help of the savages they so despised.

I can trace the beginning of my white roots back to the 1770s. My great-great grandmother, Lydia Campbell (1818-1905), wrote an account of her life, which has given us the first Native perspective on what life was like when the white men came and settled permanently in Labrador. The only way those white men could survive was to "marry" Inuit (Eskimo) women. Lydia's father would beat his wife when she ate raw meat or did anything else from her culture that he considered heathen, yet she was allowed to chew the seal skins to make his clothing and do whatever else was necessary to provide him comfort. The children of these mixed marriages were accepted as "white" by other European men, and thus worthy to be their wives or daughters-in-law. There is a story about a white man who could not find a "real" white woman to marry so he asked another man, who had married an Inuit woman, if he could marry his daughter. The girl was very young and he was afraid that if he waited until she was old enough some other white man would take her. He promised her father he would not sleep with her until she was twelve years old. The father, also very concerned that his daughter marry a white man, consented, and they were married.

As a result of the prejudices of the intruders to our land, most people of mixed blood were ashamed of their Native roots, even though it was plainly obvious by appearances alone that they had Aboriginal blood. Since the formation of the Labrador Inuit Association, more and more people who considered themselves white are now accepting their Inuit roots. It would be interesting to know how many accept their Native blood out of a growing pride in who they are and how many are doing it for the benefits membership offers them.

It seems that wherever white men have gone, they have been condescending to the natives of the countries they went to exploit. They always appeared to think they were the superior race. That attitude, though somewhat muted on the surface, still exists. Just a few years ago a newcomer from Europe questioned why I would even admit I had "Eskimo" blood if I could pass as white. How many more thousands of years will pass before humanity accepts that differences should be appreciated and not despised? As my father often told me, "We are descendants of a race that needed nobody but the Creator to survive. Be proud of who you are and never look down on anyone else!"

WHEN AN IMMIGRANT MEETS AN ABORIGINAL
PUI YEE BERYL TSANG

We stand in the elevator,
Shyly stealing short looks at each other,
Feeling strange.

She wears jade hoops in her ears.
I wear feathers in mine, there is an incongruity.
We admire each other's adornments.

She wants to speak.
So do I.
We can't, however.

What she has to say, I don't know.
I want to ask her what she thinks about me,
A yellow immigrant to a white country.

Does she think of us as thieves who stole the country from her ancestors?

I cannot, awkwardness fills my being.

She seems to sense my curiosity.
I feel the impetus to make my queries known,
She appears to want to answer. Our lips part.

The doors to the elevator open and we step out.
She's lost her opportunity to tell me.
I've lost the opportunity to learn.

PART 4
RACE, PRIVILEGE, AND CHALLENGES

I'VE NEVER HAD A BLACK TEACHER BEFORE
CARL E. JAMES

It was always offered as a credible explanation for the complaints, questions, challenges and disruptive behaviours that I would experience in my classes. It seemed that with the words—"I've never had a Black teacher before"—students expected me to understand their dilemmas and sympathize with their struggle of knowing how to relate to or what to expect from me, given that this was their first experience with a Black teacher. Why is this important for me to know? Why is my race a factor? What does race have to do with my role as a teacher, anyway?

I do not wish to challenge this comment, for it expresses the students' experiences and their reality. It is what is implied by this statement—*what is not said*—that I wish to discuss in this essay. In doing so, I will draw on my more than twelve years experience as a Black male teacher at colleges and universities in southern Ontario. Referring to their comments, I will discuss how students' (both whites and students of colour) preconceived ideas influence their expectations of, and interactions with, me as a racial minority teacher, and how these in turn have an impact on the teaching and learning process.

The fact that race plays a role in teacher-student interaction is important and must be acknowledged and examined. For as Patricia Williams writes in her book *The Alchemy of Race and Rights: Diary of a*

Law Professor, "... race isn't important because it isn't important; most of us devoutly wish this to be a colour blind society, in which removing the words 'black' and 'white' from our vocabulary would render the word, in a miraculous flash, free of all divisions. . . . Often we have to use the words in order to acknowledge the undeniable psychological and cultural power of racial constructions upon all our lives."

First Impressions

Upon entering a classroom, all teachers are subjected to students' evaluations based on their personal experiences with teachers. These evaluations will also be a result of assumptions and stereotypes based on such things as dress, sex, voice and race of the teacher. For instance, if students associate Black people with lower levels of education, crime and welfare, then this will influence how I am perceived by students. This is evident in the following opinion expressed by one student:

> My initial opinions of Carl were negative ... his black skin "surprised" me ... [and] his accent annoyed me. The idea of having a black teacher quite intrigued me, but having to cope with a poorly educated black teacher seemed to be asking a lot.

This assessment of my education has to do not only with the fact that I am Black, or with my accent, but also with my Caribbean origin. The student continued:

> I was ... surprised when I later found out that Carl has a Ph.D. in Sociology. Somehow that did not fit my stereotype of a Black person especially from the Caribbean. (However, I could picture an American Black person having a doctorate.)

Not only are students' emotional reactions ones of "surprise," but when the teacher does not fit their expectations, their reactions are sometimes angry. According to one student:

> No one in the class told me our teacher was Black and for some reason I felt angry that no one mentioned this to me. . . . Carl is very dark and black and I have had problems with dark black people in the past.

This anger not only has to do with the fact that no one had briefed the student about me before class, but because I was "a very dark and black" person. And insofar as she had "problems with dark black people in the past," she makes the assumption that she will likely

126

have problems with me. Interestingly, unlike some "ethnic group names," students cannot tell my ethnicity or race from my name since it reflects the history of British colonization. So it is not until students meet me in class that they know my ethnicity. This contributes to their surprise, and also indicates what for them represents the norm for a teacher.

As for racial minority students, because of their limited experience with Black teachers, they also come to expect their teachers to be white, so when they first experience Black teachers they too tend to be similarly "surprised" and experience the same ambivalent reactions as their white peers. As one Black student said, "In all my years of attending school I had never met a black teacher. Even though I myself am black I felt a bit uneasy, and unsure of how to react towards this teacher."

Where Are You From?

Either within the first hour of my first class or within the first two weeks, students usually ask me, "Where are you from?" or "Are you from Jamaica?" In earlier years, I used to say, "No. I'm not from Jamaica," or "I am from the Caribbean." Sometimes, students will insist on getting an answer. And when I ask, "Why the question?" or "Why do you assume that I am not Canadian, but an immigrant?" the response is, "Because you have an accent." Usually, I do not answer the question for I wish to challenge the tendency of students, like many other Canadians, to associate being Black with being an immigrant. This is an example of how individuals, consciously and unconsciously, reaffirm difference, and remind those of us who do not "look and/or sound Canadian" that we are immigrants. Is there any wonder that, when asked, we mention our ethnocultural origin, use a hyphen or continue to identify ourselves as immigrants rather than Canadians? I would suggest that this question "Where are you from?" is of course more often asked of racial minority persons, thus making race, or racial difference, the pivotal point around which interactions are built.

It is certainly possible that students ask me this question because they are interested in building a rapport with me — as a way of being friendly. For racial minority students, and Blacks in particular, asking this question might be a way of establishing connection or distance. The latter might be their way of publicly demonstrating to their peers that there is a difference between us — a way of indicating that they are Canadian (born) with no accent. Their intention might be to put me and their peers on notice that although we are the same in skin colour, there are important differences that must be taken into consideration. Thus they protect themselves from any embarrassing situation that may arise.

Some might say that not answering the question indicates that I am unfriendly, but I do not think, initially at least, that my cultural background has anything to do with the educational process. Further, I think it is important for me to challenge the not-so-subtle ways in which students make evident their privilege and power in the educational process.

My Accent

In many cases, reference to accent is another way of referring to race and masking racial attitudes. It is also the way in which students try to locate me as an outsider. For this reason they make the assumption that I have a Jamaican accent. I am not Jamaican; nevertheless, for those students, my accent is considered to be Jamaican because I am Black and an immigrant. This is a reflection of the stereotype that most immigrant Blacks are Jamaicans. But this is only one of the stereotypes that are held about race and accent. For instance, referring to accent can be seen as "acceptable social etiquette" — a permissible, supposedly neutral approach, in identifying my origin in a white society which is desperate to be "colour blind" and "non-racist." In another instance, one student associated accent with education:

> My assumption that Carl was poorly educated stemmed from the fact that he has an accent. Now, if Carl had had a British accent I would have probably assumed that he was quite well educated. British people "sound" well educated to me simply because of their accents, not because they are in fact, more educated. Conversely, Caribbean accents, which have a different grammar structure than the English I speak, arbitrarily "sound" less educated to me. In reality I know that there is absolutely no correlation between accent and level of education, but this knowledge has never stopped me from making unfounded first assumptions.

Students' feelings about my accent also help to determine how they hear me, understand what I say, and how comfortable they are interacting with me. One mentioned that it was after talking with me "one-on-one" three weeks into the course that she began to see past my colour. As she put it in our conversation, I said nothing "spectacular," I was saying the same things I "had been saying in class" but:

this time however, I was talking with a person, not the black man or professor I had heard in class. . . . I started listening to him in class as a person. I had been concentrating on the strange sounds of his accent instead of what he was saying. After a while I got used to his accent and didn't think about it any more.

References to my race and accent are ways in which students establish that in the larger scheme of things in this society, I am what is termed "a visible minority," "an immigrant," "an other"—a person whose colour and accent are indicators of educational credentials, occupational status and location in society. It is for these reasons that students would have expectations that their teachers would be "white, English Canadians who spoke with perfection." Given that I do not fit this description, they are left with a surprise. Therefore, they feel a need to not only verify how I got there, but also to ascertain that the status quo remains the same.

Equity Hire?

Students are well aware that I also represent one of the employment equity target groups. While it was never suggested that I have benefitted directly from this program, they saw me as "symbolically" representing the group of minority people—"young Black men"—who are robbing them of their chances to fulfil the career goals for which they were educating themselves. They all seemed to know some Black person who obtained a job (e.g., on the police force) and was "not qualified." So in discussing employment equity, they would display their anger and frustrations at what they saw as injustice, and they would say that they "should not have to pay for past practices." In reflecting on these discussions, one student said:

> Some anger was most likely directed towards the instructor not as an individual but as one representing all the frustrations and individuals that may pose a threat to our advancement to a career.

In these discussions, I make the point that it is necessary to give consideration to the historical and social conditions of groups that, because of discriminatory practices, have not had equal access to the educational and occupational opportunities available in society. They argue that "race does not matter" and that people are able to get jobs based on merit. This just has not happened. We cannot simply say that individuals are the same in our society; gender, race and ability make a difference. Therefore, we must always bear in mind the context from which individuals come and examine their opportunities accordingly.

129

What Am I Expected to Teach?

One of the stereotypes that students hold is the kind of course that an individual is likely to teach or have expertise in. For example, one person pointed out:

> I have never expected to be lectured in a course like this by a black teacher. Thinking back, I guess that I took it for granted that a course dealing with Canadian Culture will be taught by a person from the majority (white).

But not everyone operates with the same stereotypes. While I am perceived by some as the person unlikely to be teaching about "Canadian culture," others believe that culture, race, and ethnicity are more likely to be topics of interest to a racial or ethnic minority or immigrant person. In her words: "The moment he walked into the classroom on the first day, his skin colour was predominant and I thought to myself, 'Oh, he's Black. This course will be right up his alley.'" There is no doubt that the parents, schools, textbooks, media, etc. have played a role in reinforcing these stereotypes, by portraying certain kinds of people as having the expertise to address particular subjects.

In my view, making the assumption that I am unlikely or most likely to be qualified to teach particular courses is another way in which stereotypes or preconceived ideas will affect my interaction with students. Thus, in my classes, particularly in the earlier ones, I am faced with the challenge of whether to address directly the stereotypes that are held — those stereotypes that present me and other minorities as limited in our academic or professional capacities. For students who think that because I am a member of a minority I am most likely qualified to teach about culture, race/ethnic relations, discrimination, etc., the challenge I have is to show that my interpretations or analyses of issues (like those of others in minorities) are not only based on personal or political interest but are also informed by theory in the same way that other experts' analyses are informed by theories — same or different. Further, I take the position that whatever the analyses or interpretations I present, they have a legitimate standing in any academic discourse.

Course Content and Students' Feelings?

The topic areas I often deal with in my courses include inequality in relation to social class, gender, ethnicity, race, etc. Discussing these issues in class is often accompanied by deeply felt emotions as students struggle to understand how the structures of our society have perpetuated and maintained inequality and how mechanisms such as sexism, racism, heterosexism, classism, etc. have operated to maintain the status quo. Students claim that these issues taught by a Black person contribute to their discomfort, fear and defensiveness. One student wrote: "Carl was the first black teacher I had ever had which also made me slightly more uncomfortable. This discomfort, I believe was more a fear of what to expect." Another wrote: "I looked around the classroom and saw a number of minority groups represented amongst us, including the teacher. My immediate reaction was to feel defensive about my WASP background." This indicates that as a Black educator, not only am I to be responsible for organizing and structuring courses which challenge students intellectually, but also I am expected to anticipate and be sensitive to their feelings. While sensitivity is a critical requirement for all teachers, this prerequisite becomes more significant in this case because my race is factored into both the interactions with the students and the course content.

It is typical that teachers will challenge students to assess critically a situation or seek alternative explanations for social issues. In some cases, my challenges are seen as a deliberate attempt to "bring out individuals' prejudices," or as inappropriate, and/or reflective of my militancy or as oversensitivity to issues of prejudice or racism. Some students even go further to suggest that I am "taking out my anger on them" because of my "experience with racism." Once after a student became angry and walked out of class, he sent me a note that said:

> I found that while being in your course (not your fault) my prejudices have become stronger because I don't like breaking People down to a race or culture, skin colour or language, I accept people for who they are if they're an asshole so be it. . . . . PS. as a child did some one ever persecute you, you seem touchy.

What Is the Issue: Teaching Style or Race?

Sometimes students linked my pedagogical approach to teaching with my race. There has always been the suggestion that I was intimidating because of how I "said things," how I "arranged the classroom in a circle to promote discussion" and/or how I encouraged a certain kind of dialogue. And there was always the question of my objectivity.

> I am now sure that if a white man had stood there and talked about immigration to Canada and how non-whites were discriminated against I would have taken it much differently. I found myself saying that both his writing and teaching were clearly taken from a black person's point of view and I wanted him to be more objective. Could this . . . really mean that I wanted him to be white? I'm not really sure.

This comment illustrates that "getting beyond my colour" was important if the student were to benefit from the classes.

But it is not only the students who needed to recognize how race was operating as a factor in the educational process. The administrators also displayed a lack of awareness of how they contributed to the issues that were raised about my teaching — specifically, how they were raised and who raised them. For instance, during my first semester at one college, students complained to the chairperson of the department that they "could not understand", or that I demanded "too much of them." Because the number of complaints was highly unusual, the chairperson conducted an evaluation. He reviewed my course outline and my test questions, and visited my class to observe my teaching. In our follow-up meeting, the chairperson commented that he did not find my "teaching any different from other faculty members," neither was "my expectation unreasonable for first-year college students." He mentioned that he had had complaints about other faculty members, and new faculty members in particular, but never the number of complaints as he has had in my case, and he was unable to provide an explanation. As he and I reviewed the many variables in order to understand the problem, I silently noted that race was one difference but he said nothing of it. (I was the first and only racial minority in the department.) I remember that day. Driving home that evening, in January of 1985, CBC radio carried the news of Frances Henry and Effie Ginzberg's study *Who Gets the Work: A Test of Racial Discrimination in Employment*, which showed whites are three times more likely than Blacks to obtain employment in the Metropolitan Toronto area, due to racism and discrimination. I thought that I had a job, but was experiencing racism differently, and that my supervisor was being oblivious to the reality of racism that racial minority staff like myself will, and do, experience.

The Irony of Bias

As a "Black teacher," how I raise certain topics in class, the kinds of topics, or the arguments I might advance around some topics are sometimes seen to be related to my race, and by implication "reflect my prejudices and bias." The student in the following quote demonstrated this: "I found myself saying that both his writing and teaching were clearly taken from a black person's point of view." Evidently, hearing or reading for the first time some of these viewpoints that challenge their deeply held world views, and having them put forward by a Black man, can be, as they reported, "intimidating," or can make them "angry." The fact is, they do not see new or different information as a chance to examine their world views. For after all, as a teacher I understand that it is hard for them to simply start believing that their education to date has been one-sided and limited. Hence, it makes more sense for them to see me as misguided, biased, prejudiced, having "a chip on my shoulder," and representing a Black point of view. Isn't it ironic that they do not think of what they have learned as being a "white point of view" that they have internalized and accepted as "neutral" and "objective"? Peggy McIntosh, in her article "White Privilege and Male Privilege," makes this point when she writes: "whites are taught to think of their lives as morally neutral, normative, and average; and also ideal. . . ." This is why one person said:

> The first day I entered your class I had a really open mind. . . . When I left the class though, I was feeling really angry. In fact, when I went home that night I told my parents that I had a prejudiced Black teacher.

So steeped in their belief that "whites are more objective than non-whites," they judge me as prejudiced and biased. The following quote is illustrative:

> You came across trying to sound unbiased, however, the statements that you put forth and more importantly the way in which you worded them led myself, and other members of the class, to believe that you thought what you were saying was right. Or, put another way, that your answer was THE right one. . . . Although you are most certainly entitled to your own opinion, that is all it is, and it is not necessarily THE right answer, as you time and time again portrayed.

133

That I bring to my teaching a particular framework which informs my analysis and interpretation of events, situations and experiences is certainly expected. Insofar as students label this as bias, and therefore challenge my credibility as a teacher or the legitimacy of my argument, it is something I must contend with as long as I engage students in critical analyses. I interpret their challenges as part of their resistance to what I try to communicate. Nevertheless, I think it is important for me to challenge students to examine their "own lenses" — that which they use to label what I say as bias. My experience has shown that when students are unwilling to accept other or alternative explanations — why working-class people, women or racial minorities, for example, are justified in challenging the social and economic system that has disadvantaged them — they identify what I say as bias. Further, it seems to me that race rather than content, and students' unwillingness and/or fear of confronting issues, may well be at the root of their suggestions of my bias. Therefore, I tend not to engage in discussions that attempt to dispel the idea that I am biased. For should not students be shown that there is a relationship between attitudes held, socialization, race, gender and social class? Should not our educational process involve our intellect, biology and emotions? Is teaching merely to confirm the status quo or to challenge ourselves so that we may become critical participants in our educational process and society as a whole? If students become uncomfortable or angry as they learn about the mechanisms in society that have privileged and/or disadvantaged them, and about their role in promoting and maintaining this situation, this may well be the important starting point of the necessary self-reflective journey.

In disagreeing with their peers' suggestions that I am prejudiced and biased, racial minority students' reactions can be seen to be grounded in their experiences as minorities and their wish to be supportive. Black students, in particular, were the most emphatic in suggesting that their peers' positions were based on ignorance, resistance and racism. In the words of one female:

> I realized that our class was only acting the way they were because of their ignorance and the colour of Carl's skin. I know if it was a white teacher who was saying the same things, their reactions would have been much different. With [my teacher], it seemed that they didn't want to learn or believe that what he was saying was really true. Many people imply that he was being prejudiced and only cared about what was happening with blacks and nobody else. . . . No matter what Carl said they always had something to say trying to make it look like what he was saying was all because he was black.

One of the things students use as evidence for my bias is grades. Naturally, those students who receive low grades will always look for reasons to explain their grade attainment, and blaming the teacher is often a convenient one. In their attempts to validate their hypothesis of my grading as bias or prejudice, and if Black students are in the class, some students (usually whites) make comparisons between the grades white and Black students receive. (This is not to suggest that Black students do not do the same and claim racism when white students get better grades.)

Black Teacher, Black Students: Ambivalent and Antagonistic Relationships

I have already mentioned that for some Black students, I was their first Black teacher, and like their white peers they felt "uneasy and unsure of how to react" towards me; others felt positive and comfortable and some made public "their differences." Evidently, there is much more to the dynamics of our relationships. Some reported that they felt a responsibility to ensure that they did not make fools of themselves, because with a Black teacher, they are "noticed more." Correspondingly, they expected that my behaviour would not embarrass them. For this reason, my colour and accent, and even my dress, were scrutinized. In the words of one student:

> Our teacher walked in dressed very casually. He is also what you call a typical looking black man, with a short afro and dark brown skin. To top it all off, he spoke with an accent. I could understand, but I wasn't so sure that everybody else did.

Other Black students felt that my being Black was in their "favour" — it helped them to feel validated. This is evident in comments such as: "I suppose I felt a sense of pride and belonging because for once the person in charge was just like me — a minority. I felt like I had something over my classmates." I would often find these students to be co-operative and committed. But as one student suggested: "I actually thought that maybe I'd get special treatment because Carl is black." It seems that in return for their co-operation I was expected to show preferential treatment or "go easy on them." Fortunately, some students reason that since the majority of students are white and the majority of teachers are predominantly white, do these white students expect to be treated special because of the common colour they share with the teacher? My answer was no. They couldn't possibly expect preference after all there are too many of them for special treatment.

Where grades are concerned, Black students were very much aware of their peer group dynamics when the teacher is Black. They know that they not only have to work hard to satisfy the high expectations of the teacher (who, some claim, has expectations as high as their parents), but to prove to their peers that they deserve their grades. The following comment explains the experience of one Black student quite well:

> After our group received a good mark, the class turned around and said it was due to . . . favouritism for our group because there were two black people within our group. Boy, did that ever make me mad! I felt that I worked very hard for what I had accomplished. I took the extra time to talk to our teacher like he was any other teacher to find out what was really expected of us in the assignment.

I think that such experience might explain why some Black students "do not like" Black teachers or "prefer white teachers." In racially mixed classes, this is a pressure that the students will want to avoid. Sometimes this pressure leads to an antagonistic relationship between the Black teacher and the Black student: because being in such a class not only requires paying attention to their educational program, but also entails trying to maintain a friendly but distant relationship with me.

And then there are those Black students who are "looking for a break" from the white teachers and the educational system from which they have felt alienated. But Black teachers are not uncritically accepted as the alternative. We are scrutinized, tested and evaluated in terms of the extent to which we "ignore" or "affirm" Black students or "take the place of the colonizer." In cases where I might be (in many instances) one of few teachers who points out weaknesses to these students or from whom they receive low grades (especially if they have been "succeeding" with white teachers all along) I am perceived as imposing "harsher standards" and having "unreasonable expectations of Black students." Moreover, I am seen as "carrying on where white teachers left off"—"the continuation of colonialization but a different overseer."

So while I welcome the opportunity to be a part of the educational process of Black students, I am conscious that I do so within the context of their experiences with racism and discrimination, and within an educational system from which they feel alienated. Consequently, I cannot expect to be accepted as a teacher without questions or ambivalence, for they too have internalized the white cultural values of their schooling or have become quite cynical about the capacity of anyone working within the system to change their situation or the system. Further, I cannot assume that because I share the same history and many of the same racial experiences as these students, that they will be unquestioning or uncritical allies. For these reasons, I must be prepared to deal with their ambivalence, expectations, conditional support and doubts. Given all these, it can be expected that our relationships will often be filled with tensions.

Putting the Learning Process into Perspective

Fortunately, amid all the anxieties, frustrations, denial, anger, surprise, cynicism and hostility, by the end of the course some students reflect on what they learned and admit that my race was a significant factor in their perception of and reactions to me. They also talk about their mistakes and misdirections. As one student asserted: "I was mistaken and thought that Carl, himself, was prejudice (sic) terribly against whites. What if he had been white? Would I have had these same feelings of aggression towards him?" Another student wrote:

> As I sit and write this assignment one revelation hit me that I did not think of before. The uptight feelings I had in the class, although brought out because of the topics, were affected by the instructor. It has nothing to do with his capabilities as a teacher but rather the colour of his skin. This may sound racist but let me finish. In the eighteen years I have been in school, I have never had a Black teacher, or one of any minority. To have a Black teacher teaching race relations and the class discussing agendas that hit close to home, surely affected the way I perceived my environment.

It is knowing that eventually some students come to recognize their role in the learning process, and admit that they did learn, that gives me hope and inspiration to continue teaching. Hearing students reflect positively on their learning experience is very gratifying and helps to build confidence.

So What Does All This Mean to Me?

The issues raised in this essay are certainly not unique to me. I am quite sure that many racial and ethnic minority people, women and people with disabilities can tell of similar experiences as teachers. Experiences like these are what I see as part of the "minority experience." As a minority teacher, I must give consideration to the extent to which my race, tone of voice, eye contact, smile, how and when I introduce certain topics and what I say have an impact on my interaction with students.

My experience as a teacher is not unlike that of the young Black men and women I interviewed in 1991. They talked about having to cope with being Black in work settings in which they were the "only Black" or person of colour. Racism both among their co-workers and clients was a reality that they had to deal with. In addition to saying it was "just a part of being Black in this society," they conceded that they were not only workers, but "crusaders," "change agents," "advocates," "educators," "pioneers" and "representatives" of Blacks and other racial minorities. One respondent observed: "There is nothing that you can do except bear the brunt and go on. You have to learn how to handle and get out of that situation without compromising your dignity."

As I talked with these young people, then, and heard of their experiences, I thought of how much they reflected my experience as a teacher. Many times, in the course of my work, I have had to pretend I did not hear disrespectful comments, or I would give the impression that I am open-minded enough not to address those comments that challenge my role as a teacher. While some students boldly verbalize their challenges in class, it is in the evaluations that their anger is most often spelled out. I am sure students are well aware of the implications of such evaluations if they are uncritically used in an assessment of me.

I also see the challenges I receive from students as a reminder of the paradox or precariousness of my role as a teacher. On the one hand, I have authority vested in me by the position I hold; at the same time, this authority is mediated by my colour. This reflects the extent to which my authority is situational at best and circumscribed by my minority status in this society. Thus, when students ask, "where are you from?" or comment on my accent, teaching style, etc., these are subtle reminders that I am a member of a minority, and that they are thereby asserting their position in relation to me. In writing of this paradox of power that she experiences as a Black law professor, Patricia Williams, in her book *The Alchemy of Race and Rights*, points out: "I am expected to woo students even as I try to fend them off; I am supposed to control them even as I am supposed to manipulate them into loving me. Still I am aware of the paradox of my power over these students. I am aware of my role, my place in an institution that is larger than myself, whose power I wield even as I am powerless, whose shield of respectability shelters me even as I am disrespected."

By factoring my race into our interactions, and claiming that their inexperience with Black teachers is responsible for some of the problems they experience with me, students (both white and Black) absolve themselves of their role and responsibility in the educational process. Their strategy is to avoid the confrontation with self, and to delay the pain of knowing that they must change. Hence, to protect themselves and evade the fact that they must now confront their expectations and start to question what they have all along accepted as truths, knowledge, objectivity, morality and neutrality, they see the problem as resting with me, their teacher, not within them or societal structures and ideology. Indeed, this is an excellent example in which societal, institutional and individual aspects of racism play themselves out.

So what do I think of the comment "I've never had a Black teacher before"? I think it is understandable because Blacks make up, according to Statistics Canada, 1991 Census, only 2.4 percent of Ontario's population. (Some people, particularly community members, suggest that this is a conservative estimate and that there are as many as 300,000 Black or African Canadians living in Ontario.) Hence, with so few of us, many students do not have the opportunity to experience Black teachers. The comment also reminds me of the discriminatory immigration policies which limited the immigration of African peoples to Canada, and how structural inequalities and discriminatory practices are responsible for Black people's lack of access to teaching opportunities. I know that these points partly explain why many of the students have not had a Black teacher before. But unfortunately they do not know this, largely because it has never been pointed out to them. This is important information for them to know.

And how do I feel about being referred to as a "Black teacher" you ask? It does matter. I am a teacher who happens to be Black, and this identity informs my position in society and how I see the world. Therefore, as a Black teacher, my race operates as a significant social force, profoundly affecting my interactions with students from the very first day I walk into the classroom. Given the way society has constructed Blacks, students enter the classroom with stereotypes that mediate my qualifications, potential and expectations as a teacher. As an African Canadian, as I prefer to be identified, the role that my skin colour will play in my interactions with students cannot go unnoticed. Finally, while being Black cannot be regarded as incidental to being a teacher, it should not be the most significant factor that others use to judge me, categorize me, or deny me the privileges that other instructors receive.

WHITE TEACHER, BLACK LITERATURE

LESLIE SANDERS

When I agreed to write an essay for this collection, I thought it would be a relatively easy and interesting task. As a white person who has been engaged in research and teaching in the field of African American literature for almost twenty-five years, I have frequently had to reflect upon my position. But writing this essay hasn't come easily at all. Early drafts sounded like manifestoes or apologies. Some things I really wanted to say felt personal and private; other ideas, when put in writing, seemed pretentious. Contemporary identity politics, both in theory and in practice, now complicate how I might want to describe my position, which some formulations of Afrocentricity assert is untenable, in any event. So why and how did I become a scholar and teacher of "African American literature"? And why am I still doing it?

My reasons are, at root, intensely personal, but so, I believe, is any scholarship. I think people usually choose fields that provide them with a way to articulate their most basic questions about life. Lost in all the complex issues that could be discussed is the obvious idea that we study in order to *learn from*, and that simple notion is where I wish to begin.

This process of learning from is complex, however. We increasingly have come to understand that all knowledge is constructed from particular points of view, and relies on particular assumptions. As we study, we also make knowledge because we make connections, see significance and interpret, always from particular points of view, both individual and cultural. The history of the field of African American literature is a good example of how problematic this process can be. White scholars of Black culture have often represented the academy at its most imperialist. For example, in the early 1960s, the American sociologist Daniel Moynihan pronounced the African American family dysfunctional. His "expertise" determined conventional wisdom and government policy for the next generation, to the extreme detriment of those whom the policies purported to help. The belief that the scholar is an "authority," capable of ascertaining truth, is extremely dangerous.

White scholars in African American Studies can, however, undermine conventional views of academic authority, simply by refusing to claim it. We can, instead, be students, seeking to learn rather than to pronounce, sharing what we discover, testing its usefulness by constant dialogue with those for whom our findings, and their own, are more personal and critical. I think that I do fully understand how problematic my being in the field is for others, how it has meanings that I may not intend, but still must take responsibility for. Yet I do not think that my presence and my work are intrinsically wrong or offensive, although I must always give thought to what I am doing.

It took a while for me to understand why this field engages me so completely. African American culture permeated the postwar Long Island, New York, world in which I grew up, but I knew little about Black people and had little contact with them. I spent most of my school years in Catholic schools, and very few African Americans on Long Island were Catholic. School desegregation, the Montgomery bus boycott, the early days of the civil rights movement were events I knew about, although they did not impinge upon my reality except as news reports. In 1962 I began university in Toronto, and spent summers waitressing in a Long Island resort area. In retrospect, I was surprisingly uninvolved in protests about either civil rights or the war in Vietnam, the two upheavals that profoundly altered my generation and the United States as well.

My lack of engagement was not for want of political consciousness. In grammar school, I already recognized that home lessons differed from those at school. Memorably, in grade five, after a nun's paean to Joseph McCarthy, I said that my mother didn't like him at all. My mother's terrified response when I told her of the incident silenced me till high school. There, however, along with a very small band of "radicals" in the Catholic girls' school I attended, I spent my entire time, it seemed, arguing with the extraordinarily right-wing faculty, and also with my classmates. There was little in the society I knew that I could support, and so neither Vietnam nor the civil rights movement presented epiphanies. The first seemed simply as horrible and unjust as any war, the second was, equally simply, only right and inevitable. Again in retrospect, during my undergraduate years, personal problems and the continual need to earn money to stay in school took my energies.

In 1968, M.A. in hand, wanting to teach but back waitressing, I was invited to work at Southern University in Baton Rouge, Louisiana, a public university that is still, I believe, the largest of the "historically Black" universities in the United States. The job was in a special federal program for the "educationally disadvantaged," situated in fourteen Black post-secondary institutions. It also entailed attending eight-week summer conferences where the faculty developed curriculum, several mid-term conferences to evaluate our progress and frequent external evaluation of our teaching. Each program had an equal number of "in-house" and imported faculty. Students in the program took our courses in first year and part of second year before integrating fully into the university.

I arrived half way through a summer conference, barely knowing where Baton Rouge was and, as one of them wryly noted, hardly able to tell my new colleagues apart. And my life changed irrevocably. Why? Well, the program, which even over thirty years later is the most exciting educational experiment I've ever encountered, embodied the critical pedagogy about which Paulo Freire had just begun to write. The diverse and intense group of young Black militants, older Black scholars and preachers, young white radicals and intellectuals and the occasional older, stolid and traditional white faculty who had staffed some of the schools for generations managed, during the summer conferences, to reproduce and fight out every conceivable aspect of American race relations. The Black artists and historians whose work gave rise to the Black Arts Movement and to the field which had just claimed the name of Black Studies came to the conferences to teach and to inspire us. People were often very direct.

And so the two years I spent at Southern, reading, talking, living and teaching, introduced me to a people and a culture from whom I've never stopped learning. When I returned to Toronto to do a Ph.D., I chose a dissertation topic, the development of Black theatre in America, which allowed me to consider what I had learned and explore the things I wanted to know. One friend in particular, an African American woman from New Orleans whom I first met at Southern, was my real supervisor; our mutual boss at Southern used to tell us our stars were crossed: her M.A. had been on Bernard Malamud. But there is more to it than that.

In the U.S. much has changed in the racial politics of Black Studies in the last twenty-five years. I think it not unfair to say that Black and white scholars of Black literature before the Black Arts Movement made modest claims for a developing literature. There was little work done, and some of it, from white scholars in particular, was grounded in narrow and largely unexamined notions of "good art." By the end of the decade, young Black writers and scholars sought to develop ways of talking about Black literature that rendered such judgments moot; at the same time, of course, white scholars in the field were met with suspicion, if not direct hostility. At stake, of course, were issues of authority; a new generation of Black scholars and artists assumed the task of describing, critiquing, interpreting and developing a literature. White folks not welcome.

So why did I stick around? I stayed because nothing else drew me in the same way. Looking back I realize that my immediate and powerful engagement with this literature had to do with my feeling that the work I encountered was constantly testifying to the truth, and with an immediacy, honesty and concreteness that I had never experienced before. It consistently illuminated experience that, although not mine, clarified things I knew, or needed to know, things I needed to understand that the people I knew and the books that I read weren't talking about.

Being "different," an outsider, is an accustomed, and even comfortable position for me, and so being on the margin of my field is not difficult. Single child of a single mother in a society that saw us both as tainted; Jewish, but raised from the age of seven as a Catholic yet taught never to deny my race; isolated because of the adamant but unnamed anti-Semitism in the Catholic world I inhabited; poor in the way I only recently came to recognize through friends; that is, in the way of the child of a bourgeois refugee who never gained her financial footing in the new society; raised socialist in a Republican, if not fascist community; a woman who knew from childhood that I had to make it on my own; reared by a mother whose hostility to feminism still confounds me: combatting the elusive was, for me, a fundamental way of life. None of these things was ever named for me, so concrete issues came as a relief. You're okay, but you're white.

Yeah, I can dig that!!! Which is not to say that I didn't begin with a well-spring of racism of my own, only that it was (and still is) continually confronted in ways intense, unavoidable and cleansing. It is to say that many people taught me, helped me, gave me love and support. Sounds corny, but it still is true.

I must ask my readers to consider: if I were writing about my experiences as a scholar of Spanish, Chinese, Russian literature and culture, my gratitude for those who have and continue to help me would seem perfectly normal. My appreciation of a literature, a language, an entire culture, a people, would be a matter of proclivity. No one would question my presence in the field, nor my presence in the classroom. The meanings attached to my presence in this field are not the same, however. The politics of race relations and racism, of scholarship that has defined entire peoples into speechlessness and their cultural productions into exotic objects of curiosity, mark my presence in the field, dog my footsteps, gloss my words. Professors profess expertise; scholars aspire to the definitive articulation of their objects of scrutiny. White person (woman, American) tells people (white people, Black people) what Black people mean.

My meaning is more problematic in Canada, where there are so few academics of African Canadian/American/Caribbean origin, than it is in the United States, where the majority of academics now engaged in the study of African American literature are Black, and where African American academics are, at last and to a large measure, the arbiters of what constitutes good scholarship in the field. In Canada, few academics concentrate on the work of African Canadian/American/Caribbean writers; only a very small proportion of these academics are "people of colour"; even fewer have pursued African American literature/culture in particular. Can I make a constructive contribution in Canada (to whom and to what, this sentence does not easily finish)?

Certainly there is one way in which I cannot contribute and that is as an "authority" on anything at all. I do not mean, by this, to say that I know nothing: I would be lacking in self-respect if I claimed ignorance of what I am learning and have learned. I also believe myself able to create conditions in which people can, if they wish to do so in a class I teach, learn from and about African American people and their culture. Claiming authority, however, suggests one has the right to create, to define, and to defend against counter claims, what will, even what ought to, constitute knowledge about a subject. In the context of the liberal arts, in particular, authority also suggests the right to speak for those about whom one claims, "I know." That is not an authority I can ever claim.

In my practices as a teacher in this field, I try to make clear to students that I can only act as a resource for them, offering what I know as only one of the many resources available to them in their own process of knowledge making. I find that Black students and white alike are astounded at what their schooling to date has hidden from them. They are amazed at the material that is available, material I make them seek out with massive bibliography and other assignments. In other words, my goal is that they leave my courses with the sense that they have only scratched the surface, and that the entire field is there for them to pursue and advance in their own fashion. It is painful to see the tremendous hurt that the Black students feel when they realize how cheated they have been. I see my role as trying to create an environment in which they can transform this pain into the energy to take charge of this process of knowledge making.

I look forward to a time when there will be, in Canada, the kind of academic community now emerging in the U.S., filled with people who can legitimately claim authority, and whose work will challenge and enrich us all. Encouraging students, changing curriculum and altering hiring practices are contributions I can make towards this goal. Yet I am also concerned that a kind of institutionalized "intellectual multiculturalism" will surface, without effecting the radical change necessary in the composition of the academic community. This version of multiculturalism confines people to studying their own lives, and sees them as suspect when they pursue and speak about issues other than their "own." It is, in a way, but not entirely, the flip side of what renders me problematic as a white scholar of African American culture. Fields such as African American literature are in themselves massive and complex. They also fundamentally alter what scholars now call "dominant narratives," and if these remain unchanged, we are not much further ahead. This knowledge is critical to us all, not just to those for whom it is of particular interest and relevance, be they teachers or students.

What is at stake is power: who gets to say what about whom, and who gets to decide what is true. It seems to me that only in a truly diverse academic community can these problems be resolved. In the meantime, the problem isn't resolved simply by insisting that, for example, only Black people should teach Black Studies. Certainly the opportunity to pursue the field should exist even when no Black teachers are available.

Getting where we need to go isn't easy. These days, I sometimes wonder how I will feel if what I hope for becomes true: that way before I'm ready to retire, my students will be ready to replace me. It will be a joyous day, certainly, and it will also be hard. I really love my work. Perhaps they'll invite me to give a guest lecture . . . maybe even two.

WHITE PRIVILEGE
WHAT'S IN IT FOR ME?
KAREN LYNN

Waking in the morning I am confronted by a tousled mass of thick brown hair and sleepy lines on the face of a middle-aged woman in a mirror. I hastily fulfil the obligations of my culture by transforming my features with makeup, my body with the right clothes. Studying my face critically, I strategize to survive the day. It's not so difficult any more, now that my son is no longer a baby and I have found my niche in society, a job that I love and think I can do fairly well.

I am an equity worker. I work to promote human rights. But I seldom have to deal with any human rights issues on my own behalf or that of my children because we are able-bodied, middle class and white. Herein lies a dilemma. I live in the castle of my skin and accrue all of the implicit benefits of being white, including having this job. Every day I advocate on behalf of people who experience a lack of these same benefits because of their skin colour, yet I can never hope to understand their experience adequately. I am restricted to *identification*, the indirect, but only way, that human beings can empathize with one another when they don't share a specific source of anxiety, in this case, oppression due to skin colour.

But in light of the blaze of white privilege illuminated for us by Peggy McIntosh in her article "White Privilege and Male Privilege," once again I find myself examining a new face of white privilege and studying my own image in the reflection. The awareness of my own white privilege is for me both painful and magnetic. What follows is an attempt to analyse my experience of white privilege so that I can further understand the extent of racism and participate in its dismantling.

It is fairly easy to understand the pain. I had always thought that I deserved whatever status or benefits that I have because I struggled for them and overcame the great disadvantages of being female and a single mother. However, what I have learned from thinking about white privilege is the part that I didn't deserve. I have colluded with the meritocracy in believing that if you work like hell you can get what you deserve regardless of race, class or gender. This is only part of it. The most difficult aspect has been giving up my position of moral superiority, which was based on my being a woman. I hadn't considered that the privilege of my race, unexamined, seriously challenged my claim to understand racism.

I am not used to this feeling of, dare I say, guilt. Some of the victims of male supremacy, white women, are also often the perpetrators of white supremacy. Guilt is not supposed to be part of anti-racist education; we are supposed to recognize that we did not consciously support racism and therefore feel no guilt. But sometimes I wonder if a manageable amount of guilt is necessary to promote social responsibility. Isn't this what Freud called *thanatos*, the very foundation of civilization?

I am momentarily comforted by the thought that there is another group of people, some of whom have been through a similar experience: that is, men of colour. Some of them have challenged their own sexism, found it to exist, and may also have experienced feelings of guilt similar to mine when I observed my own privilege.

None of us can afford to feel comfortable about oppression. In fact white women are sometimes the victims of the strange concoction of racism and sexism when they are chosen by racial minority men for their enhanced status as whites, not their real selves, and then later used as recipients of bottled up anger and aggression against whites, as if they were solely responsible for white supremacy. But in spite of this unfair practice of using white women, it pales in the face of sexist activities practised against racial minority women by men of all colours. Anita Hill's response to Clarence Thomas's sexist behaviour was countered by cries of racism from his supporters. *Miss Saigon*, which opened in Toronto in 1993, inflicts the continuing stereotype of hooker upon Southeast Asian women. White men frequently choose racial minority women for their "exoticism," another painful stereotype.

150

Last January I was propelled into this analysis of my own white privilege when I was invited to speak to a group of women on International Women's Day. The topic was racism. My reaction was angst. What can a white woman say to a group of racial minority women about racism? Explaining my dilemma to the woman who was making the request, I refused. But she was persistent. She said that she trusted me. Why should she trust me? What have white people done for racial minority people that wasn't to their own advantage? But then, who am I to be suspicious of such a person because she trusts me? And if I refuse her request, what message does that send back to racial minority people? That racism is their problem and not mine? I agreed to speak on the condition that I could only speak from my own experience, white privilege, and that I had no advice to give to the audience since I strongly felt that it wasn't my place to do so. But my problem then became that racial minority people usually already know about white privilege. And why should any non-white audience care that I now knew about it too? I concluded that we all need to recognize that white privilege is a barrier and that white people need to acknowledge this to all racial groups in order for all of us to learn how to dismantle the system of race-based privilege.

I began to seriously debrief my own personal white privilege and try to understand my own relationship with it. It may be obvious that I didn't do this alone. I had lots of help from people who have been living the other side of the coin of my privilege all their lives. This isn't an armchair activity. It is a synthesis of my personal (white, female) experience, others' experience and my logic. It's hard to determine one's own white privilege because, as Peggy McIntosh says, it is invisible. For example, a Black friend told me that she was unsuccessful in finding a specific Black doll for her daughter. The doll had been advertised, but was unavailable, since shipments of the doll from Hong Kong only randomly contained the Black doll. I had no such problem finding the right doll for my daughter. It would never have occurred to me that easily finding a doll for my daughter was a privilege conferred on me because of my skin colour. Another young Black friend told me that when he goes shopping he is frequently shadowed by sales clerks, who apparently imagine that he will steal something. This is a fact of his life to which he became accustomed when he was very young. Yet I have rarely had this experience; when I shop people leave me alone, a privilege which I would never have known without the benefit of this comparison.

I seem to relinquish some of this privilege sometimes when I am in the company of racial minority people. For example, when I was

151

driving my car accompanied by a South Asian (male) friend, a police officer, for no apparent reason, asked to see my driver's licence. This had never happened to me before. Instead of being viewed favourably, or at least indifferently, as I am seen when walking with a white man, I have received strong looks of disapproval from strangers when I walk with a racial minority man.

You may ask why I bother to go through this, or you may despair if you think that understanding white privilege is too difficult for the broad community of white people. White people *en masse* may see no advantage in changing just for a principle. But I think that there is a tangible advantage to be offered to white people.

Eros, the pleasure principle, is what really drives me. In imagining a reinvented world in which there is no privilege based on skin colour, I am more than tempted, I am compelled by a feeling of utter sensuality to embrace a society of invisible systems in which individuals confer love and appreciation on one another. In the dream, we value both racial differences and similarities. With all barriers removed, healthy unbruised spirits would interact selflessly, buoying each other up, teaching each other, learning egolessly from each other, wanting the best for each other. There is no room for privilege or hate. People would no longer be retreating to heal and return to the centre of the ring of our world, ready to come out fighting in the endless boxing match of life. There would be no people on the inside and no people on the outside. All of us would have, as April Burey, a wise woman I know, describes, "the power of the spirit."

At first glance it would seem that this particular vision of eros is unattainable in my lifetime. But I try to create it in my relationships with my friends, in my daily life. In that way I can, albeit imperfectly, participate in the dream. And of course there is joy in the process of trying to bring life to the vision, the thrill of painting the picture.

It seems to me that this is an accessible post-liberal position for anti-racist white people to take. The liberal position is uncomfortably benevolent, seeking to satisfy "the other" and not one's self, ultimately a dishonest and untenable position. Liberals would not see that they have to change in order to dismantle their privilege, nor would they acknowledge that there is any inherent personal value in redistributing race privilege. But I think that there is a great advantage for everyone in removing racial barriers and that no one should feel selfless about taking care of this anti-racism business.

It may be that the tendency on the part of some white people to deny the benefits of white privilege stems from their liberalism and the fear that sacrifice is required. Liberalism may act as a perceived safety zone, making real change unnecessary. Possibly some people who are not white may also buy into liberalism, causing them to be grateful for improvements to their status, an unnecessary attitude if the bestowers of the improvement are actually the beneficiaries as well.

As a white anti-racist educator I sometimes encounter racial minority people who are suspicious of my motivation. I expect that they smell liberalism and don't want any favours from someone who might get cheap thrills out of "helping" people. Or maybe they fear cultural appropriation by people who are alienated from their own culture by virtue of privilege and need to borrow identity from others. All of this is true and possible. White people have been so busy studying "the other" that we have forgotten how to look at ourselves. Or if we do, we may not like what we see — white privilege.

It might be useful to relate this idea to a practical issue of our times: employment equity. We have a new law in Ontario which requires most organizations to implement an employment equity plan. This means that organizations must attempt to change the profile of their workforce with respect to four designated groups — Aboriginal people, people with disabilities, racial minorities and women — to match the community. The resistance to this always implies that a sacrifice is required on the part of the people who have the power in the present system. For example, some white men are afraid that they will not be able to find a job. Or white people say, "But what about my son?" I think they miss the point. Our collective humanity will be better served by employment equity. Yes, my son will have a tougher time applying for and getting a job. He will have to hone his skills better, and perhaps improve his education to be more competitive. But finally, when he is employed, he will have the pleasure of working with a more representative sample of the whole of humanity. He will be more able to access the wealth of knowledge and experience of our complex human community.

It is clear to me that we can't even approach this vision if we merely seek to end white privilege. The other forms of privilege must go too: class, gender, able-bodiedness, etc. The list is a problem for philosophers, lovers of logic, ethics, our children. I only know that we must dive between the "isms" to wrench the truth, sibyl-like, from the bowels of knowledge.

I know that the gulf between the vision and reality seems unbridgeable, but our human condition requires growth that must at

153

least be progressive. Why shouldn't we, then, develop in this way to promote the well-being of our most valuable asset, ourselves, our collective spirit?

The first problem is sharing the vision. Most whites do not see their privilege. It is as invisible to them as germs were in the eighteenth century. Much is said these days of paradigm shift. I think that this is what is required to expose the present system. Yet a paradigm is more than just a system, it is an abstract way of looking at a complex of systems. An anti-racist paradigm would present a new vision, a seductive image, which would motivate participants. There is no doubt that many people who are not white share much of this vision already and that it is white people who most need the vision in order to want change.

Anti-racist education should provide the vision. To forget this would be to deprive white participants of a reason for being there, for engaging in personal change, for understanding their potential contribution to the human ecosystem. In this way, understanding white privilege is no longer a barrier, a superficial balm, a chore to be accomplished for humanitarian reasons.

The second problem in dismantling resistance to white privilege is concerned with changing people's own daily lives. Surely if people are involved in the vision, and if the invisible systems are made visible, people will change very readily because they will see that it is to their own advantage. The real challenge of change lies in bringing reality to the vision, convincing the caterpillar to become a butterfly, the rock to be a gem.

My reason for suggesting this is simply that this has been my own experience in coming to seek anti-racist change. Experience has told me that although I seem to be a person who embraces social change, when personal adjustments are required I can be as recalcitrant as the worst of them. Logic tells me that my experience is roughly similar to the rest of my species, who pattern their behaviour according to prevailing paradigms. And so I will retreat and muse some more — this time about strategy.

LEARNING FROM DISCOMFORT
A LETTER TO MY DAUGHTERS
BARB THOMAS

Dear Karen and Janette:

A few weeks ago, Janny, we had a conversation at a friend's cottage — two of us well over forty, three of you twenty and under, all of us white. You were talking about the huge chasms between kids with different racial identities in high school — how you felt unwelcome when you went to the Afro-Can club and you never went back; how old friends from as far back as daycare got pressured by their peers to avoid you as a friend because you were white; how you experienced the different clubs in the school as being divisive and exclusive. Your stepsister got angry with me when I started to talk about the reasons why these clubs might be a place of relief and comfort for kids who experience racism in the school and society. She said I was always "sympathizing with the Black kids," but what about a white kid's feelings of being excluded and laughed at by a group of Black kids? I said that both kinds of pain could be happening at the same time, and that it wasn't necessary to deny Black kids' realities in order to pay attention to the feelings of exclusion she as an individual might feel. And this is, of course, not simple, because she, as a Jew, also experiences a form of racism in anti-Semitism.

I've been thinking about the many times we've talked about these questions, trying to hold different truths in our hands at the same time without smashing the ones we don't like. And this cottage conversation has some of that same spirit. But it also has some ech-oes — uncomfortable for me — of the louder, more strident pro-nouncements out there in the streets, organizations and newspapers about "white people's pain," in particular "white women being si-lenced."

It is important to acknowledge and address your own hurt; and there are different kinds of hurts, different scales of hurt and wounds. There are also different kinds of power to ignore others' wounds, or get your hurt recognized. We've got some names for those huge wounds — words like racism, sexism, imperialism, poverty. These wounds are not accidental — they are done to some people by other people. And the damage has been, and continues to be, massive.

Right now there is an enormous denial of the big wounds, in par-ticular of racism, by the people who are not on the receiving end. You'll hear such people say they're tired of "hearing about racism," or "listening to women griping" or reading newspaper stories about child poverty. "What about my job, my problems, my freedom of speech?" They'll talk about something called "political correctness," which is a label slapped on anyone who feels and expresses revulsion against the big wounds. They'll rail about "angry women of colour who hurt my feelings when they said I was racist."

As white people, we have the immediate luxury of saying these kinds of things and actually getting listened to. But I don't think we have the long-term luxury, not if we want things to be any different for your children. When people who are not the targets of racism get that uncomfortable and angry, and are that determined to trivialize enormous social problems, you can bet there's something substantial to look at and change. And when people can't see what's right around them, there's some effort being exerted not to see.

I didn't always think or feel this way. In fact, you've witnessed some of my awkward, stumbling journey thus far, often to your em-barrassment and inconvenience. However, the times I've learned the most have been when I managed to stay with my moments of dis-comfort and learn from them. And I'm distinguishing here between the constant discomfort zone where I live as a woman in which sex-ism is directed at me, and the less pressured unease I feel as a white person where I am not the target of racism. It's this second type of discomfort I want to explore from my own experiences. And you'll de-cide, as you always do, what is useful to you. I'll organize these mo-ments around four of the questions you have put to me from time to time.

You asked me what, in my growing up, affected my learning about the world.

My parents — your grandparents — and the communities from which we came, gave me both the nourishment to be critical, and the reasons not to be. You know that we emigrated from England after the war, when I was two, and my sister three months. My dad is English. You know that my mother was born in Canada; her grandparents on her mother's side emigrated from Scotland; her family on her dad's side descended from United Empire Loyalists. This ancestry was unremarkable in downtown Ottawa of the fifties and sixties, and unremarked. I didn't ask about it; I was "normal"; I didn't have to think about it. I only discovered this much later, when I heard other children, who had to know so much more about their histories in order to survive here, talk about their families. It was then that I realized my ignorance.

What I knew was that my sister and I were deeply loved, and that my parents deeply loved each other. This I learned, quite early, not to take for granted. This knowledge both helped and hindered me in my later rebellion against them.

Indeed, your grandparents were both very present in my life as a child. Dad's office was at home, and his and my mother's preoccupations were transparent, part of our everyday lives. My parents' travel and their opinions on international events had a profound effect on the questions I asked or didn't ask, and on my views on the world.

I was the child to whom Dad showed his stamp collection, and to whom he explained, with the help of a map, how the world was organized. From his point of view, the most significant part was the British Empire. Your grandfather had been a British officer with the Gurkhas in India from 1936 to 1945. We had many photograph albums of him in India and in Burma. His own father had owned a colonial outfitting business, equipping English people "going to the colonies." There were photographs of my dad on horseback, or being served tea. The people in the foreground of all these photographs were white. Sometimes, in the background, there were Indian people, serving and carrying. (These are later reflections on something I took for granted at the time.) When I was a child, I loved these photographs of my dad in earlier moments in his life.

I first heard of Aden (which became Southern Yeman and is now the Republic of Yemen), Antigua, Australia, Bahamas, Barbados (where we were later to live), Bechuanaland (now Botswana), Bermuda, British Guiana (now Guyana), British Honduras (now Belize),

157

Ceylon (now Sri Lanka), right through the alphabet to the Turks and Caicos Islands and Zanzibar (now part of Tanzania) from the meticulously groomed stamp collection which my father helped me to continue. Together we would send for the prettiest ones (which always came from places other than England or Canada), or the special commemorative ones. In his book, these included the Bahamas 1942 stamps celebrating "450 years after the landfall of Columbus"; or the gorgeous 1906 Barbados stamp commemorating the "tercentenary of annexation" (I had no idea what this meant); or the 1939 royal visit to Canada. The same king or queen's head appeared on stamps from all these countries. We were all — including Canada — part of the "family of the Empire."

I felt these connections with "another home" at Christmas time particularly. In late October, we would pack up an enormous cheddar cheese, a big fruitcake and other goodies to send to my aunt and cousin in England. And we would await the package of hand-knitted sweaters and books that would arrive every year. The books were Enid Blyton adventure books, or *Girls' Annuals* in which comics and stories were set around the world. Young white people (although I didn't see them as white then; they were just people) my age strode across countries, solving mysteries in jungles and deserts. They seemed to do so with resolve, cunning, and more compassion than their "enemies" — usually the people who lived there — appeared to deserve.

On Christmas Day we would count down to 10:00 a.m. for the Queen's message — a voice struggling through underwater cables and transmission problems; a voice heavy with responsibility, overseeing the Empire, urging compassion, harmony, enrichment together; a voice calming in its assurance that things would get done. There must have been messages before 1952 when she abruptly became Queen, but I don't remember them. I do remember the death of King George, and trying to imagine what a king really did. My parents were of the opinion that he was a "good king," whatever that meant, and that this was a very sad occasion indeed. And so the Queen's coronation was a grave and dignified event — a young woman assuming "enormous responsibilities." In order to help me imagine what these might be, I was equipped with lots of books about the Royals — the Queen and Princess Margaret as young girls, their education, their travels, their horses, their parents, lots of people in carriages. I was taught respect for the monarchy and a sense of being part of a benevolent "Commonwealth" where people treated each other decently and responsibly, but where sometimes things went amok. I never questioned that the words "empire" and "commonwealth" could be used interchangeably.

And then there was the BBC at 8:00 every morning—that garbled, pebbles-in-the-mouth voice crackling through the seawaves—pronouncing on Ceylon, Tanganyika (now Tanzania), Malaya (part of what is now Malaysia), the Mau Mau Rebellion and India. My father and mother had a sustained and intense interest in international news, and always tried to develop my own curiosity in "world events." But as a child, I never made the connections between these countries and their struggles and my life in Ottawa.

I think I had more daily experience of, but no words for, class differences. There were the "kids from Heron Park" who invariably became the "tech kids" at our high school. We were exhorted to be friendly, but to stay away from these kids. I had a friend, Sandy Olsenberg, who got talked about differently than anyone else. I was aware of differences between us, but didn't grasp their significance. Her parents listened to Johnny Cash; her dad was often unemployed; they moved a lot; she got to eat more junk food than I did; Sandy had lots of responsibility; she looked anxious much of the time. I once brought home a boyfriend from university who named himself as a working-class kid. My parents were concerned about "important differences between us." It appeared we were not working-class. However, at the same time my father would get angry with me for using words and references designed to make my father himself feel stupid. He would warn me about the social folly of "my pseudo-intellectualism"—quite rightly I now think—but also because he shared the anxiety that many self-taught people have that they will appear unlearned to those with a few more years of school. I was the first in our family to go to university.

Unlike your experience in Toronto, my Ottawa childhood was filled with the static noise of worlds outside my neighbourhood, and, at the same time, devoid of real, daily contact with the people in those worlds. But that doesn't mean there was no contact. I think it was my fifth birthday party. My parents borrowed the movie *Little Black Sambo* from the library along with a projector and screen and set it up in a neighbour's house. I remember this movie vividly. I felt wonder, curiosity, derision, anxiety. Were there creatures in the world like this? Were there really jungles? Is this who lived here? Why were children my age having to deal with tigers? Was this a human child? There was nothing and no one to help me answer these questions.

159

There was no respectful, authentic representation of African peoples, Native peoples, Asian peoples. Most white children like myself, growing up in Canada in the fifties, "met" the other four-fifths of the world through comics; through movies such as Walt Disney's *Song of the South* (see Alice Walker's essay on how this movie hurt her and other people in her community); through radio programs such as *Amos and Andy* (now satirized, sort of, in the movie *Amos and Andrew*); through the countless westerns on radio and TV, such as *The Lone Ranger*; through missionaries at church; through the limited range of people authoring the school textbooks and novels; through the narrow world view of teachers; and through the garbled voice of the BBC. Almost without exception, these versions of the rest of the planet were written and directed by white people.

This "absent presence" or "present absence" of four-fifths of the world, characterized what "contact" I had with people who *did* live in Ottawa and environs at the time. When we went for picnics with my grandparents to see the site of my grandfather's family farm that is now buried by the St. Lawrence Seaway, we did not talk about the Aboriginal peoples who lived there before the Loyalists, or whose land may have been taken to give to the Loyalists. It was not in the school books, and it was not part of my family's consciousness at that time, either. It is only this week, in the summer of 1993, that my mother recollected why her father's family never relied on store-bought drugs. She was reminiscing that her father and aunt always looked for boneset and other plants good for stomachache. She told us that when her father's family migrated to Canada as Loyalists, they learned about the healing properties of local plants "from Indian people who lived here."

In Ottawa, I was more specifically aware that French people and Jewish people "were not like us." French people were "poor and less educated"; Jewish families "had lots of money." Face-to-face contact was sporadic, guarded, unequal, and just enough to reinforce these powerful stereotypes. Certainly, nobody named social class, ethnocentrism or racism as factors affecting people's lives, or shaping what we learned to see and hear, and not to see and hear.

In these years of my youth, I was self-absorbed and protected from trouble in ways that neither of my parents had been. I had the choice to stay unconnected to the larger world I inhabited. At Queen's University, I remained unaware of even the mild political activity on that campus. There was evidence of people's pain, oppression, and resistance all around me. Their muzzled voices were present in the events that one *could see*, like the civil rights marches on television, or the sustained and vicious forms of contempt expressed towards Aboriginal peoples; and in the things that one couldn't see, such as the exclusion of most people who weren't white from the university; the all-white teaching staff; the total European focus of all studies; the strange silence, even during those civil rights days, concerning race and racism in Canada. I walked around as though vaccinated from the disturbance that these real people and these real struggles might make in my life. This kind of blinkering and ignorance, this distortion of the world, is one of the chief effects of a racist environment on white people.

And yet, I must have been exerting some effort to not see/hear what was around me, because I had some indefinable unease, some snuffling sense that there was more to the picture, some curiosity and some fear about how it was with other people, whomever they were.

I'm reminded, as I read the above again, that I have really only begun to answer the question June Jordan poses: "What took you so long?" In her essay "On Listening, A Good Way to Hear," she challenges a white American activist to explain what took him so long to "very very very very slowly realize that something is hideously wrong."

You asked me what I learned when we lived in the Caribbean.

I had to leave Canada and live and work in Barbados for two years to see what Ms. Jordan was talking about. It was there that things came unravelled — quickly, it seems now — but in identifiable stages. Barbados was one of the places behind the beautiful stamps; a place that had celebrated a "tercentenary of annexation," a part of the "family of the Empire."

I was twenty-four, your father was twenty-five and you were two, Karen. I remember sitting on a bus to Speightstown in the first week we were there. I was looking at the skin on my arm and thinking, "I'm white. What took me so long to name this?" This sounds so elementary now. It wasn't to me then. I remember thinking that "white" was less my physical colour (indeed, I was a violent pink) than it was my "social" colour, if you know what I mean. It had everything to do with the mixture of deference, resentment and polite distance that I felt from so many people — the effort people had to exert to see beyond my whiteness to whatever qualities they might find

161

attractive in me. This awareness emerged in little lurches. I'm sure I whined, initially, about people not seeing the "real me."

And I was learning, through Caribbean writers, that the Empire was not a happy family. I read about Europeans exterminating Arawak and Carib peoples to clear land for European plantations; Europeans capturing African peoples to provide a pliant labour force; Black and indigenous people resisting this sustained brutality against them; the legacy of this history economically, socially, psychologically; and the current, continued struggles of Caribbean nations to forge authentic, new, democratic paths for themselves.

My learning was stimulated by more than books. I could see the effects of colonialism in every aspect of daily life. Observations, and frequent conversations with friends, neighbourhood children and students, many of whom you met, Karen, raised whole new questions for me. There was one exchange in particular where fifteen-year-old Anthony Griffiths told me that he really liked me because I was white. I was startled and hurt. Didn't he like me "because of me"? I racked my brains for a question that would explain this to him, and settled on, "How would you feel if I told you that I liked you because you were Black?" He replied in a deeply wounded voice, "I'd think you wanted me for a puppy dog." I looked at him helplessly. He was not talking about individual hurt caused by a comment; he was talking about what white people could do to him and other Black people. I realized, then, I had no notion of the scale of damage which had been done to him. The effects of racism on me were not "equivalent" to the effects on him. And, whether I liked it or not, I could not filter out my whiteness from Anthony's responses to me. Anthony Griffiths helped me to begin to analyse power, in particular, the power behind the exercise of racism. In the world as it is, Anthony Griffiths can hurt my feelings, but he has none of the social power, none of the weight of history that would help him, through the exercise of racism, to reduce my circumstances, my life chances, my sense of myself.

These everyday moments forced me to examine what "white" represented, what white people had done, and were continuing to do to Black people in Barbados. And from Barbados, I had to think about the rest of the Caribbean, and the United States, and Africa, and other parts of the world, and eventually, Canada. What had taken me so long? I was furious at the information I had been denied, and ashamed of my own collusion in the situation.

At the same time I was reflecting on my situation as a woman and developing questions about feminism. I was young, married, with a small child — you, Karen. A white American anthropologist was also living in Barbados at the time. She was there with her child — defiantly not married — investigating why Barbadian women would not participate consistently in the birth control schemes that proliferated there. She would express exasperation with the women who were my neighbours. She saw them as taking abuse from their men, getting pregnant when it wasn't necessary, and not fighting for their rights. She saw part of her job, in addition to her research, as "promoting feminism." It seemed there were certain ways you showed that you were a feminist. It seemed that neither myself nor my neighbours were feminists. It was in Barbados that I learned something else that now seems obvious — that women's struggles are shaped by race and class. I had struggled to prove that I could both have children and go out and work. Some of my neighbours would have loved such a choice. They were fighting to put food on the table for their children. For them, working outside the home was a given. Women carried loads of sugar cane and food on their heads for miles. This was everyday life since slavery. They took care of middle-class (usually white or light-skinned) women's children to the detriment of their own. Many of my neighbours did not see birth control as some kind of liberation; some of the birth control experiments made women sick and unable to have children; in the absence of old age pensions, children were their security. And women looked out for each other's children, including you, Karen, in ways I had never seen in Canada. I had to ask myself whether Canada was as child-loving as I had thought; I was forced to broaden my understanding of women's rights; I had to question a feminism that only acknowledged some women and some rights.

Some of these issues were only half-formed insights and questions when we returned to Canada in 1972. But the two years in Barbados made everything different. Toni Morrison, in her book of essays called *Playing in the Dark: Whiteness and the Literary Imagination*, has a wonderful passage which, for me, names this shift in my vision:

> It is as if I had been looking at a fishbowl — the glide and flick of the golden scales, the green tip, the bolt of white careening back from the gills; the castles at the bottom, surrounded by pebbles and tiny, intricate fronds of green; the barely disturbed water, the flecks of waste and food, the tranquil bubbles traveling to the surface — and suddenly I saw the bowl, the structure that transparently (and invisibly) permits the ordered life it contains to exist in the larger world.

Having seen "the bowl," I now had a responsibility to chip away   163 and widen the cracks in it. And the biggest cracks came, I discovered, from people who were outside the bowl, who were organizing to make a different structure that would meaningfully include them.

You'll hear that not much was going on in the seventies or even the eighties, but this is someone's wishful thinking. Over the next years I learned a great deal from efforts to organize non-profit daycare, to get our voices heard as parents in schools, to support farm workers and domestic workers in their organizing, to build community and coalition, to expose racism and get new policies and practices in public institutions. When I came back from Barbados, I "discovered" — I guess a bit like Columbus — what had been happening for some time. Native peoples, lesbians, women, poor people, artists, workers, South Asian people and others had formed organizations, were talking back and were making a difference.

For a number of years after Barbados, I was furious with my father and ashamed of my family's participation in this Empire — this "fishbowl." My father and I had fruitless fights in which I disparaged him cruelly for the criminal activities of the British, for what he had done in India, for American imperialism. We managed to hurt each other a great deal, I think, before we made peace with each other's lives. I know that is part of what has taken so long. Another writer, Minnie Bruce Pratt, says a helpful thing for me:

> When we discover truths about our home culture, we may fear we are losing our self; our self-respect, our self-importance. But when we begin to act on our new knowledge, when we begin to cross our "first people boundaries," and ally ourselves publicly with "the others," then we may fear that we will lose the people who are our family, our kind, be rejected by "our own kind."

I both feared and wanted this as a way of distancing myself from my own shame at not seeing, earlier, what was all around me. But my parents never let this happen. You'll remember the painful time in 1983 when I was working in Grenada and the U.S. marines invaded. There was a handful of us who came back to Canada choked with rage, and incredulous at the lies that were passing for news. We spoke about what we had seen, and we went on a cross-country tour to make sure that other people heard about it, too. My parents found it really difficult to believe that the Americans would have deliberately done something that wasn't for the protection of all of us. However, whether or not they agreed with our analysis of what the Americans were actually doing there, they did believe that the Americans had contributed to my immediate physical danger. They collected all the news clippings, and soon after our return went to a party with the clippings, as usual, tucked in my mother's purse. They were assailed by criticism from old friends, angry that I was misleading people and that I was saying all these "Communist things." Your grandparents tried to defend me by accurately quoting from the clippings, and they were supported by another friend who loudly and contemptuously dismissed the entire gathering. Shortly after this, my parents attended a little photographic exhibit on Grenada, entitled "A Small Revolution"—wonderful photographs documenting the extraordinary achievements of Grenada from 1979 to 1983—the real reason for the invasion. They gave me a poster of this exhibit for Christmas. I was more moved by the love in this gift than anything they have ever given me. And I stopped arguing with them.

You asked me how the two of you helped me learn.

You were constantly brushing me up, uncomfortably, with my ignorance, and my unfamiliarity with the world. I'm grinning as I remember you, Karen, on the back steps, your two-year-old fist clutching the hair of your friend, her fingers stroking yours, both of you quite entranced with each other. And when she pushed her finger into your arm it left a white mark momentarily. Why was that? Why didn't her brown skin do that? Why did the water leave your hair all lank and plastered against your head? It didn't do that to Sophie's. And while I rushed around trying to find out about melanin and skin colour, you'd come up with some harder question. Why was Sophie's mother upset because we gave Sophie a Black doll? Why, when you wore clothes that a relative had outgrown, did Sophie's mother throw your perfectly fine, outgrown clothes back on our doorstep calling them "dumps?"

And just when I thought I was on the right track, a reaction from one of you would shake things up again. How was I to comfort you, Janny, when you were five years old, and we had just read the book and sung the song the "Drinking Gourd"? You began to sob that you were frightened that they would come and catch your friend, Fran. I tried, awkwardly, to explain that slavery was over, but that its legacy was not. And I also fully realized something, at that moment, that I had only partially grasped before. You needed to know more about how Black people had fought back, and continued to do so. We read

Harriet Tubman; we talked about South Africa. And you needed to know that some white people resisted being caught into a set of oppressive relations with their Black neighbours.

And when you were seven, Karen, there was the day I heard you calling, taunting, "nigger, nigger," to your friend, Connie, next door. Before I reached the back door, I realized that my rage was also about my failure, and would not help Connie or you. And so we talked about that word, about where it came from. And we went to talk to Connie and Connie's mother. I'm not sure whether your friendship survived that day. But it was an important jolt to my liberalism. It was not enough to have a variety of books, exposure to different music, or to live in a cosmopolitan neighbourhood. Contact between people was still not equal. There were weapons you had in a fight with Connie, that she didn't have against you, and you had, at seven, learned to use them, as I had at seven. Resisting white supremacy required an everyday, active set of interventions. There was no such thing as "non-racism," only "anti-racism." This was a very important lesson for me, and one that directly influenced my increasing focus on anti-racism work in my job at the Cross Cultural Communications Centre.

Indeed, at ten years old, Janny, you already grasped that inaction about racism by adults had left kids on their own to fight it. Do you remember sitting at the dining room table eating supper—you, your friend Fran and I? You were congratulating Fran on the damage she had inflicted on the eye of one of your classmates, Louis. Fran nodded. I, of course, asked what happened. Fran responded economically that Louis had called her "nigger" and she had punched him out. I asked, in my law-and-order way, if there hadn't been some teachers around who could have helped. You two looked knowingly at each other, and Fran began explaining—slowly and carefully, because clearly I wasn't too swift—that if teachers did hear that word, they always found something else to do, or pretended they didn't hear. If you reported the incident to a teacher or principal, they either asked you what you had done to provoke it, or they punished you for being a tattle-tale. "So," concluded Fran, slowing down to let me get the point, "if you're going to get punished anyway, you might as well have the satisfaction of punching the guy out." I had no response to this inescapable logic. This was just another incident in the daily series of child-wise nudges that shook up my comfortable edges. What took me so long, anyway?

Meanwhile, you were making your own paths. I still remember

your march home from a grade nine science class, Karen. You asked whether the Board of Education had a policy that could stop teachers from being racist. It seemed that your science teacher had slipped into the classroom at a raucous moment. Everyone was acting up, but he had swooped down on your classmate, Bao, and sneered, "What's the matter with you? Your kind are well-behaved and quiet, so what's your problem?" In the uneasy silence that followed, no one had spoken up — for Bao, or for themselves. You returned to school the next day, having read the Board's race relations policy. And you went to the science teacher at break and told him that you now knew there was a policy that said he couldn't say the things he had said to Bao; and that your parents knew what you were doing; and that if he ever did that again, you would report him. In mentioning that your parents knew about this, you were demonstrating your growing strategic sense that when you speak up you risk punishment, and where possible, you need to protect yourself.

Always, the two of you have challenged me to "make the way by walking." You never allowed me to hoist some politically cleansed flag, and hitch myself to it. Daily living is so much more messy, and if you're paying any attention at all, that living is constantly throwing up new questions. After watching the movie *Jungle Fever*, Janny, you and I spent three hours analysing the powerful scene in the middle where a group of Black women talk about their experiences with Black men, and with white women. They don't mince words. You felt uncomfortable and accused. You had already seen the movie once with a male friend who was Black, and the two of you had struggled for adequate words to talk about questions of sexism, racism and sexuality without hurting each other.

And there was the youth meeting at a local high school that you attended with a friend, Karen; you were one of the few white people there. You wondered whether you were intruding; you tried to watch alertly for signs that your presence might be inappropriate and hoped you'd be able to read the cues. There is a politic to respecting people's need for caucusing and organizing, while at the same time continuing to learn and do your share of the work to make things better. It's important to keep wrestling with that balance and not give up trying because you're afraid you'll get it wrong. There are other questions. What am I responsible for? What will others hold me responsible for, whether it's fair or not? How do I claim the parts of culture(s) that help me be whole, while at the same time opposing those many aspects that oppress, divide and diminish? How do I both protect myself

167

against malicious and small-minded attack, and leave myself open to continued challenge? These questions take me to the final part of this letter to you.

You asked me what role(s) white people have in fighting racism.

In a certain way, this entire letter is an attempt to answer that question. I can't speak for anyone else, but the efforts I feel best about are those which don't, in themselves, reproduce racism, that build coalition, that acknowledge leadership from activists who experience racism, that ensure that I speak from where I am, and that I move things forward and not back. This is everyday work; I haven't found this easy. I know you two haven't either.

There's a prevalent notion around that white people can choose to fight racism, or not, and people of colour don't have this choice. Let's start with the first part of this statement. It's true that white people are not the targets of racism; and that indeed, many whites have benefitted, and continue to benefit, from dominating and excluding others. Many white people not only do not acknowledge racism as a system of domination, but also choose to do nothing about it if they do. "Having a choice" makes us suspect, because we might pack up anytime the going gets tough. History is littered with examples of people from the power group taking their ball and going home when they're "misunderstood," when they're accused, when the consequences are distasteful, when people "aren't grateful" for their efforts.

We'd better be clear about the reasons we fight racism and other big wrongs. This is where I have come to at this point in my life; I fight racism because I can't be with myself in the world without trying to do so. I fight racism, as I fight other forms of domination, because it has killed millions of people; because it has totally messed up relations between people(s) on this planet; because it forces me into oppressive relations that I reject with other people(s); because it lies about who is in the world and who has made what happen; because it has limited what I have been able to see and know; because it diminishes the friendship and community that I seek, with others, to build; and because I learned through the two of you that inaction is complicity. When I'm clear about that place in myself, I can, as bell hooks says in her book *Black Looks*, "be capable, via *my* political choices, of working on behalf of the oppressed." But I can't work on behalf of anyone else until I know where I am.

And what about the second part of this statement of who has choice about fighting racism? People of colour and Aboriginal persons do not have a choice about being the targets of white domination. However, each person makes decisions about what their stance towards this will be. Not all persons of colour or Aboriginal persons fight racism, any more than all women fight sexism. Certainly there are different consequences and risks for people of colour who fight racism than there are for whites. In your classrooms and workplaces, you will sometimes hear people of colour deny racism, and its effects on themselves and others, just as you'll hear women trivialize sexism. And you will hear white people welcome these pronouncements. In these situations, you will have to speak from your own rejection of racism, and not what you think or hope others will say.

As you already know, there are consequences to speaking and acting against injustice, just as — I believe — there are consequences to not doing so. For people of colour daring to name and challenge racism in a workplace, reprisals are often swift and brutal, crude as well as subtle. Colleagues shun you, talk about you behind your back, suggest that you're crazy and too angry to have any perspective; information about new training, developmental assignments, promotions and new job postings reaches you later than anyone else; decisions affecting you are made at meetings where you are absent; job vacancies you apply for which were previously permanent become temporary; hiring selection teams ask questions about your personal life and views. And on it goes. I personally witnessed all of the above and more in the government workplace where I just finished a contract. These stories are not peculiar to this workplace. It is a serious decision for a person of colour or an Aboriginal person to confront racism — in the workplace or in the streets. It's a serious decision for anyone who's the target of those big forms of oppression to fight back. In lots of places, including Canada, people have been killed for doing so.

Are there consequences for white people fighting racism? Yes, but they're usually of an entirely different order. In my last job, my contract was not renewed. Management didn't like being reminded and challenged about acting on their stated commitment to fighting racism. But this happens less to people who are not at the receiving end of the hurt that you're fighting — men fighting sexism, for example, or straight people insisting on rights for gay people. Indeed, white people challenging racism are often met with an admiration and surprise that can be seductive. "What got you into this anti-racism thing?" I've been asked with interest by people of different racial

169

backgrounds. This applauding of white people's anti-racism efforts is not confined to individual interactions. "Association with anti-racism work" can actually help white people get promotions and jobs, if they are careful, tactical and "not too noisy." In an anti-racism pilot school project on which I worked a few years ago, several of the white teachers included their participation in the project on their resumés and in many cases this "experience" assisted them in securing a vice-principalship or consultant's job in a Board of Education anxious to appear anti-racist. Contributions to this project produced none of the same benefits for Black and East Asian teachers whose efforts were critical to the work. You will encounter this in your work as a teacher, Karen. There is — still — a prevalent notion amongst white people that Aboriginal persons and persons of colour should be challenging racism; and that therefore their efforts and the risks that they take are unremarkable. Co-existing with this fiction is the puzzling view that Aboriginal persons and persons of colour cannot be "objective" when it comes to racism, are likely to overreact and get angry, and are therefore highly suspect when it comes to fighting racism. The corollary to all of this is that white people are best placed to get paid to do anti-racism work, and they are more likely to get recognition for their work. This is, in fact, a microcosm of how racism works. These are some of the ways in which racism can co-opt anti-racism efforts, and any white people who do anti-racism work.

Needless to say, this situation has justifiably ticked many people right off. In this climate and these circumstances you need to pay attention that when you talk back to racism, you aren't benefitting at other people's expense. Indeed, there are jobs you may have to let pass, or opportunities that are exciting to you that someone else would really do better. This is not about condescending to someone, or pushing someone forward "just because she's Black." This is about making sure that the old affirmative action for white people isn't still in operation, with you as a key beneficiary; it's about really trying to get the work done with all the wits, skills and different kinds of knowledge we can assemble.

And you'd better not expect people to be grateful for your efforts. In fact, the more you work on trying to make things right, the more mistakes you'll have the chance to make, and the more you'll get criticized from different people. Sometimes their criticism will be useful, and even if it's hard to listen to, supportive of you and of more effective work. You're lucky when you get that kind of challenge. But sometimes people will try to tear you down, and erode even useful work. Watch out for that; distinguish between the two.

Sometimes, you will feel shame at being white; you will feel uneasy about being middle-class and without disability. It's not easy to embrace who you are, to find models you are proud to claim, and, at the same time, to continue resisting the most abusive aspects of the culture of which we are a part. However, in the long run shame doesn't do you or anyone else any good. Shame is immobilizing unless you use it as information to move on and to change things. Part of being in the power group—whether you like it or not—is being the target of anger when people start to analyse how they are being mistreated by "your" group of people, and to demand that things change. As white women, we live with oppression as part of the "oppressor" group and as part of the "oppressed" group. These are different places to be, and we occupy them at the same time. There are different challenges to being a socially responsible person with these simultaneous identities.

There are moments when you can become just another white person, even to people who love you, know you, want you in their lives. (You know yourselves, that there are times when our anger at men's violence against women, and men's power to avoid changing anything, can extend to all men—our fathers and other loved males. And sometimes, intimate men *do* collude in our oppression. Sometimes we *do* collude, as white people, in the oppression of people we love.)

Do you get the picture? It's what you know already; life is a messy, challenging business. Mostly, you walk one day at a time, clucking over mistakes, and being prepared to make some new ones, trying to leave your little corner of the world in slightly better shape than you found it.

If you take nothing else from all these words, take these five ideas and use them in your own ways. First, remember that *you are not responsible for wrongs committed before you were born, but you can't escape the legacy of those wrongs.* You need to understand some history in order to understand your current position in the world and other people's perceptions of you. *And you are responsible for what you do now.* In this regard, *there's no such thing as "doing nothing."* You two and others have taught me that. Even indecision, or unconsciousness, results in some action or inaction which has consequences for you and other people. The question is whether you're going to take responsibility for it.

171

Second — in whatever situations you experience it — try to *use discomfort to pose new questions to yourself, and to seek new insights.* I'm not talking here about an informed fear of physical danger or attack from other people; I'm speaking of the discomfort resulting from avoidance, silence, or the challenge posed by people seeking justice for themselves. Try to ask, even when it's inconvenient, "What and who is missing from this picture? Who else should be saying something about this? What's behind what's going on here?" (This last question could be about what's going on inside yourself, as well as an event in the world.)

Third, *distinguish between, on the one hand, hurt feelings that a person with privilege might feel at being excluded, and on the other, the sustained, systemic, and pervasive damage inflicted on all parts of the self, by the big wounds* — racism, sexism, class, imperialism, ageism, heterosexism, oppression of people with disabilities. As white people, and as women, you will experience both. There is a backlash against people who are organizing against these big wrongs. Part of that backlash trivializes the damage of these injustices and inflates the personal feelings of those people who are being challenged to change.

Fourth, *value your own experiences as sources of learning and wisdom about yourself and the larger society*, even if those stories are painful. The tensions in our personal lives, whether they are economic, social, and/or in our psyches, mirror in some way the tensions and contradictions in the larger world. This is not the same thing as thinking that your experience is everyone else's experience. My stories here are about some moments when I managed to be more "accurate about myself and to force my mind into a constantly expanding apprehension of my political and moral situation." (These are not my words; they're June Jordan's, but I like them as one descriptor of what I'm trying to do, what I've seen both of you try to do.)

And finally, *make the most of who you are without damaging other people with less social power than yourself.* This means being self-aware, and self-critical. It means using what you know and acknowledging and being curious about what you don't know. It means living as truthfully and as consciously as possible with all your social identities as young, white, middle-class women, but not being reduced by them. It means not being apologetic for who you are, but being responsible for what you do.

As Bernice Johnson Reagon (of the singing group Sweet Honey in the Rock) says, "Most of the things you do, if you do them right, are for people who live long after you are long forgotten. That will only happen if you give it away. Whatever it is that you know, give it away." And that is what I'm trying to do here. To put it mildly, you haven't always warmly welcomed the knowledge I wanted to give to you at different moments in your lives. But I feel some urgency now about what I've tried to say in this letter. Please take these thoughts with you as you decide how you will travel these roads.

Loving you in all the ways I know,

Your mother.

PART 5

STEREOTYPING IS A
COMMON PRACTICE, BUT . . .

STEREOTYPING

KAI JAMES

Stereotyping is a common practice, but
If stereotyping remains unchallenged
Doors of opportunity will slam shut.

It is often just a habit,
And a bad one at that
Because it can lead to hurt and misunderstandings
And who knows what.

We often indulge in stereotyping
Simply because it's knowledge that we lack.
And reliance upon inaccurate portrayal by the media
Just will not help.

Fulfilling stereotypes is an overwhelming temptation,
One which must be avoided.
Therefore, we must be aware and open-minded,
For knowledge is the key to resisting the enticement.

I DIDN'T KNOW YOU WERE JEWISH . . . AND OTHER THINGS NOT TO SAY WHEN YOU FIND OUT

IVAN KALMAR

Imagine that you and I have been acquainted with each other for some time. And now you learn that I have written this article. You are surprised, and you say: **I didn't know you were Jewish!** Really? How touching. What would you have done if you had known? More important still, what are you going to do now that you do know? Watch yourself when you feel like saying something anti-Semitic? Not criticize other Jews? Avoid speaking about the Middle East? Not tell Jew jokes? Hide your doubts about the Holocaust?

Perhaps you mean to compliment me. I am not loud and aggressive. I am not interested in "jewing" people I have financial dealings with. If you are politically conservative, you might mean that I am not a subversive pinko radical, or a big-city sexual and cultural pervert. If you are on the left, you might mean that I am not a Zionist Imperialist. In either case you mean, ultimately, that I am "Jewish but nice." But I don't need your compliment. To me, "Jewish" and "nice" are not opposites.

Notice: you did not simply ask me, "Are you Jewish?" I could take that; it is an ordinary question of personal information. You said, "I didn't know that . . ." and you said it because you don't speak to Jews

179

the same way you speak to non-Jews. If you had known that I was Jewish, you would have treated me as a Jew, rather than as a human being.

Let us go through some other things you may have said instead. I know you do not feel that you are an anti-Semite. If you give some consideration to the issues to be raised, then you will not *appear* to be an anti-Semite to Jews like me, either. I cannot speak for all Jews, of course, but I do know that many would agree with me on much if not all of what I am going to say.

I don't care if a person is Jewish; to me all people are the same.

Maybe you think if you had said this, I would have been happier. Sorry. Yes, there are many Jews who would enthusiastically accept being "just human beings" rather than "Jews." In my book, *The Trotskys, Freuds and Woody Allens: Portrait of a Culture,* I call such people EJI (pronounce it "edgy," an acronym for Embarrassed Jewish Individuals). Jean Paul Sartre simply called them "inauthentic Jews," and pointed out that there were no human beings who were not also French, English, Black, white—and/or Jewish.

I am not an EJI. No, I don't want you to treat me as a Jew rather than as a human being, because that implies that a Jew is not fully human. But I also don't want you to treat me as if I were not a Jew. I want to be treated as a Jew *and* a human being. I would like you to understand that being Jewish is a normal thing for a normal human being to be. It is, unfortunately, true that some of us Jews do not understand the point either, but it does not excuse you from trying to be more sensitive to the legitimacy of human differences.

What's the JAP's idea of an ideal home?

"Six thousand square feet with no kitchen or bedroom." Very funny. So you find out I am Jewish and you tell a "Jewish" joke. Why not, you think, the Jews are so funny. In one episode of the BBC television series *Alexei Sayle's Stuff,* the board of directors of a corporation is meeting to welcome Mr. Gold, their new accountant. They are told by the very "Aryan" looking new arrival that, despite his name, he is not Jewish. Though this happens to be the truth, everyone takes it to be a funny Jewish joke. The distinguished directors break out in inextinguishable guffawing. From then on they greet everything the accountant says with wild laughter. "Jewish humor," the chief executive exclaims, "very funny . . ."

You want to please a Jew, you think, with a Jewish joke. And you choose a JAP joke. A JAP is, of course, a "Jewish American Princess." There is not a more vicious anti-female stereotype around. It is no compliment to Jewish men to have invented these vicious insults to Jewish women, who are portrayed as lazy, frigid, spoiled and stupid. Indeed, the JAP is everything a woman means to a frustrated macho misogynist. I suspect the Jewish men who make up JAP jokes are unconsciously using a subtle and rather effective argument: "Look, our women are just as despicable as your women and in the same way; and we put them down just as much as you; therefore you, goyish macho chauvinists, and us Jewish macho chauvinists have much in common." It's like the old Jewish saying about Sammy Davis, the Black comedian who was Jewish: "Get *him*, he's both!" A Jewish woman is both: a Jew and a woman. But the Jewish teller of a JAP joke wants you to hate the woman, not the Jew.

When you, a non-Jew, tell it, a JAP joke becomes not just anti-female, but clearly anti-Jewish. For you are not laughing about your own women (which would certainly be bad enough) but about ours. You are contradicting the Jewish JAP joke teller's intent. You laugh not only at women, but also at Jews.

It is not in good taste for a non-Jew to tell any joke whose butt is a Jew. Some fat people and bald people like to joke about their physical characteristics. They hope that way to preempt any aggression or derision on your part. It is often for the same reason that Jewish jokers tell a joke that puts down the Jews: a "Jew joke." (Anti-Semites love the adjective, "Jew," rather than "Jewish": Jew woman, Jew doctor, Jew boy.) Would you tell a fat joke to a fat person? Why then would you tell a Jew joke to a Jew?

You meant to be friendly by telling the kind of joke you feel you hear Jews themselves saying. But you ended up merely sounding inconsiderate again: to Jews, and, if it was a JAP joke you told, to women.

My mom's such a Jewish mother.

For decades American Jewish comic performers have won great fame putting down their mothers. Telling their inanities in the first person, they have convinced the public, Jewish and Gentile, to think that Jewish mothers are nagging, guilt-inducing monsters. I cannot really

181

blame you for picking up a stereotype that is aggressively marketed by Jewish entertainers. By telling me that your mother is a Jewish mother, you wanted to say that we have much in common. But I hate the "Jewish mother" stereotype, another misogynous insult dressed in Jewish garb.

That mothering can be smothering is well known from all cultures. Just like the JAP concentrates the hostility of all misogynists against wives, girlfriends and daughters, so the "Jewish mother" is the anchor for all anti-mother resentment, felt just as much by Jews as by Gentiles. Indeed, "Jewish mother" has become a normal English expression for a passive-aggressive, guilt-inducing female progenitor. But please. Some Jewish mothers are "Jewish mothers," just as some non-Jewish mothers are. I don't know if the percentage of "Jewish mothers" is higher among the Jews, but I doubt it. Even if it is, could you please not generalize? My mother is not a "Jewish mother" and I'd like you to leave her out of this.

What about the Palestinians?

Now I feel you are not even trying to be nice. Your expectation is that your question might irritate me. It does, but not for the reason you think: not because I hate Arabs, or because I oppose the Palestinians' legitimate rights.

Of course, I have views on the Arab-Israeli conflict. And, of course, as a Jew I am ultimately on the side of Israel, the Jewish state. I am emotionally bound to Israel, a realization of a dream that my ancestors have held for centuries. Moreover, Israel seems proof to me, like to most Jews, that another Holocaust would not be possible. This time we know how to use arms. If, God forbid, we have to go again, we will not go without a fight and we will not go without taking our enemies with us.

I also do happen to believe in the rights of the Palestinian people: rights to self-determination, and possibly a right to a state of their own, as long as its aim is not to take our state away from us. I deeply regret and am ashamed of the human rights abuses committed by the Israelis.

But I do not want to talk about this with you, because your question, coming on the heels of my revelation that I am a Jew, makes me fear that to you "Jew" recalls "abusive Israeli occupier" (i.e. Zionist Imperialist). If so, chances are you know little of the complexities of the Middle East; little of the large and widespread opposition, not only among world Jewry but also among Israeli Jews, to the Israeli army's practices; and little of the abuse committed by Palestinian terrorists, not only against Jews but also against fellow-Palestinians as well.

When you know me better, I will be ready to discuss this issue with you. But not unless you accept the following disclaimer: I hereby declare that any resemblance between me and the prime minister of Israel is purely coincidental.

We all believe in one God.

OK. This time you truly mean well. You want to show me that you and I are both God's children. True, those of us who are religious, Jews, Christians and Muslims, believe in one God. Yet I don't think it is true that we believe in the *same* God. Now I know that many rabbis would contradict me on this. But they just want to be nice, whereas I want to be frank.

Our God does not have three persons like the Christian God: the Father, the Son, and the Holy Ghost. He did not become incarnate in Jesus. He has no human form at all; indeed, nowadays it bothers many of us a lot that we refer to him with the masculine pronoun, as if He were a man.

We associate God with the history of our people. We thank God for taking us out of slavery in Egypt, and have trouble not blaming Him for allowing the Holocaust to happen. He speaks to us immediately, without the mediation of a Jesus and his family, or of saints (though some North African Jews do worship the memory of some sages as if they had been saints).

Our Gods are similar, but not the same. I would say the same to you if you were a Muslim, a Buddhist, or a follower of any other religion. I respect your tradition and I expect you to respect mine. But to equate all religions is not the same as to respect them. A religion for all people would have to be a new religion that means to replace all previous ones, and it is implied that this new religion would be more perfect than the old, "particularist" ones. Of necessity, religious universalists believe that their view of religion is better than that of the "particularists," and therefore create their own brand of religious one-upmanship. The universalists feel superior to the "particularists" just like the Christian missionaries felt superior to the pagans. (*Iglesia catolica*, after all, means "universal church.")

What, however, distinguishes our Jewish religion and has distinguished it since the Middle Ages is that we are proudly particularist. We do not think that our religion is better for everybody, just that

183

it is better for us. We are more tolerant of other ways of thinking about religion than the "universalists." We wish to keep our religion and let everyone else keep theirs.

There can and ought to be a brotherhood of religions. But there is not and cannot be a universal religion, any more than there can be human beings who are not also French, English, Moroccan, etc. — or Jews.

Do you eat ham?

When you invite me for dinner and ask me if I eat ham, you mean to show your understanding of the fact that traditional Jews do not eat pork. You want to make something I will eat; I understand and appreciate your concern. You mean to be considerate.

But remember this. If it is true that those of us who are religious have a concept of God that is not the same as that held by non-Jews (although there is a great variation among us in terms of religious belief, just as there is among you), it is also true that many, perhaps most of us, have no concept of God at all. Quite a few Jews do not believe in God; I am still not sure if I do myself.

Those who are observant of the ancient behavioural code known as the *halakha* are a rather small minority. Even many of those who are affiliated with Orthodox synagogues don't really keep it. The Conservative, Reform, and Reconstructionist congregations, which comprise the great majority of synagogue members in North America, have all modified or at least reinterpreted the *halakha*.

"Eating kosher" is a practice prescribed by the *halakha*. It means much more than just not eating pork. For example, meat must not be mixed with milk. Also, nothing must be served on plates that were ever touched by non-kosher food, unless a special cleansing ritual is observed. This means, of course, that even if you don't serve ham, your kitchen is automatically disqualified. To put it simply, no strictly Orthodox Jew can eat with you unless you buy ready-made kosher food, or unless you serve only vegetables (which are always kosher) and you serve them on plates and with utensils that had never been used before. In practice, the problem can be solved by using paper plates and plastic utensils. But you're better off not inviting an Orthodox Jew for dinner at all. Think of coffee or a ball game instead.

However, the great majority of us are not Orthodox. Jewishness is a matter of much more than religion: a culture, an ethnic identity, a shared history, family memories. It is perceived by us as a sort of

184

magical identity, which we do not understand ourselves. Even Freud, a master decipherer of the mind's subtleties, could not manage to spell out just what it was that made him Jewish. He was, he wrote,

> completely estranged from the religion of his fathers — as well as from every other religion — and [one] who cannot take a share in nationalist ideals, but who has yet never repudiated his people, who feels that he is in his essential nature a Jew and who has no desire to alter that nature. If the question were put to him: "Since you have abandoned all these common characteristics of your people, what is there left about you that is Jewish?" he would reply: "[What is left is] a very great deal; indeed, probably, my very essence."

Jewish identity consists of much more than Judaism. For many of us, Judaism is not even a very important part of it at all.

At any rate, you can quite reliably tell an Orthodox male by the skull cap on his head, although even some people with skull caps make compromises like eating kosher at home but not outside (a fairly popular practice, though not officially approved by their rabbis, among Conservative Jews). Women are harder to pinpoint, although the most traditional wear wigs. If you don't see these outward markers of Orthodoxy, chances are you are dealing with someone who is not strictly traditional. You are probably dealing with a Jew who is quite comfortable eating what you serve him or her. I certainly would be.

So when you ask me if I eat ham, I am not offended, but I feel a bit taken aback. Perhaps a better way than asking me about ham would be to just invite me. If I were Orthodox, I would tell you what my religious practices require.

What do you think of Jesus?

And while we're dealing with religion, what about Jesus? Here and there I meet a religious Christian who longs to find out how it is possible for me, a member of Jesus' people, to "reject Him." So I am asked what I think about him (big "H" for Christians, small "he" for us). The simple answer is that I don't. I don't think about Jesus.

I happen to be a devoted lover of Christian art and music. And I often find images of Christ deeply moving, a genuine symbolic depiction of the divine spirit. I am similarly touched when I see some images of the Buddha or of Hindu gods. But Jesus is no more an issue for me than Shiva is for you. I am not for or against Jesus, and I have not rejected him. I have read the New Testament, and I find some of

185

it quite interesting, and other parts quite stirring. But I am a Jew, and happy to be one. I am not asking you to be a Jew; please don't ask me to be a Christian.

The problem is that if you are a Christian then Judaism *is* an issue for you. After all, Christianity started as a Jewish sect that opposed mainstream Judaism. (The early Christians' opposition centred mainly around Jesus: the Christians believed he was the Messiah, and the rest of us did not.) But Judaism did not start in opposition to Christianity. We have no beef with Christianity at all.

Medieval myths libeled us as desecrating the Host, for the primitive Christian's image of the Jew is that of a Christ-killer, whose religion is devoted to opposing the concept of Jesus as the Messiah. This attitude reads into Judaism much more preoccupation with Jesus than there ever has been.

But even sophisticated and enlightened Christians are puzzled that we don't accept Jesus as the Messiah. They want to know why. Indeed, Jewish-Christian dialogue groups often break down when the Christians bring up Jesus. Some Christians simply refuse to understand that the relationship between Jesus and Judaism is an issue for them, but not for us.

We are not "the people of the Old Testament." Our religion has evolved throughout the centuries, just like Christianity, though ours has done so without Jesus. When Christianity added the New Testament to the Old, we added the Talmud. I am told that there is one line in the Talmud about Jesus, though it is of no importance at all. Our religious texts, ancient, medieval, and modern, ignore Jesus almost totally. They say nothing important at all about him, pro or con.

We respect Christianity, like we respect all other religions. But Jesus is to us simply a foreign religious personage. Next time you want to ask me what I think about Jesus, ask yourself what you think of Krishna.

Merry Christmas and Happy Hanukkah.

Now here is one that most other Jews not only appreciate, they are positively thrilled by it. When you say Merry Christmas and Happy Hanukkah, you are recognizing that not everyone is a Christian, you are noticing me as a Jew, and you wish me to share in the cheers of the holiday season. So why should I object?

I do not consider your greeting offensive, but I would like you to spend some time thinking about what it really means. You might then reconsider whether you want to wish me Merry Christmas and Happy Hanukkah next year again.

Let us start with the issue of Christmas. In public many Jews love to praise Christmas to the hilt, to make absolutely sure that they do not appear "different." Only in private, among other Jews, do some of them admit that their enthusiasm may have been a bit of a show.

I am reminded of the merchant that I visited one December to arrange for a print to be framed. He had beautified, indeed overdecorated, his store with innumerable wreaths, pine-tree branches, and pendants for Christmas. He expressed his intense disappointment with the fact that it was too late for him to finish my order by the arrival of Yuletide. And he topped up the transaction by wishing a merry Christmas to me and mine. He appeared quite shaken when I revealed that I did not celebrate Christmas because I was Jewish. "So am I," the storekeeper replied dejectedly, and added—"I hate Christmas."

Talking about Christmas is one of the truly favourite devices by which Jewish speakers wish to bridge the gap between themselves and the Gentile audience. When the pioneer American-Jewish cineaste George Cukor made his first movie, it was a tearjerker about a poor child at Yuletide. And not everyone remembers that the all-time hit "White Christmas" is a composition by Irving Berlin, who also created "Easter Parade" and "God Bless America." It is in the tradition of these great entertainers that the mainly Jewish army of Hollywood sitcom writers churns out, year in and year out, their obligatory sappy Christmas episodes.

Being nice about the Christmas spirit has a triple objective. First, it may steer attention from the fact that the speaker is not a Christian. Second, if it does not do so, the speaker will at least have made an appeal to the Christmas spirit of tolerance. And third, the speaker will have demonstrated a positive attitude to the one holiday that makes all Christians and Jews acutely aware of following different ceremonial traditions in the most intimate circle of their family.

But I hate Christmas. I hate Christmas because during the Christmas season I am put upon, time after time again, by well-meaning non-Jews to declare my difference from them. When I am wished a merry Christmas, what am I to do? If I return the greeting, my Jewish conscience accuses me of not having the *chutzpah* to say "I do not celebrate it." If I do say so, however, I get into an unwanted discussion, often with someone I do not really wish to chat with; or I might

187

spoil the holiday mood for someone I do care for. I am also not a little upset by the arrogance of people who think it a matter of course that *everyone* celebrates Christmas. To hear them talk about it, Christmas is as naturally part of December as snow in Minnesota. I don't care if the Japanese or the Indians have bought the idea and, though not Christians, welcome Santa and erect Christmas trees. We don't have to.

I certainly do not hate Christmas for what it means to Christians. I like togetherness, I like peace on earth, and I like presents (so do the Jewish merchants in shopping malls). I just wish it wasn't rubbed in my face, when I am not part of it. For let's face it, the reason many of us Jews do not like Christmas is that we are jealous. Worse yet, we fear that our children will be jealous, that the presents their Gentile classmates receive will make them want to become Christians, like the natives who join the church because the missionaries give people bicycles.

So what do we do? We come up with a Jewish version of Christmas: Hanukkah. Hanukkah is probably traditionally the least significant of Jewish festivals. Unlike major holidays, for example, on Hanukkah it is permitted to work. Yet the majority of non-observant Jews, the EJI, who do not even know the dates of such major festivals as Sukkoth or Shavuoth, do not fail to observe Hanukkah. This is profoundly ironic. The events that Hanukkah celebrates are not even in the Hebrew Bible, but in the Greek-language Book of the Maccabees. The "zealots" of Israel, armed Pharisee fundamentalists, rose against the Graeco-Syrian rulers of the land, who were amply assisted by "assimilated Jews." One of the things that most shocked the zealots were Jews who ran and exercised naked in Hellenic stadiums in the Holy Land. Hanukkah or Rededication commemorates the zealots' victory. This resulted in their recapture of the Temple, where they relit the "eternal flame." (The little consecrated oil they had for the purpose miraculously lasted eight days — hence the eight days of the festival.)

How much Hanukkah has become a Jewish Christmas is demonstrated by office workers who put up "Happy Hanukkah" signs next to "Merry Christmas." Once I was at my office when a non-Jewish employee was posting up a "Happy Hanukkah" sign as part of the "festive season" decorations. I politely reminded her that Hanukkah was already over. Since the holiday is observed according to the lunar Hebrew calendar, it does not always coincide with Christmas, and sometimes, as was the case now, comes much earlier. So what sense

188

did it make to celebrate Hanukkah after Hanukkah has ended? My mild protest was not at all well received. It was hushed up almost as an indecent remark, not only by the Gentiles, but by the Jews as well.

As far as the kids are concerned, Hanukkah has allowed us not only to match the *goyim*, but to trump them. Non-Jewish children get presents on Christmas. But many Jewish children get one every night for the duration of the eight-day festival!

The farce of Hanukkah as a Christmas substitute was revealed a few years ago, when an ultra-Orthodox group erected a twenty-eight-foot-high Hanukkah menorah in a strip of parkland near the municipal centre of Beverly Hills — and no Christmas tree! Four Jewish residents of the posh and very Jewish Southern California township protested. With the official support of the American Jewish Congress, they went to court to have the menorah removed. The resulting litigation lasted for years. There has never been such trouble in the thousands of places all over the United States where there was, along with the menorah, also a Christmas tree. What the neighbourhood EJI were up in arms about was, in the last analysis, not the menorah, but the lack of a Christmas tree next to it. The ultra-Orthodox had the guts to try to recapture Hanukkah as a Jewish holiday, rather than as a symbol of non-difference between Jew and non-Jew. Merry Christmas and happy Hanukkah; we are just like you. You celebrate, we celebrate.

When you said "Merry Christmas and Happy Hanukkah," you did help me avoid the tensions of Christmas; you made sure I did not have to identify myself as "different" from you. But I would rather be uncomfortable than phony. As far as I am concerned, Merry Christmas posters will do just fine at the office, without Happy Hanukkah. It would be nice, though, if next fall, when we really celebrate a major holiday, someone put up a sign saying Happy Rosh Hashanah.

By now you might be feeling overwhelmed. "Is there nothing I can say to a Jew without being considered insensitive?" you might ask. Relax. If you take what I have just said into consideration, chances are you will no longer say things that offend me. But if you slip up, don't worry. I know you mean well. Remember, I am not only a Jew. I am also a human being, like you.

BUT YOU ARE DIFFERENT
IN CONVERSATION WITH A FRIEND
• • • • • • • • • • • • • • • • • • •
SABRA DESAI

Sabra: So, you think I'm not like the rest of them.

Alex: Yes, you are different. Well, you know what I mean.

Sabra: No, I don't. Tell me exactly what you do mean.

Alex: Well, when I see you, I don't see your colour. I don't see you as a South Asian. You're not like the rest of them. I'd like to think that I judge you through my own personal experiences with you. I don't judge you on the basis of your culture, colour or class for that matter. I refuse to see you as being different. You're just another human being.

Sabra: First you tell me that I'm different, and then you say that you refuse to see me as being different. So, which is it? Let's try to unravel this.

Alex: Well, I meant that you're more like me, you know, like one of us.

Sabra: Oh, so, I'm more like you and less like, should I say it, "a real South Asian." You see, although you're not saying it, your statement reveals that you have some preconceived ideas of South Asians, the people that I'm supposed to be so unlike. This means that whatever your preconceived ideas are of South Asians, they make South Asians less acceptable, less attractive, and less appealing to you than I. Well, this is not just stereotyping, it is racist stereotyping.

Alex: Well, just wait a minute, Sabra, you're accusing me of being a racist. You're taking my statement entirely out of context and you know that isn't what I meant. I really don't appreciate the implication that I am being racist.

Sabra: Before we get to unravelling the implications of the statement "but you are different," let me ask: are you upset that I'm challenging your thinking? Would you feel better if I were grateful for being "accepted" by you and less analytical or critical of your reasons for doing so? I think that part of what might be upsetting you is that for all your willingness to "accept" me, you're not ready to accept me as a South Asian.

Alex: By saying that you are different, I assumed that the senseless stereotypes of South Asians do not apply to you. I thought you'd appreciate my comment, but you've surprised me. I thought that coming from a society where you were very much defined by race, you'd want people to ignore differences and treat you the same as everyone else.

Sabra: You obviously don't recall asking me this very question once before. You once told me that you thought that having come from a country as racist and as segregated as South Africa I would endorse the concept of "melting pot." To that I said: in spite of the fact that I left such a racist society, where race was all that mattered, in my mind to say that one's ethnicity or race does not matter is still racist.

So goes one of the many conversations I have had with Alex and a number of other friends. One tires of these exchanges after a while, for it seems that I can never be accepted as the person that I am, but only as what my friends have made me out to be. I at least expect my "differentness" to be acknowledged, although I really want it to be appreciated or, if they genuinely care, to be explored. I wish that Alex and company would recognize that I am a member of a marginalized minority group and that as "mainstreamers" they have a tendency to negate, romanticize or stereotype our experiences and differentness. I am a South Asian human being, but there appears to be some difficulty or reluctance on their part to accept me as such, to try and understand what being South Asian is to me and then to try and come to grips with that reality rather than attempting to make themselves comfortable with some sanitized image.

    I think that one may be "different" by degree within the context of one's ethnocultural group but it is not possible to be different from something which, by definition, one is a part of. So, perhaps because I do not fit Alex's preconceived notion of what a South Asian should be, she doesn't think of me as one, she sees me as the preferred anomaly. My ethnicity, culture and colour do not matter to her. She says that she sees me only as a human being. For me, the implication of this is that being a South Asian somehow devalues me and lessens my humanness. So, in order to relate to me she remakes me into her image; she whitens me so that I can be like her. Alternatively, she is suggesting that if I change the colour of my skin I can belong, as she does.

Let's talk further . . .

Before talking further with you about Alex, I should tell you that I grew up in South Africa, where every aspect of my life was mediated by the colour of my skin and by my ethnicity. As a person classified Indian, and of course non-white, whether it was the privileges that were denied or the ones that were granted me by both statutory and informal laws, they were all arbitrarily applied to me because of my colour and ethnicity; nothing else mattered. For example, where I could go to school, where I could live, where I could receive medical services or for that matter be hospitalized and what jobs I could aspire to were all dictated by the laws of the country. Where and with whom I could play were all largely predetermined for me because of my skin. What my white counterparts—yes, I dare say counterparts—could take for granted I could not. Where I could shop, whether I could try on the garment before buying it, what restaurants I could eat at were all considerations to be taken seriously. One small infraction could, in fact, mean that I was breaking the law.

All this is part of me. It is central to who I am. I am a product of that social context; it is part of my cultural identity. Saying that I am different does not change the fact that my ethnicity and race are used to set me, like other South Asians, apart from whites. I say that because in my experience these labels are reserved to describe the "others," most often "minorities," across the divide, who are referred to as "them," "they," and "those people." We are different when society wants to exclude us on the grounds that we do not fit, we do not know the rules, we do not speak the language, we do not sound Canadian, or we are not desired as neighbours. Yet, paradoxically, we are perceived and seen to be the "same" by some, particularly when we are to receive certain long overdue rights and privileges such as equal access to jobs, housing, culturally sensitive social services, education and heritage language.

Recognizing my differences is in a way acknowledging the irrefutable and undeniable power of racial construction and culture on all our lives. Therefore, words like "brown," "black" and "white," referring to the race of a people, cannot be simply dismissed to suggest that one does not see colour. The very act of not referring to my race or ethnicity, when it is central to the discussion or context, renders me invisible. The omission, in fact, gives a powerful message that colour, culture and ethnicity must be ignored.

In saying this, I can hear you ask the question, as others have so often asked, "But don't you think that this constant reference to skin colour or one's racial identity by minorities reinforces the racism in our society? It might, in fact, reinforce the existing stereotypes." To this I say: not recognizing that things such as gender, race and ethnicity mediate one's life chances in our society is like burying one's head in the sand. Any denial of the significance of race or skin colour implies that skin colour poses a problem or is an obstacle for those who wish to avoid it in their interactions with people of colour.

Wishing that we lived in a colour-blind society is not necessarily a virtue. Colour-blindness, as I come across it, means a denial of the differentness in culture, identity and experiences of those who are less valued in society. This denial reflects the tendency of the oppressor to minimize and deny the impact of the oppression. The oppressors can afford the enormous luxury of ignoring the formative and fundamental influences of social context and history on "other" people's lives while remaining keenly aware and protective of the benefits and privileges of these same influences on their lives and the lives of their descendants. An African Canadian friend of mine once said, "When you see me and do not see my colour, it is just as problematic as when you see me and all you see is my colour." Colour-blindness is an illusion in the minds of those Canadians who like to think that as a nation we are not racially hierarchical. Until very recently, in spite of the hundreds of years of domination, exploitation and oppression of Aboriginal peoples, the prevailing idea concerning race and ethnic relations was that racism did not exist in Canada. It has been documented and ought to be obvious at this stage that social divisions based on colour and ethnicity are a fundamental characteristic of the political and socio-economic configuration of our country.

Getting back to my differentness from mainstream society, I am variously referred to as an immigrant, visible minority, racial minority, "paki," ethnic, coloured, and East Indian: loaded labels decided for, and applied to, South Asians in general. It is also mainly people like myself who get asked: "Where are you from?" or "What are you?"

These questions always remind us of our status and the inherent "otherness" and inferiority associated with it by mainstream society. Such questions also imply, of course, that members of the dominant group do not have an ethnicity and/or that people like myself are not of this land.

Perhaps by challenging the connotations associated with ethnic and racial stereotypes, particularly negative ones, an individual like me forces "mainstreamers" to confront their stereotypic images and biased attitudes, and presents them with the dilemma of holding onto "old ways" in the face of refuting evidence. Stereotypes, as the victims know all too well, influence attitudes and actions towards the members of the disadvantaged group in very real ways. For example, in a society where negative social stereotypes and biases towards a particular group are prevalent, access for members of that group is restricted or even denied altogether. Stereotypes, therefore, serve a social, economic and political purpose for oppressors. Some people cling to these stereotypes quite steadfastly because it is easier to discriminate against someone who is seen as being inferior since by virtue of that inferiority the person is not deserving of equal rights and privileges.

When people say that I am different, they usually mean it as a compliment, and fail to see the inherent racism in their flattery. An encounter with another friend, Jane, is a case in point. Jane describes herself as a feminist who understands the systemic inequalities in our society and the patriarchal system as well as the prevailing attitudes that maintain the status quo. Given her understanding and analysis, she sees herself as always standing up for the rights of minorities because she understands the issues. Some time ago, during our conversation about the opera we had just attended, Jane remarked that she was not sure I would have accepted her invitation to attend, but she now recognizes that I am different. I said to her, "As a feminist, how would you feel if someone said to you, 'Oh, but you're different, you're not like the rest of those feminists.'" She replied that she would be offended. "It's a sexist remark. Feminists are not a homogeneous or a monolithic group." This is precisely my point. Her statement indicates that differences are not to be found among the South Asian monolith, we are not heterogeneous like the majority group. Furthermore, in this context, I find the cliché "but you are different" particularly self-righteous and condescending. I thought, "What privilege, what power, what arrogance! She defines me, imposes her definition upon me and presumes that I am complimented by her statement."

In conversations like these I am usually told, "You make it all so

195

serious. You should learn to relax, you take life too seriously. You must admit that things have improved a lot for racial minorities. Relax! Lighten up!" But I have to be serious. Life has made me acutely conscious of the inequities and indignities that people like myself have to endure and resist every day. Jefferson said, "The price of freedom is constant vigilance." How can I relax and lighten up when the situation demands that I maintain my vigilance? It is difficult to relax in the margins. Yes, we have made some progress, but both Blacks and whites have to be vigilant to maintain the gains we have made.

This struggle is very much in evidence even with programs such as employment equity that have been instituted to break down barriers and make employment opportunities more accessible. Without getting into the assumptions surrounding employment equity and my understanding of it, I think the following incident nicely illustrates one of the paradoxes of life for racial minorities in racist societies. About two years ago, at the end of a presentation on employment equity, a participant came up to me and said, "I am not a racist, but I really think that women, minorities and Aboriginals should not get a job just because of their race. I think that we should all be treated equally. If I came to your country, could I get a job regardless of my skills and qualifications?" I said, "Well, in Canada aren't we all entitled to a job?" To which he said, "That's not what I meant. I didn't mean Canada. I meant where you came from originally." And I said: "The truth of the matter is, in the country that I come from, you would enjoy more entitlements and privileges as a white visitor than I as a native-born South African." He did not expect such a reply and I hope that he has been cautioned against making such assumptions. I suspect that one such assumption was that I came from India and that, of course, with such a caste-based society, how could I be so bold and impudent as to question the benevolence of my adopted country?

The second assumption is that employment equity means giving jobs to members of racial minorities and other groups who by definition are unskilled and/or unqualified; and in this way the overall standards of "our country" are being lowered by "those people." Thirdly, there is the assumption that by treating everyone "equally," that is, in the way we have been doing things over the years (status quo), we are in fact being just and equitable; this is, after all, a free and democratic country.

The truth is, there is a large gap between the rhetoric of democratic equality and its day-to-day realization. It is just like saying, "Well, I am not prejudiced, children are children, I treat them all the same," not an uncommon attitude in social and psychological services as well as in education. This implied neutrality epitomizes the equality of treatment which is supposedly granted all citizens of a democratic country. It is thought that neutrality means equal opportunity since preference is not given to anyone; neutrality is supposedly the ultimate in equality. It suggests that we should be blind to colour, gender and class. Anything that goes contrary to this ideal is reverse discrimination. This is a paradox for minorities. It suggests that when it is useful for members of mainstream society, those who are normally seen as different are conveniently perceived to be the same. I once heard someone comment that race and gender discrimination was the oldest and longest form of affirmative action going for white middle-class males.

I have another example to relate. Once when I was asked to be interviewed for a job, a male acquaintance said to me, "Well, congratulations. I hear you're short-listed. You stand a good chance. You have a lot going for you as a woman and a racial minority." I responded by saying: "What I am about to say is not from a position of arrogance but from a position of confidence. You have just rendered all my schooling, professional training and ability to zero. You have devalued everything I have strived for and achieved through hard work and perseverance. I'd like to think that if I do join the group not only would I add some colour (smile, smile) but that I will bring a fresh and different perspective to the position I am hired for."

Sometimes, I have challenged the implication that employment equity means taking jobs away from white middle-class males and giving them to minorities who are unskilled by asking, "Are you suggesting that I should not have been given an opportunity to have this job because I do not have the skills?" or "Are you suggesting that I do not have the skills to do this job that I am doing because I am a minority woman?" To this, I usually get the reply, "But you are different, you are qualified, you can do the job." Then I'd respond by saying, "Thank you for your keen observations." These kinds of seemingly complimentary remarks are in fact indicative of the pervasiveness of what one might call "innocuous racism." However, there is no such thing as innocuous racism or being "a little racist" in my mind. Racism is racism. I am South Asian and have no desire to separate myself or have others separate me from "my people" or from my group of ethnoracial identity.

So when I hear "but you are different," I think that I am being judged and evaluated in terms of how closely I reflect the generalized preconceptions of my ethnic group. The person, me, to whom these stereotypes are applied becomes the focus of a judgment, while the judge does not take a moment to think about how flawed her/his thinking may be. Perhaps, part of the problem is because those who make this statement are not aware of how their privilege and power as well as their location have brought them to their definition of difference. Moreover, it is uncritical, evaluative and judgmental in that it implies that being different from one's ethnocultural group is somehow possible and desirable when in fact being different, as is suggested, is also to be an anomaly or an aberration.

Implied in this statement is also the notion that difference means being deficient or being culturally deprived. This notion is underscored by the assumption that the standards of the dominant society, that is, white middle-class culture, represent the norms by which all other cultures should be measured. It is taken for granted that deviations from the white middle-class norms mean cultural deficits. Therefore, the closer one is to these norms the smaller the deficit, and of course the further one is from these norms, the larger the deficit. In other words, one becomes whiter, "more normal," as one renounces one's culture. The cliché "but you are different" is loaded with many racist assumptions. One assumption is that the minority person wants to be taken into the proverbial fold, to be an honorary member of the dominant group and be grateful as well as proud that she has made it, "I am one of them." Often the cliché seems to be proclaimed with a liberal self-confidence that makes the speakers totally oblivious to the condescending, patronizing and moralistic implications of their statements. I often bristle as I listen to the self-righteous confidence with which people unconsciously exercise judgment over me. There is no sense of the flawed thinking, or a recognition of the prejudice and racism in their statements. Nevertheless, I still find it useful to engage my friends in these discussions because, by engaging in an open and honest dialogue, we are able to unravel our inextricably linked realities regardless of where race and cultural politics situate us. A line from a poem by Miguel Algarian sums up quite well what I think my friends and I should strive for in our conversations and interactions, indeed in our friendships: "When I see what you see, the distance between us disappears."

198

PART 6
CONFRONTING RACISM

THE "RACE CONSCIOUSNESS" OF A SOUTH ASIAN (CANADIAN, OF COURSE) FEMALE ACADEMIC

ARUN MUKHERJEE

Two years ago, as I was walking to my class, a South Asian male, probably in his mid-thirties, asked me for directions to a building. He had chosen me for his informant, I thought, because of our common past: we both could tell by looking at each other that we were South Asians. Anyway, he looked lost and I was only too happy to instruct him. Now, such a nondescript encounter would surely have faded from my memory except for this man's next question: "So what courses are you taking?" Why, I asked myself, had this man decided that I could only be a student, despite my very gray head of hair? The answer I gave myself was painful to articulate and is painful to write about: he could not imagine a South Asian woman in the role of an academic because they are such a rarity on Canadian campuses.

After this internal debate, I told my compatriot, "I teach here." There was surprise and contrition writ large on his face as we parted after he had said his "Oh, I see." And as for me, I pondered the complexities of my answer for the next few minutes. Although the man's facial expression had changed from registering a desire for familiarity to a combination of awe and admiration, I felt that his admiration would soon disappear if he were to know that I only taught as a part-timer, liable to be hired and fired at the whim of the people who made those decisions.

I still have to pinch myself to remember that my fortunes have changed since then. In fact, as I write this on 1 July 1991, the first day of my first full-time tenure stream job, the one-hundred-and-twenty-fourth birthday of Canada, I cannot help but connect my personal fortune with that of non-white Canadians in general. For I am fully aware that my present success is the outcome of not just my "merit" — that hallowed principle so often invoked by those who claim employment equity will flood our institutions with "inferior" appointees — but of the anti-racist struggles waged across Canada by communities that have borne the brunt of racism in Canada.

My active involvement in this ongoing struggle and my memory of the past struggles are the factors that constitute my race consciousness. Some celebrity academics put the word race in quotation marks because there is no such thing in biology as race. We all share the same blood types and the same gene pool. They warn us about essentialisms if we talk about race: things like Black people having rhythm in their blood and Asians being good at math.

My race consciousness, my awareness of the fact that I am non-white in a white country, is certainly not essentialist. I am conscious of being non-white, of being South Asian (I cannot call myself Indian in Canada though that's what I really am), of being "Paki," to the same extent that white Canadians are not conscious of their whiteness. They would rather be "just Canadians."

But being "just Canadian" is a privilege only white people enjoy in Canada. It is we non-whites who are seen as deviants from the norm. So we are tagged with identity cards, some worn proudly, others with resentment. I can't, of course, speak for all non-white Canadians (we even disagree with the words that are used to mark our difference: some find "non-white" totally unpalatable because it is rooted in negation; some love to use the term "people of colour," others hate it because, in their mind, it obliterates our heterogeneity; some have no problem with "visible minority," they say, because one should call a spade a spade, whereas others find it a term imposed by a racist state), but I am always conscious of my being non-white and how that fact determines my total life experience. I doubt that I will ever become "just Canadian," whatever that means.

As to the negative qualifier in "non-white," I have absolutely no problems with that. After all, terms like "non-violence," "non-cooperation," and "civil disobedience" also use negation. Moreover, "non-white" is only one aspect of my multiple identities, for I am also a woman of colour, a Third Worlder, a South Asian, an East Indian, an

Indian, a Punjabi, and a Mukherjee (my patronymic caste marker). What term I use to describe myself and my subject matter depends on whom I am speaking to and what I am talking about. (Some white academics have told me that I cannot be a Third Worlder and a South Asian at the same time. One has gone so far as to write that since I have a comfortable tenure-stream job, I cannot claim a Third World identity. If I were to use an analogy, this kind of thinking suggests to me that one ceases being a sister or a daughter if one becomes a wife or a mother.) I use the term "non-white" in order to talk about the binary relationship of power where "white" is the dominant term because there is no denying the fact that we live in a racist world order.

Being non-white in an academic setting means, or has meant thus far (I am banking a whole lot on employment equity) being the single non-white, male or female, at departmental meetings or social get-togethers or conferences. It has meant a tremendous loneliness of spirit because your white colleagues don't seem to notice that there is any thing abnormal in a meeting room or a plenary at a conference where only a handful (or less) of non-white people are present (I deliberately use the words "white colleagues" because the non-whites present at such gatherings always talk to each other about the "absence" of people of colour).

My having entered through the gates that have been locked to people who have dark skins, then, becomes an existential and intellectual problem for me. How have I managed to get in, I ask myself, when so many of my non-white contemporaries with academic ambitions did not make it? And now that I am here, what do I intend to do?

First of all, I intend to survive. In fact, I am here because I knew how to dissemble, to give them what they wanted so that they would give me my degree. That meant never reading a book by a non-white writer as part of the curriculum during my entire education in English literature, both in Canada and India. I try to look back on those days of my studenthood and reconstruct what I thought about the absence of non-white authors in the curriculum. I think again and again of the all-white American Literature courses that I was taught, both in India and Canada, and my unproblematic acceptance of their normalcy.

I realize now the power of the teacher as authority figure. My teachers made the racist, exclusionary curriculum normal for me. They made it normal by convincing me that the curriculum was composed of the "best" works ever written by "man." And whatever did not make it in the canon was not excluded because of racism or sexism but because of objective criteria that measure excellence. Not that I, or my classmates, ever asked any questions about why so and so was not on the book list. Messages about exclusion and inclusion, however, were embedded in the discourse of critical theory that we got in the class and in the books we were asked to read.

Racism has a long reach and my soul trembles to think of how much I had imbibed unconsciously. For example, during all my twenty-five years of living in India, I never knew that the United States (Canada was not part of my curriculum at all) also had people of colours other than white. No one, that is my parents, teachers, media, ever told me of the existence of these non-white Americans. The pictures in the papers and magazines were always of white Americans and the books in my curriculum were the same. (Here I can't resist a story Marie Marule, a Native woman from Alberta, told me. When she told people in Zimbabwe (then Rhodesia) that she was a Native Canadian, i.e. "Red Indian," they responded, "But you are extinct"!) Well, that was the silent message my anthologies of American literature gave me too. And it was reinforced by the white visiting professors of American literature and white Peace Corps volunteers.

As a non-white female academic, I intend to make sure that my students will not go away with such unconscious racism unchallenged. Even when I have had no control on the design and content of the courses, I have told my students what I thought of the materials I had been assigned to teach. I began a course I taught on "American Literature" as a part-timer by telling my students who was not on it: Native writers, African American writers, and women writers, both white and non-white. And I made the absence of these writers on the prescribed curriculum a constant presence by invoking them as we read the sanctioned writers. (When I read the course evaluations later, there were two that said that there was too much about racism in the course and not enough about "technique.")

I have had to resort to similar strategies when faced with "Women's Studies" courses that did not include a word about the histories and texts of non-white women. I have told my students to be wary of accepting the experience of white women as the "universal" experience of all women. I have told them that I cannot rejoice with the celebratory histories of Canadian women that present white women getting the vote as "women get the vote," ignoring the fact that Canadians of Native, Chinese, Japanese, and South Asian ancestries, both male and female, had to wait another forty years to enjoy voting rights. I have told them about the racism of such prominent feminist foremothers as Charlotte Perkins Gilman and Nellie McClung, whose racism is the reason I can't feel as enthusiastic about Persons' Day as some white feminists. Such questioning of the curriculum leads my students to think about the enveloping cloud of racism in which we live as a society. It makes them suspicious of the curriculum that their society, in the shape of their schools, universities and teachers, imparts to them.

In fact, some time during the course of teaching, the question always crops up if any of my students have had non-white teachers before taking my course. The number of students who say yes to this question has been infinitesimally small thus far. That question leads us into another: who controls knowledge and how do they define it? We talk about the Eurocentric nature of the Canadian university and how few and far between are the courses offered on non-European (read non-white) cultures. We talk about whether it is possible to read texts by non-white writers, both male and female, in the framework of aesthetic theories developed in Euro-America.

I am delighted to see that the work we do in my classes also rubs off on the other work my students do. For instance, while reading Attia Hosain's *Sunlight on a Broken Column*, we noticed that the plot treated the servants in the household as characters in their own right. We went on to discuss such classics as Jane Austen's *Pride and Prejudice*, where large dinners are eaten in feudal homes with not a servant in sight, as though the dinner had cooked and served itself! We also discussed Virginia Woolf's *To the Lighthouse*, where servants can appear only off stage and not as part of the plot.

The South Asian text, thus, helps my students envision other ways of writing, other ways of creating and responding to art, and other ways of living. It takes them away from the "universalist" aesthetic norms that actually theorize on the basis of hand-picked "great" works of Euro-America, albeit with my theoretical help. It is not the text itself that can help them reach across the cultural barriers, for texts can be completely misread. (As Chinua Achebe tells us, a letter from a New York high school student, who had just read his classic text *Things Fall Apart*, thanked him profusely for writing such an informative book on the superstitions and customs of an African tribe.) So it is my responsibility to challenge my students, both through my teaching and my research, to stop applying "Western" norms and "Western" values as though they were true for all times and all places. Because when one does that, one does not really encounter the complexity of cultural diversity across our planet, but only stares at

205

oneself in the mirror. My goal as a teacher and a researcher has been to challenge this "Western" narcissism, this fake universalism which is really Euro-American ethnocentrism talking about itself in the vocabulary of "the human condition" at the same time that it denies the humanity of others.

I am, thus, always conscious of the "difference" that my being South Asian in a white Canada continuously produces, both inside me and outside of me. I am conscious of the fact that until 1947, the year of India's independence, the doors of Canada were closed to me. I cannot forget that Canada's racist immigration laws pertaining to South Asians were repealed only after the Indian Prime Minister, Jawahar Lal Nehru, personally asked the Canadian government to get rid of them if they wanted a friendly relationship with India. I cannot forget the Komagata Maru incident, when Canada quarantined four hundred South Asians on this ship for two months, denied them food and water rations and a fair judicial process and finally sent them back, some to their death at British hands. I cannot forget this incident, even though I did not read it in Canada's history books.

I won't forget these facts, and other such facts pertaining to Native Canadians, Chinese Canadians, African Canadians and Japanese Canadians until I begin to see real changes happen. I won't forget them until I see Canadian schools teach about all Canadians, something they didn't do in my son's case. I won't forget them until I see Canadian universities open their doors to all Canadians and teach and produce research about all Canadians.

It is funny how some things stick in one's mind while so much else disappears with the flow of time. Twenty years ago, soon after my arrival in Canada as a student, I was asked to visit an elementary school. The children I spoke to were grade four and five students, no older than ten or eleven years. One of the very first things they asked me was why India didn't solve its food problem by eating all the cows that wandered everywhere in the country. I must say that I was absolutely stunned by the question and the way it was phrased. It assumed that Indians were so foolish that they could not see a solution to their problems that was staring right in their face! It showed a total disregard of the economy and culture of the country that they knew nothing about and it showed an arrogance about their own intellectual superiority. For instance, it would not occur to these children, and their teachers, that the cows may not be "wandering" but "foraging." And that, of course, changes the whole picture. (For those wanting to know more about India's cow-based economy, I recommend Marvin

Harris's *Cows, Pigs, Wars and Witches: The Riddles of Cultures*. Harris shows that a living cow in India is far more valuable economically than a dead cow.)

I learned more about this arrogance when I read Ontario's secondary school textbooks to find out how they represented my part of the world. They told the students about the customs and superstitions of the Indian people and blamed these for India's poverty. I learned that it was the idea of rebirth, as propounded in the *Gita*, that kept India from making progress. I also learned about the wonderful things the British did for my country. My rebuttal of these representations in *East Indians: Myths and Reality* was the beginning of my struggle as an anti-racist scholar.

I continue to teach and research in an academic environment that retains much of the arrogance displayed by the children in the school I visited. Its cultural and curricular practices militate against assigning more than a marginal space to non-Western, non-white cultures and societies. Such a skewered power relation with the dominant system makes me aware that I cannot do "disinterested," "objective" research that those in power loudly proclaim as proper "academic" research. I must fight politically and in solidarity with other anti-racist struggles to bring about admission equity, curriculum equity and employment equity on Canadian campuses. I hope my teaching, research and political action will help to bring the day closer when universities will consider all cultures as equal and valuable and all human beings as equal and valuable.

ONE FAMILY. INDIVISIBLE?
OR ME, AND TWO OF MY CHILDREN
• •
BOYCE, ROBERT AND BELLE
RICHARDSON

Boyce (Caucasian male)

Early in 1992 I suggested to the *Canadian Forum* magazine that I write an article on race relations. I did so because I have concluded, after nearly fifty years as a scribbler, that there are two pre-eminent issues in the world today. The first is equity between nations, and between peoples within nations. And the second is the maintenance of amicable relations between different races. For what on earth would be the use of creating a Canada that is efficient and productive as all Tories want us to do, if we descend into such mutual antagonisms that we are armed and shooting at each other, as seems to be happening in parts of the United States, where conservatism rules?

I asked my son Robert, who was at that time chairperson of the Coalition on Employment Equity in Toronto, how he thought I should approach such an article, and his response was immediate. "First, you should ask the magazine why a minority person has not been hired to write this article," he said. This led to a lively debate, and a lot of soul-searching. Joined by one of his Black friends, we argued for hours in a Toronto restaurant, an argument that stopped just short of acrimony. While acknowledging that there are minority writers who should have the chance to write about this subject, I was unable to accept that their existence implies that the subject should be out-of-bounds to me. The most extreme form of their argument was that I had been able to utter as a writer throughout my lifetime only because of my privileged position as a white Anglo-Saxon male. They said there must have been minority people who were denied this privilege, but who, like me, could have written thousands of articles, if they had had the chance; therefore, my time was over, or should be.

I could not, and do not, accept any of this. Although it is true that I can never understand racism as does my son, who must be prepared to deal at any moment with being patronized, insulted or slighted because he is Black, can this possibly mean that only he, and other victims of racism, can express an opinion on the subject? I think not.

The result of our discussion was a compromise. My son and I agreed we should each have our say. My daughter, who is also Black, wanted to have her say, too.

✦ ✦ ✦

The social climate in which Robert joined our family in England nearly thirty years ago was spelled out on the day we brought him home. The janitor of our building was a retired auto worker, a poor man who was looking after four apartments in return for a free flat in the basement. He and his wife were excited about the proposed addition to our family, and when we arrived home they hurried upstairs to have a look. He peered into the crib, and without a moment's hesitation said, in the kindliest of voices, "Ah, he's a little nigger!" Eventually, we became a family of six, four children, two adults, born on three continents, comprising three races — Caucasian, Negroid, and Polynesian — and with parentage stemming from six countries. As a result, it's become a deeply held conviction for me that, as Rodney King asked in Los Angeles, "Guys, can we all get along?" Simplistic, maybe. But without it, what sense does life make?

We soon found that small Black kids are regarded by everyone as cute; as they grow, those who are prejudiced find them threatening. Twenty-one years after he became one of us, in 1984, Robert was constantly being hauled over and checked out by Ottawa police, and finally was arrested ("for suspicion," said the policeman) while walking home. We wrote a letter to the mayor accusing the police of racism (his two white brothers were never checked out). The police inquiry was over in two hours. They completely exonerated their officer although he had done, by our reckoning, three illegal things. Welcome to the farcical world of the police complaints procedure. The mayor set up an advisory committee. Seven years later, an unarmed Black man, Vincent Gardner, was shot by a Nepean policeman, for no apparent reason. "They haven't changed," said my son, when I mentioned the incident to him.

Robert (Black male)

The image of Black people I grew up with, as a Black child in a white family, a white community, and a white school, was the cartoon character Little Black Sambo. He was the guy who looked most like me. Of course, I didn't have a bone in my hair, my lips didn't reach my belly and my skin was more brown than Black, but all the same Sambo was my representative in the world. If it weren't for Sambo there wouldn't have been anyone at all. Even though one's family may have a positive image of Black people, being a Black child growing up in a white family in Canada has problematic effects on one's self-image.

The problem at home stemmed not from negative images but from no images of Black people. Black images at home existed only in the odd visitor to the house, or television specials depicting some exotic tribe from the dark continent, or Saturday morning cartoons with Sambo and Bugs Bunny. If you told a Black child growing up in the sixties and seventies in Canada that he was an African you would more likely than not get a punch in the nose. It is confusing and hurtful for a child whose dominant images of Black people are those of the caricatured African to be told he is Black.

Canadian society is racist, its predominant images of Black people negative. Perhaps in a home with strong, positive Black role models the effects of this negative propaganda can be negated. However, for a Black child in a home with no Black role models the question of trying to ameliorate society's negative image of Black people becomes academic.

As a child, I went to a summer day camp. As in most of my childhood experiences I was the only Black child at this camp. One year the camp hired a Black man, Charles, as a counselor. Charles was young and strong and everyone seemed to like him. He taught me how to lift weights and play ball and was generally someone I could look up to. It was a great summer. The next year, looking forward to another summer and another year with Charles, I showed up at camp. Charles didn't. I remember being told that Charles had been

211

caught robbing a shoe store over the winter and was spending that summer in jail. I remember all the kids at camp were talking about it. None of them seemed to remember Charles as the man who had taught us to play games and lift weights. They remembered him only as someone whom they never felt they could trust anyway. They all knew he would do something like this: he was Black. I didn't say anything and tried to be as white as possible, hoping no one would notice that I too was Black.

To complicate matters my parents adopted another child, a little girl, a Black girl. She was blacker than I was! Friends came by to congratulate my parents and tell them how pretty their little Black baby was. She grew up much the same as I had, but seemed to succeed where I had failed at being accepted into the community. She came home from school one day singing a new song, "Nigger nigger pull the trigger." I felt like throwing her out the window: she was whiter than I was!

I think school was a constant source of frustration for us both. For me, because I didn't accept anything, and for her because she did. She came home from school one day happy to have a role in the school play. She was to be a railway train conductor. Her happy mood was quickly broken by a barrage of criticism from her family. I don't know if she ever did understand why we were all so upset.

Since school, I think my sister and I have both changed. While in school, she had been accepted as long as she acted white and kept her eyes closed. For her these terms had been acceptable, a condition I envied. She had little contact with her heritage and possessed an ability to substitute that of others for her own. For her it didn't matter that Black people were missing from her life, her books, her history, or were portrayed as criminals, or caricatures. It seemed that to her being Black was cosmetic and no different from having big feet, or little feet, blue eyes or brown. Her history and heritage were white and no one need tell her differently. It was when she left school and lost her honorary white status, that it hit her. Beyond high school the rules had changed: her threat to others as a Black and as a woman was now real, whereas as a child she had been just cute.

My sister's seeming indifference to being a Black girl in a white man's world was a trait to be envied. I was "oversensitive." I couldn't let someone call me a nigger without hitting them (unless they were bigger than me). By the time I reached high school I had had it. I had been disciplined for fighting in every school I had ever been to and was considered an academic problem by all concerned. My ability to fit in was nearly nil and my ability to articulate this was less. I dropped out. I should say that these are my perceptions, while those of my sister may well be quite different.

The methods my sister and I used are manifestations of living in a society that is inherently racist. Growing up, we were both taught that colour is only skin deep. But while biologically we may be the same, our heritage is vastly different and the treatment outside the home is so disparate as to create a gulf in understanding not easily bridged. Growing up Black in Canada is very different from growing up white and as a result we become very different people.

Belle (Black female)

Woman. Adopted. Canadian. Black. Ghanaian. Barbadian. New Zealander. Had I spent my life consumed by one or more of these labels, all of which could apply to me, I would have taken precious time away from the much more worthy experience of being a human being. That's not to say that gender, roots, birthright, nationality, skin colour and heritage aren't important. To be sure, they are all elements that make me who I am. I think I am sufficiently proud of each of them, but they are factors over which I have no control.

I was fortunate to become part of a family that didn't perpetuate racism. My white parents didn't ignore that prejudice existed. They simply sent me into society with no prejudices of my own. Because I wasn't raised to watch for it, I sometimes missed what might have been offensive to others, but I also didn't find it where it never existed.

Certainly racism did exist, and I didn't miss all of it. As I child I was called "spear chucker" and "jigaboo" by some of my white friends, and considered it a compliment until I was told otherwise. When I was a teenager an elderly white man yelled at me in the health food store where I worked, "Go back to Africa, and sink lower than a ship can sink!" As an adult I had a role in a national commercial, but it was downgraded because the company decided it didn't want a "person of colour" in the lead.

Conversely, in Los Angeles, many African Americans have criticized me because I do not know much about the American civil rights movement. While walking among the diverse crowd on Venice Beach with a white male friend, I have been harassed by Black men who have felt that — because we share the same skin colour — they have a right to judge my choice of companions.

213

My brother says that I had "honorary white status." That makes a good debating point for him, but I don't think it has ever been true. As far as I know, I have been Black since the day I was born, and I fully expect to be Black until the day I die. Consequently, everyone who has known me has had no choice but to treat me as a Black person. The difference between Rob and me lies not in the colour of our skins, or the way we are treated, but inside our heads. Rob has even called me an "oreo." Oreo! Black on the outside, white on the inside—no great compliment!

Only one thing is certain. We may all look different from without, but if we were cut open, within we would look pretty much the same. What matters is our humanity.

Boyce

I started out to write the usual journalistic article, dealing with what we have done in race relations, where we have failed, and what we should do next. In fact, I started the ball rolling by doing just that. I went to Toronto and talked to some visible minority people, in and out of government, and tried to figure out what they thought we should be doing and where we should be heading.

I was impressed by something told me by Enid Lee, chair of the Black Secretariat, a grass-roots clearing house for information and action, of which Robert was then a board member. She complained that the media take little if any notice of the ceaseless work being done by Blacks and other minorities, day after day, week after week, month after month, to overcome their problems. "If you were to take a camera," she said, "and go around Toronto on a Saturday photographing every Black person who is working as a volunteer with children, you would really have a lot of photographs. No one ever gives us credit for doing that. When you read the press you get the impression we are not doing anything to help ourselves."

A common theme among those I talked to was that most formal solutions have proven to be inadequate. Racism is, as Robert says, pervasive. Even organizations set up to combat racism have had problems of racism on their own staffs. Even having more resources does not always help. For example, many resources have gone into cross-cultural training, but grass-roots activists complain that the money has gone mostly to mainstream organizations who are then, once again, in a position to impose their own solutions.

214   I wrote something along these lines, and much more. My usual

journalistic schtick, you might call it. But Robert found it "too imper-
sonal." He spoke from being deeply involved, day by day, in efforts to
combat racism against Blacks in Toronto. For him, the latest racist
outrage, the most recent random cop shooting is not just yet another
deplorable anti-social occurrence — as it tends to be for me — but a
personal insult and threat. For him, all this reflection on this or that
solution doesn't get to the guts of the issue. I began to realize that
just by opening up this article within my own family, I was introducing an intensely personal dimension that makes my usual flow of information, my facts and figures and carefully noted contexts, seem
almost irrelevant.

Robert

The Canadian way is to deny the difference between Blacks and
whites, to act as if all people are the same and should be treated as
such under the law. The multiculturalism policy and Charter of
Rights and Freedoms recognize diversity while attributing to all persons equal treatment and responsibilities. But these laws are not
enforced. Even if they were, the rights and responsibilities of the descendants of the invaders who now control most of the economic and
political power are very different from those of the people whom those
invaders enslaved, or whose lands were first invaded. Multiculturalism in Canada has come to mean the celebration of diverse cultures
through special events that display different foods, clothing and
dances. But for most of Canada's history, being other than European
in origin has meant being other than human, and like other non-hu-
man creatures, our only recognized value has been in our ability to
produce product. These conditions have continued officially and legal-
ly well into this century. Oppression is an ingrained part of Canadian
history, as is its denial.

Recently a vacuum-cleaner salesperson came to my house. Making small talk, he asked me where I was from. I responded that I was
Canadian (a lie — I was born in England).

"Yes," he said, "but where were you born?"

"In Canada," I responded.

"But where is your family from?" he persisted.

"We have been here for three hundred years," I persisted.

"I see," he said. "My family is Irish so I guess we are all immigrants; they came over two hundred years ago. Where did yours come
from?"

"Jamaica," I lied.

"I thought you were Jamaican," he said, and continued with his demonstration.

I have had similar confrontations with bank managers, teachers, store clerks, apparent friends and others. What each seems to want is to take me out of a country seen to be white and into a country seen to be Black. I vary my country of origin from time to time, but I have found that people will continue to ask me where I am from until I give them a country in Africa or the Caribbean. They will not accept that I could come from Europe or North America. There seem to be two reasons for this. The first is a simple denial that I could have roots similar to their own, since this would put me on a par with them in terms of levels of civilization as measured by their standards. And secondly, if they were to admit that my roots might be as I say, then they would have to admit the history of oppression for which their families are responsible. Interesting to me is how the myth of Canadian tolerance and acceptance can be so effectively sold to people on a national and international level.

Western history and culture is based on the belief that white northern European values are superior to those of other cultures, and in this society whites have gone to incredible lengths to prove that other cultures are inferior, thus to justify the unequal privileges they themselves enjoy. Until whites accept the fallacy of this, the pain and suffering they inflict will continue. I am talking here not only of the overt white supremacists but also of those who claim to be outraged by them. These are the truly dangerous individuals, for while they preach equality and tolerance they continue to accept and use their privilege without question. They speak with righteous indignation when confronted with individual instances of discrimination, but do little to counter the systemic forms of discrimination that exist everywhere in their society. In Canada there is a passive acceptance of the philosophy of white supremacy while at the same time a denial of its existence to any significant degree.

There are plenty of questions white people could ask of themselves: How often do white customers in a store ask the salesperson why they are following Black customers around, while allowing white customers to go unobserved? How often do parents ask the school why their children are graduating, while Black children are not? How often do they question why Blacks and Aboriginal Canadians fill Canada's prisons, far out of proportion to their numbers in the general population? How often do they question why their child gets probation while a Black child committing a similar crime gets a prison sentence? Or why high school history books lie about the development of the nation? Or why they themselves were singled out for promotion, while their Black counterparts with seniority were ignored? Or why whites are continually asked to speak about the oppression of Blacks, and Blacks are rarely, if ever, asked to speak about the tyranny of whites? How many ask why so few Black people work in their organization, live in their neigbourhood, or are part of their government?

Race is a social construct. Racism is a reality supporting a system founded on inherent inequality. You can either attack the construction of race, or the structure which cultivates this form of oppression. If you choose to eliminate the construct, the structure will still exist. There is no reason to believe that the elimination of race as a category would substantially change the fate of those presently suffering from the effects of racism, for the structure of this society is such that it will find a new way of oppressing these same people. If you attack the structure, you attack the principal foundation of our society.

By challenging the structure you question your own privileges and rights and the very foundation of your moral and value systems. The primary question then is: *What are you willing to do/give up, to help create a society founded on justice and equal rights?*

Belle

I am no less Black because I was raised by white parents and speak with a Canadian accent than is a person who has been brought up in south-central Los Angeles. Similarly, a farm worker in Alabama is no less Black than an Ashanti tribesman.

No one Black experience can be called *the Black experience*, or the correct Black experience. No one can be the judge of what is Black. Black like whom? My skin is darker than most, but that doesn't make me "more Black." The Black experience worldwide is rooted in being a minority. It would seem logical that Blacks, of all people, would be tolerant of people with experiences different from our own.

I am anxious to discover my African/Caribbean heritage, as much as I am my parents' roots in New Zealand. I empathize with those who have been oppressed, but all I can do is provide an example for what I believe our world should be — a place of inclusion, whose strength is in its diversity.

217

Bitch. Bastard. Nigger. There will always be excuses for people not to love me. I am obligated not to be insensitive to those who do not share my attitude. But I feel I owe it to my parents and myself not to use ignorance and segregation as an excuse for not succeeding.

Boyce

I think I will abuse my privilege as father of this outfit to have the last word.

I did not expect this article to take this form. I have always avoided writing about my family, for fear that I might seem to be drawing attention to myself, and have fallen into it on this occasion really through no wish of my own. Since Robert tried to elbow me aside as an inappropriate person to write an article on race relations, I have found the whole process revealing, and at times painful. I had expected that he would use the article to outline what I might call "the Black activist political agenda," to tell us what he and others in the Black movement think should be done, what measures they hope that those of us who are not minorities will support. To describe Canada as a country devoted to a doctrine of white supremacy, as he has done, is to betray a millenarian attitude: anything short of perfection is worthless. If Canada is a white supremacist country, how would one describe South Africa?

Though I am not by nature an optimist, I find Robert's pessimistic rhetoric depressing, perhaps because I was brought up at a time and in a place when we believed that human society, if not exactly perfectible, is at least susceptible to constant amelioration. My first memory as a sentient political being is of a Labour government whose fundamental purpose — especially when examined in the light of what is now common — was to improve the welfare of people. It became a matter of faith for me that great social movements, beginning with the labour movement, have struggled for generations against the implacable hostility of those who control wealth, towards the attainable goal that human society can be decent and can offer to everyone the prospect of a creative and fulfilling life. According to this view of the world, social action and political action for change have gone hand in hand, the one inevitably leading to the other. I have always counted racism, along with class privilege, economic and social inequity, censorship, and colonialism as social diseases that human beings can cure by using all the political and social tools available.

This faith has been severely shaken in the last decade since

Reagan, Thatcher and their clones such as Mulroney and Bush have worked to destroy what I have always considered to be the finest achievements of modern society—those measures of welfare that have rescued people from slum, sweatshop and workhouse.

To the extent that the ethic of collective social responsibility seems to be in full retreat in the industrial world, I share Robert's pessimism. But if the last decade has taught us anything, it is that we must hang on for dear life even to the imperfect measures of social improvement that have been so laboriously put in place by people working together over the last hundred years.

We have to accept that all our solutions will be less than perfect. The people I spoke to in Toronto, who are working to combat racism every day, were generally agreed that racism will always be with us. The objective has to be, not so much to eliminate it—an impossible goal—but to moderate and control the anti-social behaviour that stems from racist attitudes. This is not going to happen overnight, but we have to hang on to the faith that people of goodwill, working together, can do it. As Robert suggests, profound attitudinal changes are needed. Our laws against racism are far from being adequate. We have to push on until racist behaviour becomes as unacceptable as rape or murder.

When I began to write this, I put to paper 3,000 words of information: the history of racism against Aboriginals; the changing nature of Canadian society as more people of colour come from the Third World; the many warnings we have ignored from reports and committees of inquiry; the need for more resources to combat prejudice and keep racism in check; the persistence of Canada's damaging "two founding nations" ideology, which denies the place of Aboriginals and other minorities; the passive acceptance of a growing race-based economic underclass; the need for stronger laws and greater political commitment.

But I have jettisoned all that. It might all be very interesting, but I feel that Robert's anger will give readers a better feel for what is involved than my comparatively detached journalism. And maybe Belle's calm tolerance will suggest the human possibilities.

THERE'S A WHITE MAN IN MY BED
SCENES FROM AN INTERRACIAL MARRIAGE
•••••••••••••••••••••••••••••••••••
PUI YEE BERYL TSANG

Sunday I woke to discover a white man in my bed. Once I got over the initial shock, I took a closer look and realized that the stranger sleeping in my bed really wasn't a stranger at all. He was my husband of seven years. Why had it taken me all this time to realize he was white? Was it near-sightedness, the desire not to see his colour, or just plain colour blindness? Why did this realization hit me at this precise moment? Was it that this awareness would somehow change the nature of our relationship, hurt or even end our relationship? He—the white man in my bed—kept sleeping through my minor brainstorm. Once, I mused, I would never have paid serious attention to any of these questions; they were too deep and profound for me to ponder. On that Sunday morning, however, they seemed so pressing that I had to take the time to reflect on them.

As I threw the covers off and opened my eyes to the bright sunlight filling our bedroom, I started thinking about my realizations. In the process I couldn't help but notice the whiteness of the white man in my bed. His skin was more than just white, it also had a translucent quality. Just beneath the surface of his skin I could see the blue traces of his veins, the purple fibres of his muscles and the delicate red etchings of his blood vessels. Lying next to him, I could see how truly yellow my skin is, with a deep opaque richness that hides everything beneath its surface.

White skin, I thought, is different in other ways. Sunlight scorches it faster and with more vengeance than it does other skins. Illness is more easily revealed in it than with other skins. It is even injured more easily and takes longer to heal than other skins. I looked at my arm where there were scratches from our cat; they are no longer visible. I look at the white man's skin; the scratches from our cat are still there, even though we received them at the same time. What is it about white skin that puts me on edge? How did these feelings arise in me?

Then I remembered . . .

The night before, the white man and I had gone for drinks and dinner at the home of a distinguished Canadian poet who was also white. Most distinguished Canadian "anythings," I have come to understand, are usually white. I didn't want to go, I didn't have to go, but I went to show the white man that I supported him. After all, he had spent nearly every weekend of the last month going to rallies, marches and conferences for yellow, red, brown and black people.

"These people," he told me, "are very important. They can help me publish more poetry and reach wider audiences with my existing work." "I'm not sure I'm going to like them," I confessed. "It's going to be okay," he reassured me. "Just be yourself."

"That's what I'm afraid of," I commented to myself.

It began auspiciously enough. There was the mandatory ritual of "Welcome to my home. Let me take your coat." Then it moved onto the obligatory "What would you like to drink?" More people arrived and the usual "Hi, I'm so-and-so, I write such-and-such. I've recently been published in XYZ journal" took place. Things were going relatively well. They were actually not bad company. They were witty, erudite and undeniably brilliant. Their white skin, however, reflected the light in such a way that it cast an uncomfortable feeling on me.

We were having a good time discussing our various travels around the world, the weather and the quirks of our respective cats. (It is a stereotype to say that poets are fond of cats, but many are.) Then conversation moved on to the Ontario Minister of Culture's new initiative to fund artists, filmmakers and writers who have been traditionally excluded from participating in the cultural life of the province. The new measures that he enacted were meant to benefit Aboriginals, Francophones, immigrants and visible

222

minorities. Everyone in the room, with the exception of me, was white. Everyone in the room, with the exception of me and my husband, disagreed with the objectives of the new programs.

They didn't like them because it meant that the Ministry of Culture would stop funding existing writers, most of whom were white, and start funding other writers, most of whom were non-white. But the white men and women in the room were not willing to own up to this. Instead, they claimed that Aboriginal, Francophone, immigrant and visible minority writers did not produce quality work. The whole notion of granting people money to write about their experiences as "minorities" in this country was a bogus one. "If these people were any good they could get money and get published," the white men and women said.

I challenged these people on their notion of what was quality. "How do you define quality?" I asked. "Does it have to follow European or North American notions of what is considered good?" They looked offended and asked me what I meant by that. I could feel my yellow skin grow more yellow and bristle, but I remained unrepentant.

"What I am suggesting," I patiently explained, "is that the writers' community in Canada excludes non-white people. It was initially created for white men and changed to include white women. It judges the quality of literature in terms of white European or North American literary traditions. When it does embrace non-European or non-North American cultures, it does so by appropriation. Look at the way writers like Robert Kroetsch steal Aboriginal legends to add spirituality to their books. Your organizations don't recognize the existence of racism and the way that it shapes the experiences of non-white writers. You invalidate non-white writing because it focuses less on the intellectual European tradition and more on personal experiences, which most non-white literary traditions—Aboriginals, African, Asian, and Caribbean writing—value. When we confront you about your exclusionary actions and your subtle but vindictive racism, you use elaborate, theoretically constructed arguments to show that racism really doesn't exist; it is merely a figment of our imagination. So what are we supposed to do if we can't convince you that racism exists? Suffer in silence? Support your appropriation of our cultures in the hopes that we will gain a foothold in the literary community through your exploitation of our traditions? Throw off our conventions and traditions and embrace yours? What the Minister of Culture is trying to do is make room for us in the art, filmmaking and

223

writing communities, and I think it's about time room was made. This country has never been entirely white but its culture always has been. It cannot remain that way. It is becoming more and more non-white by the day, and it is important that we recognize and accept this fact. If not, we will face race and ethnic war."

I took a deep breath and sat back to see their reaction. In challenging them I was only being myself, a yellow woman. My points were grudgingly acknowledged by some, but were ignored by others who went on talking about how culture in Ontario is going to the dogs. (Are the dogs us, the non-whites?)

I AM FURIOUS. This kind of reaction is typical. I have learned, as an anti-racist educator, that it is meant to invalidate and segregate the non-white minority from the white majority. What they didn't know was that I wasn't going to let them get away with it. Whether they wanted to or not I was going to make them admit and confront their racism.

I spoke up and said, "This is silencing and I will not tolerate it. What I said must be addressed in your community. You must think about it."

The responses ranged from "I don't know what to say — you're right — but I don't know how to change them," to "It's certainly interesting but you really don't know anything about the writer's community," to "Look, I've had a bad day and I really don't care to get involved in your petty problems about white people." These people were in no mood to talk about racism and I knew it. It was time to stop.

The distinguished Canadian poet, though, thought that it was time to put me in my place. "I don't see," he said angrily, "what gives you the right to come here and call us all racists."

"I didn't come here to call you racists," I replied. "But when racism comes up, I call people on it. To tell the truth, though, I did expect you to be racists, given your reputations for consistently slagging non-white writers."

"Why did you bother coming, then? You had a choice not to come," was the nasty rejoinder.

"That's like saying that because I'm yellow I should stay in Yellertown." I bit off each word. "You're all racists. I'm leaving." Tears flooded my eyes as I left. Damn it! Why did I let him get the best of me?

As I walked out the door, I realized there was a presence behind me. It was a white man. The white man I came with. Then I felt sorry. I wasn't sorry for standing up for myself, but I was sorry for him, sorry that I might have damaged his career as a writer. These people were important, influential, significant. They could have helped him with his writing career. With their sponsorship—why did I have to ruin it for him?

Something moved.

The white man woke to find me watching him and thinking. Pulling the covers closer and squinting his blue eyes against the sunlight, he grinned and said, "It's early, go back to sleep." He reached for me and pulled me close. He was no longer a white man. He had become my husband again. Being so close to him revealed the contrasts in our skin even more, and the memory of the previous evening began staining my mind with worry.

"We need to talk," I said.

"Okay," he muttered.

"It's about last night. I'm sorry I ruined your chances to get more writing published, but I was right, they were racists," I explained.

"It's okay, you were right, they were wrong. Can I go back to sleep?" he groaned. He dozed off, but his arms were still around me, trying to pacify me. I didn't feel like going back to sleep. I struggled free and heard my skin separate from his as I rolled away. I got out of bed. I glanced at him as I left the room. Even sleeping, his white body exudes a strength that is foreign to me. As I walked down the hall to the bathroom, I pondered the source of his strength.

I know where my own power came from. It developed through a combination of experience and education. New things lived and new things learned have all helped me to form my character and outlook. They made me aware of who I am, and I am a survivor. I have survived the racial inequities of this society. I have survived them with my dignity intact and I have survived them with the desire to eliminate all forms of social injustice. His strength, though, does not come from survival. It was not acquired through knowledge or reflection, but through something deeper, something that suggested a sense of self that comes from a sense of belonging.

I turned on the shower. Stepping into the steamy spray, I soaped myself. The bar of soap was blue, the lather white, but it should really be green since my skin is yellow, and blue and yellow make green. The lather, however, remained white. As I watched, the white bubbles slipped from my breast, making my body seem white. I wondered if it is the whiteness of his skin that gives him the sense of belonging he possesses. Could his white skin be a protective shield which, despite its frailties, allows him to exist safely and comfortably

225

in the white world? Most likely. No one questions his right to be there. He can make what he wants out of his life. He can become a writer and people can admire his brilliance or condemn his impracticality. He can pursue a professional career and people can applaud his ambition or criticize his desire for respectability. He can tune out of society altogether, and people can think he's enlightened or view him as "out to lunch." No one, though, will say that all white people are like that because he's like that. He is never asked to prove his worth as a human being to anyone. The only person he has to satisfy is himself. He is secure and happy with the world.

For me the standards are different. My skin, in spite of its resiliency, is a target, drawing attention and arrows of scorn from others. People question my right to be here. I cannot do what I want. I have to agree with the existing order or else others will assume that people like me are lazy. I must become a professional or else others will conclude that people like me are stupid. I need to work hard or else others will think that people like me are useless. Everything I do has a bearing not only on me, but also on other yellow people. I am constantly asked to prove myself. I am unsure about myself and my place in the world.

Steaming water continues to spray from the silver shower head . . .

I pour the pink shampoo out of its equally pink bottle and lather my hair. The bubbles are also white; they should be a deep burgundy because pink and black make burgundy, but they remain white. There seems to be no way of getting around the whiteness of the world. The world is white, through and through. White men and women created the world in their image to nourish, perpetuate and sustain themselves. The institutions they developed only made room for them, for them and no others. Those who controlled these institutions, as I witnessed the previous evening, were intensely protective of them. They had to be defended at all costs. After all, they were proof to white men and women of their power.

As I was thinking about these things, my husband came into the bathroom. He stepped into the shower as I was rinsing off, the white soap suds sliding off my body and down the drain. I made space for him, but he said there was enough. As he soaped himself, the white lather disappeared against the white of his skin.

"I'm sorry about last night," I said, "but I couldn't stand by and let them oppress me."

"It's okay," he answered, "they were wrong. Do you think that white people have a monopoly on being right?"

226

"But you're white," I remarked.

"Yeah, but I'm not that kind of white person."

"What kind of white person is that?" I asked.

"The kind that thinks only white people and white culture matter."

"What's it like to be white?"

He stopped washing and replied, "Embarrassing, guilty. Not very good sometimes."

"Why?" I wanted to know.

"Because you have power," he answered, "a lot of power and sometimes you don't want it. After all, you didn't ask for it. It's part of your birthright. But what the hell does that mean? Does it mean you have the right to treat 'coloured folks' like shit?" He kept on washing as I stepped out of the shower to dry off, running the yellow towel over my yellow skin, refreshing it.

All through the day I watched him as he ate, puttered and worked. His white skin reflected light and cast an uncomfortable feeling on me. Short, fast flashes of the previous evening's events streaked through my mind all day.

When we married, I knew that racial differences would emerge some day. I just didn't expect them to erupt in such an "us-shaking" manner, forcing me to confront the difficulties of an interracial marriage.

I was worried that my belief in a racially equitable society, which was based on my experiences as a non-white minority, had cost him his dream of being a writer and would mar our relationship forever. I didn't want him resenting me for spoiling his golden opportunity. I might have swallowed the other writers' racism, if only to support him, but I could not do that and still live with myself. I know that he supported my actions and my motivations, but my uncertainty of his sincerity jabbed at me all day long. I kept asking myself what was going to happen to us.

I tried to think about times in our relationship when the question of race came up between us, but I could think of none. When we are by ourselves we think we are the only two people in the world. There is no racial dynamic, just the silly giddiness of loving each other. We can afford to be colour-blind, to ignore our differences and even make jokes about them. Once we get out into the real world, though, it is hard for us to be equal. He will always be treated one way, based on his colour, and I another, based on mine. His colour allows him to be accepted everywhere, mine only in some places. My marriage to him will grant me grudging acceptance in some places, but I will always

227

resent the fact that this "privilege" is not accessible to everyone. Does he really understand the complexities that being married to a non-white woman can bring? Can our relationship survive the social pressures of an inherently racist society?

I'm not sure, but as I catch him looking at me, I am reminded of the things that we have been working for. He knows that the power and privilege he possesses are often unearned and must be relinquished if there is to be racial equality. This he does without hesitation. When confronted with a racist situation, he usually speaks up. (The only time he doesn't is when I am there to beat him to the proverbial punch.) Yet when he is confronted with the choices of joining the white establishment to do something he really wants to do or of denouncing it as racist, is it fair for me to insist that he take the moral high ground? Am I the one who is putting pressure on him or is he making his own decisions about what is right or wrong? Would he be anti-racist without me?

Questions flash in my mind in a brilliant kaleidoscope of colour. The pastel shades of the answers elude me. Only the colours remain.

Later that evening we watched a movie on TV, cats sleeping on our laps, a bowl of over-buttered popcorn between us. It looked like a scene from *House Beautiful*. The only difference was that such magazines show only couples who are white, not couples who are white and yellow. My husband had chosen the movie; it was about a Chinese American family trying to make it in 1949 New York. It was touching, poignant, all those words that describe good G-rated movies. This particular film made me laugh and cry at the same time. It uses every Hollywood cliché to depict people about whom Hollywood would never even think of making a film.

I looked over at my husband. He smiled. He knows me well. He understands how important it is for me to watch films like these, because they give me a sense of identity. The movie made me forget my bitter thoughts, and for the moment I felt as if we were the only two people in the world.

My doubts about our relationship returned later that evening. We were in bed. I was trying to sleep but my husband's white skin glowed dimly in the dark and made me think about our racial differences again. The white man had returned to my bed and I didn't know what to do with him. Tired, I tried another solution to my problem.

"I love you," I said.

"I love you too," he said.

"Is my being yellow a problem for you?" I ask.

"No, not really. Is my being white?" he asks.

"Yeah, sort of," I reply.

"Oh, how?"

"I don't know," I said. (I did know.)

"So what's the problem?" he asks.

"It sometimes creates conflicts for me. Like last night. I wonder — marriage is hard enough. I don't know if the added pressure of racial difference is worth it for us," I said.

"It'll be okay. Let's take it one day at a time, alright?" he replied.

He becomes my husband again. The questions of interracial marriage still wander in my mind, but I will think of them on another day.

BLACK NATIONALISTS BEWARE! YOU COULD BE CALLED A RACIST FOR BEING "TOO BLACK AND AFRICAN"

HENRY MARTEY CODJOE

I'm sometimes embarrassed to admit that I learned more about myself as a Black man and an African in Canada, a traditionally white country, than in my native Ghana. Until coming to Canada, the question of my racial identity was not something that I had thought about. After all, I grew up in an all-Black country where the issue of race or racism was not something that was on my mind. My language, culture and customs celebrated my blackness, and I didn't see any struggle for my racial identity.

I guess I first began to think about the subject of race relations in secondary school. Just like many other Black colonial territories, Ghana was affected by its British colonial experience. There was a high premium placed on things European or white, especially in schools. European culture and ideas were considered superior and had to be mastered. The *obroni* became our frame of reference. In fact, one acquired or gained social status by going to *Ablotsiri*, or the white man's country. I had therefore viewed the prospect of coming to Canada as an opportunity few of my friends or relatives had. I was emigrating to a country that, as one India-born writer in the U.K. put it, "signified, to colonial subjects such as myself, progress, both material and intellectual." According to William Cross's model of Black racial identity development, the state of my condition at that time can be described as "pre-encounter," which meant, according to Beverly Tatum in her book *Talking About Race, Learning About Racism*, that I had "absorbed many of the beliefs and values of the dominant . . . culture, including the notion that 'white is right' and 'Black is wrong.'"

Indeed, before coming to Canada I didn't know what it meant or felt to be discriminated against as a Black person or an African. I hadn't developed any kind of Black consciousness. I was unaware of the U.S. civil rights movement in the 1960s and other Black struggles for liberation around the world. I had not heard of Martin Luther King or Malcolm X or Marcus Garvey. I didn't even know that President Nkrumah had invited the great Black scholar and intellectual W.E.B. Du Bois to come and live in Ghana. One would think that growing up in Nkrumah's Ghana I'd at least be aware of or knowledgeable about global issues affecting Blacks in Africa and the diaspora. Whatever I learned in school was learned in order to pass my exams and move on. It was not an attempt, as the late Bob Marley wrote in one of his songs, to "emancipate myself from mental slavery."

Coming to Canada heightened my awareness of racism. I quickly noticed how race and colour were factors in social interactions in North America. During my first few months in the country, two incidents occurred that made me think seriously for the first time about questions of race, identity and white supremacy ideology. It was also my first experience with racial humiliation and abuse. The first related to the time I offered to help an elderly white woman carry her bags of grocery. As soon as I asked if I could help, she clutched her bags close to her chest and yelled, "Get away from me, you darkie!" I was visibly shaken. For a moment I froze, clasped my hands tightly as if praying and let some distance come between me and the woman before continuing my walk home.

The second incident was more subtle, but the message was loud and clear. I had worked in the storeroom of a downtown hotel where I was in charge of supplying produce and drinks to the staff when they produced requisitions for whatever was required. I had noticed that the kitchen helper who each morning came for the produce for the chief chef would always gaze at me in some kind of disbelief as I read and checked off the items on his order. When I finished he would swear at me in Italian and leave. I wondered why. One day after I had finished his order, he asked me where I learned to read and write. I said Africa. He then pointed his finger at me and said how come he, the white person, couldn't read and write and I, the "Negro," could. It shouldn't happen that way. I was shocked. I never thought I'd see a white person who was illiterate — in Canada!

Related to these incidents and others was the constant reminder of my African identity. I'd always responded to the often-asked question "Where are you from?" by saying I'm from Africa. The mere mention of Africa and I'm looked upon with some mixture of pity and bewilderment. Oh, look at this poor African — he must be hungry or something! And then of course it is followed by some of the most embarrassing and ridiculous questions: How did I get to Canada, did I fly in a plane? Are there airports in Africa? Did I live in a house or is it true that Africans lived in trees? What foods did I eat? What's my tribe? Did I play with lions? Did I come from a large family? How did I learn to speak English so well? I didn't look African! Was I sure I was an African? And more. By this time, I just couldn't stand and take the way Africa and Africans were depicted in the media.

What was wrong with being Black or African? Why the daily discrimination and humiliation of Blacks? Why was I always asked what I was doing in Canada? And why wasn't I back in Africa where I belonged? I started to think more about these questions. I began to explore the whole issue of blackness: what it means to be Black or African. Given no other choice (my colour and accent always gave me away), I felt I had to be secure in my *African-ness.* I had to affirm my sense of self.

I embarked on an intellectual journey — to, using Amilcar Cabral's expression, "return to the source," so to speak. What are the history and heritage of African peoples in Africa and the diaspora? This came easily for me because of my love for books and reading. Within a few years, I had bought and read books on Black and African culture, history, politics and literature. When I graduated from university I had read books by C.L.R. James, W.E.B. Du Bois, Amilcar Cabral, Marcus Garvey, Malcolm X, Richard Wright, Basil Davidson, Kwame Nkrumah, Langston Hughes, Walter Rodney, Ali Mazrui, James Baldwin, Frantz Fanon, Cheikh Anta Diop, J.A. Rogers, John Henrik Clarke, Martin Luther King, Jr., Lerone Bennett, Chancellor Williams, George Padmore and many more. I had made the transition from a "coloured intellectual" into a "Black intellectual." I had reached the racial identity stage described by Cross as "Immersion/Emersion," or as Tatum aptly describes, "the simultaneous desire to surround oneself with visible symbols of one's racial identity and an active avoidance of symbols of whiteness." As Thomas

233

Parham notes in his *Cycles of Psychological Nigrescence*, "At this stage, everything of value in life must be Black or relevant to Blackness." But nobody told me that my newfound Black pride and identity would be threatening to the dominant white culture, or that I would be called a racist for expressing my Black cultural identity.

In graduate school I had a white roommate. For a while we got along quite well. We discussed and talked about various political and current events. But as time went by, he stopped talking to me. He tried to avoid me as much as he could. I decided to find out what was the matter. When he returned from classes one evening I asked him if something was wrong. He told me he was not happy with our living arrangements and that he was considering moving out so I could find a Black roommate. "A Black roommate?" I asked with some discomfort. "Yes, isn't that what you want? I don't think you like white people. You must be a racist!" His response completely took me off guard.

"What makes you say that? What makes you think I'm a racist?" Visibly upset, I demanded an answer.

"Well, come and I'll show you." He led me to my bedroom. "Look at all these books and posters on your wall," he said, picking some books off my bookshelves and throwing them on my bed. "Malcolm X, Walter Rodney, Marcus Garvey, Kwame Nkrumah, Stokely Carmichael, and all these Black radicals," he continued as he looked for more book titles. "And look at all these posters on your wall: Great Kings of Africa, maps of Africa, Nelson Mandela, Steve Biko, Malcolm X, Walter Rodney, Kwame Nkrumah."

"And this makes me a racist?" I asked, totally flabbergasted.

"Well, yes. All you read are these Black books, you listen to all that African music, and most of the friends who come to visit you are Africans."

"Wait a minute," I shot back. "Let's go to your room." I followed him to his bedroom. "What are these?" I pointed to some of the books in his room. "Titles by Euro-American authors and tapes and records of white musicians. And the walls of your bedroom are also covered with maps of the United States and Europe. Do these make you a racist? I don't think so. Tell me: why is it okay for you to read books by and about Europeans and Euro-Americans and it's not okay for me to read books by and about Blacks and Africans? How dare you call me a racist?" I left his room.

Now as I reflect upon this incident I'm always confounded by the charges of racism leveled against Blacks who try to assert their identity through knowledge of their culture and history. Why is it fine for peoples of European descent to know and appreciate their histories and cultures and abhorrent for peoples of African descent to do the same? And who decides whose knowledge and culture is legitimate? I remember very well when Vice-President Walter Mondale chose Geraldine Ferraro as his running mate in the 1988 U.S. presidential election. The media and commentators made many references to her as an Italian American, and Ferraro was proud of her Italian identity. Presidents Reagan and Bush went to the United Kingdom to affirm their Irish and British roots. But when Jesse Jackson tried to assert his African identity and said American Blacks should call themselves African Americans, he was branded a racist and a troublemaker who wanted to divide America.

Recently I read the story of PBS television reporter Charlayne Hunter-Gault, who changed the way she wore her hair by adopting what the reporter called "a tightly braided African style." Apparently, this didn't sit well with the white viewing audience. Hunter-Gault was said to have received "the most abusive, racist correspondence" ever. How dare she become "too Black and African"? Harry Belafonte echoed this sentiment when he told the New York Times: "By and large, as [Black] people, we've had to be more like what white people want us to be than we've been able to be who we are and express ourselves openly and honestly." When I gave all my children African names, a white colleague asked why I didn't give them European names. I told him they were not Europeans. I then asked him if he would give his children African names. Oh no, never, he said; they are not Africans. This is what Professor Henry Giroux has called "the hegemonic notion that Eurocentric culture is superior to other cultures and traditions by virtue of its canonical status as a universal measure of Western civilization."

It's very clear that notions of white supremacy run very deep in North American society. The absence of Black knowledge in our schools and cultural avenues is not a simple oversight. Its absence is an instance of racism. All too often, what is considered "legitimate" knowledge does not include the historical experiences of Africans and other "visible" minorities. It can really be disorienting to sit in a class when a teacher describes North American society and history and you're not in it. You're invisible. You don't matter. And when as "visible minority" you try to do something about it, you become a racist. In effect, "Be Black, but not too Black."

BIBLIOGRAPHY

Anzaldua, Gloria. *Borderlands/La Frontera. The New Mestiza*. San Francisco: Aunt Lute Books, 1987.

Armstrong, Luanne. "Being White." *Tessera*, Vol. 12, Summer 1992.

Arnold, Rick, et al. *Educating for a Change*. Toronto: Between The Lines, 1991.

Bannerji, Himani, Linda Carty, Kari Dehli, Susan Heald, Kate McKenna. *Unsettling Relations: The University as a Site of Feminist Struggles*. Toronto: Women's Press, 1991.

Barndt, Deborah. "Putting Ourselves into the Picture: Recovering History through Images and Stories." Unpublished Notes for Talk to Critical Pedagogy Series. Toronto: OISE, 17 Feb. 1993.

Carty, Linda, and Dionne Brand. "'Visible Minority' Women — A Creation of the Canadian State." *Resources for Feminist Research/Documentation sur la récherche féministe* (RFR/DRF) Vol.17, No.3, 1988.

Estable, Alma. "Immigration Policy and Regulations." *Resources for Feminist Research/Documentation sur la récherche féministe* (RFR/DRF) Vol. 16, No.1, 1987.

Henry, Frances, and Effie Ginzberg. *Who Gets the Work: A Test of Racial Discrimination in Employment*. Toronto: Social Planning Council of Metropolitan Toronto, 1985.

hooks, bell. *Black Looks: Race and Representation*. Toronto: Between the Lines, 1992.

James, Carl E. "Getting There and Staying There: Blacks'

Employment Experience." In P. Anisef and P. Axelrod (eds.), *Transitions: Schooling and Employment in Canada*. Toronto: Thomson Education Publishing, 1993.

Jordan, June. *Moving Towards Home: Political Essays*. London: Virago Press, 1989.

Joseph, Gloria I., and Jill Lewis. *Common Differences: Conflicts in Black and White Feminist Perspectives*. Boston: South End Press, 1981.

Lorde, Audre. *Sister Outsider: Essays and Speeches*. Trumansburg, N.Y.: The Crossing Press, 1984.

MacKinnon, Catharine. "From Practice to Theory, or What Is a White Woman Anyway?" *Yale Journal of Law and Feminism*, Fall 1991.

McIntosh, Peggy. "White Privilege and Mail Privilege: A Personal Account of Coming to See Correspondences through Work in Women's Studies." In M.L. Andersen and P. Hill Collins. *Race, Class and Gender: An Anthology.* Belmont, CA: Wadsworth Publishing, 1992.

McIntosh, Peggy. "White Privilege: Unpacking the Invisible Knapsack." *Peace and Freedom*, July/August 1989.

Morrison, Toni. *Playing in the Dark. Whiteness and the Literary Imagination*. Cambridge and London: Harvard University Press, 1992.

Ng, Roxanna. "Immigrant Women in the Labour Force: An Overview of Present Knowledge and Research Gaps." *Resources for Feminist Research/Documentation sur la récherche féministe* (RFR/DRF). Vol.16, No.1, 1987.

Page, Joanne, ed. *Arguments with the World: Essays by Bronwen Wallace*. Kingston: Quarry Press, 1992.

Pratt, Minnie Bruce. "Identity: Skin Blood Heart." In *Rebellion: Essays 1980-1991*. Ithaca, N.Y.: Firebrand Books, 1991.

Ramazanoglu, Caroline. *Feminism and the Contradictions of Oppression*. London and New York: Routledge, 1989.

Razack, Sherene. "Storytelling for Social Change." In *Returning the Gaze: Essays on Racism, Feminism and Politics*. Toronto: Sister Vision Press, 1993.

Reagon, Bernice Johnson. "Coalition Politics: Turning the Century." In *Home Girls: A Black Feminist Anthology*. Barbara Smith, ed. New York: Kitchen Table/Women of Color Press, 1983.

Rich, Adrienne. "Notes Toward a Politics of Location (1984)." In *Blood, Bread and Poetry*. New York: W.W. Norton, 1986.

Said, Edward. *Orientalism*. New York: Vintage Books, 1979.

Scheier, Libby, Sarah Sheard and Eleanor Wachtel, eds. *Language in Her Eye. Writing and Gender: Views by Canadian Women Writing in English*. Toronto: Coach House Press, 1990.

Schoem, Davd, ed. *Inside Separate Worlds: Life Stories of Young Blacks, Jews, and Latinos*. Ann Arbor, MI: University of Michigan Press, 1991.

Schuster, Charles I., and William V. Van Pelt. *Speculations: Readings in Culture, Identity, and Values*. Englewood Cliffs, NJ: Blair Press.

Walker, Alice. *Living by the Word*. San Diego: Harcourt, Brace, Jovanovitch, 1988.

Williams, Patricia. *The Alchemy of Race and Rights: Diary of a Law Professor*. Cambridge: Harvard University Press, 1991.

Williamson, Janice. "Jeanette Armstrong: What I intended was to connect . . . and it's happened." *Tessera*. Vol.12, Summer 1992.

BIOGRAPHICAL NOTES

Carl E. James holds a Ph.D in sociology and teaches in the Faculty of Education at York University. He lectures in the areas of culture, race, ethnicity, anti-racism, and urban education, and his work examines race, class, and gender inequity in social relations, educational processes, and outcomes. James is the author and co-author of several books and articles, including *Seeing Ourselves: Exploring Race, Ethnicity and Culture* (1989), *Making It: Black Youth, Racism and Career Aspirations in a Big City* (1990), *Career Equity for Youth* (1993), and, with Rick Arnold et al., *Educating for a Change (1991).*

Adrienne Shadd is a feelance researcher-writer working in the area of Black history and culture in Canada. She has been research editor and contributor to *Tiger Lily,* a journal by women of colour, and guest editor of a special issue of the *International Review of African American Art* entitled "Celebrating the African Canadian Identity" (October 1992). She is co-author of *"We're Rooted Here and They Can't Pull Us Up": Essays in African Canadian Women's History* (1994) and is working on several additional books, including a history of Black women in Canada. Ms. Shadd has an M.A. in sociology.

Susan Judith Ship is a lecturer in the political science department at the Université d'Ottawa where she teaches on women and politics. She is also involved in developing anti-sexist and anti-racist education projects for children in Montreal and Ottawa.

Guy Bédard is a lecturer in the political science department at the Université du Québec à Montréal where he teaches methodology and statistics. He is currently completing a doctoral degree in political science; his thesis is focusing on the National Question in Quebec.

Katalin Szepesi was born and raised in Toronto. Educated at York University, she taught with the North York Board of Education before going into missionary training. She lives in North Dakota with her husband and hopes to go overseas to do missionary work.

Valerie Beassigae Pheasant is a member of Potawatomie Nation (tribal affiliation). She is originally from Wikwemikong and is now a member of the Whitefish River First Nation (political/physical). Valerie is a staunch advocate of First Nations education and is currently completing her Ph.D.

Lawrence Hill lives in Oakville, Ont. His novel, *Some Great Thing* (Turnstone Press), was published to critical acclaim in 1992. His children's history text, *Trials and Triumphs: The Story of African Canadians* (Umbrella Press), was published in 1993. His short stories have appeared in various magazines and anthologies. He is currently completing a history of the Canadian Negro Women's Association and is at work on a new novel.

Jerry Diakiw is a doctoral candidate at the Joint Centre for Teacher Development at OISE. He is a former Superintendent of Schools with the York Region Board of Education, and has written several articles on multiculturalism.

Shyrose Jeffer-Dhalla was born in Tanzania in East Africa and spent her early years in Pakistan and the Middle East. In 1982 she immigrated to Canada with her parents and sister. She has a B.A. in psychology and is pursuing a Masters of Education degree at York University. She also works as an anti-racist educator in Toronto-area high schools.

Stanley Toshiaki Isoki was born in a Japanese internment camp in Lemon Creek, British Columbia, in 1945 to second-generation Japanese-Canadian parents. His family emigrated to post-war Japan when he was two years old. When they returned to Canada in 1951, they settled in Thunder Bay, Ontario. In 1958 his family moved to Toronto and he graduated from York University in 1968. Mr. Isoki currently lives in Toronto and works as a teacher/counsellor in a large, urban, west-Toronto secondary school for the North York Board of Education.

Denny Hunte was born in Barbados, the Caribbean. In 1967, at the age of twelve, he immigrated to Canada with his brothers and sisters and joined his parents in Toronto. He holds a B.S.W. from Ryerson Polytechnical University in Toronto and works in the Community Services Department of Metropolitan Toronto. He is interested in writing prose.

Kai James is in grade eight. James says he likes to write poetry because it is a creative way to express his ideas. In his poetry he explores identity as well as social and cultural issues.

Didi Khayatt teaches in the Faculty of Education at York University. She is interested in issues of gender, race relations and sexuality. She is the author of a number of articles and her first book, *Lesbian Teachers: An Invisible Presence,* was published by SUNY Press in 1992. She is currently involved in research in the area of sexual categories.

Lillian Blakey is a third-generation Canadian of Japanese origin, born in 1945 in rural Alberta where her parents went after they were forced to leave British Columbia during the war. Most of her family returned to Japan after the war, but her parents chose to stay in Canada. In 1952 they moved to Toronto where she received her education. Currently, she is a teacher for the North York Board of Education and works with teachers and children in all three levels, developing strategies for integrated models by teaching in a culture context.

Gottfried Paasche has lived in Toronto for over 25 years and is a member of the faculty of York University.

Doris J. Saunders has lived her life in Labrador. She is the editor of *Them Days*, an oral history magazine begun in 1975. She has received the Order of Canada and a Doctor of Letters from Memorial University in Newfoundland for her dedication to Labrador.

Beryl Tsang holds a Master of Arts degree in East Asian history and lives in Toronto with her partner, writer Rob Lohin, and their son. She is a writer, historian, and community activist.

Leslie Sanders teaches at Atkinson College, York University. She is the author of *The Development of Black Theatre in America* (1988) and has published articles on African American and African Canadian writers. She is a Canadian now.

Karen Lynn is the manager of Workplace Equity at Humber College,   243 where she also administers the Workplace Equity Training and Consulting Program and the Race, Culture, and Empowerment Program.

Barb Thomas is an educator, activist, and writer with extensive experience in anti-racism work and popular education. She has worked with community organizations, unions, women's groups, and non-governmental organizations in Canada, the Caribbean, and Southern Africa. In 1986 she co-founded the Doris Marshall Institute for Education and Action in Toronto where she has since worked doing social change education. She is the author of three books.

Ivan Kalmar is an associate professor of anthropology at Victoria College at the University of Toronto. He is the vice-president of the Toronto Semiotics Circle and the author of *The Trotskies, Freuds, and Woody Allens: Portrait of a Culture.*

Sabra Desai is a human rights, gender, and ethno-racial equity educator and consultant. She has worked in the field of equity, organizational development, and change from a race, class, and gender perspective for over fifteen years, presented workshops at several national and international conferences, and taught at York University. Currently a doctoral candidate in applied psychology at OISE, she also teaches in the social services department of Humber College.

Arun Mukherjee was born in Lahore, in pre-partitioned India. She came to Canada as a Commonwealth scholar to do graduate work at the University of Toronto, and has taught at several Canadian universities, including York University where she is now teaching post-colonial literature and women's studies. She is the author of two books and an editor of one anthology.

Boyce Richardson is an Ottawa filmmaker and writer. **Robert Richardson** has been a community worker in Ottawa, Sudbury, Toronto, and Halifax for almost twenty years. **Belle Richardson** is a part-time actress, bartender, and office worker living in Los Angeles.

Henry Martey Codjoe was born in Ghana and is a policy consultant with the Alberta Department of Education. He is also an independent researcher and a budding writer on Black and African affairs. He lives in Edmonton.